Barefoot Irreverence

A Collection of Writings on Gifted Child Education

Barefoot Irreverence

A Collection of Writings on Gifted Child Education

James R. Delisle

PRUFROCK PRESS, INC.

Book Design by James Kendrick
Cover Design by Marjorie Parker

Printed in the United States of America.

ISBN 1-882664-79-5

"Roger and Jim" originally appeared in 1980, *Media and Methods*, April, pp. 20, 69. Copyright © 1980 by James R. Delisle. Reprinted with permission.

"Gift Rapping: Children Speak Out" originally appeared in 1983, *Gifted Children Newsletter*, October, pp. 1–3. Copyright © 1980 by Gifted-Children.com. Reprinted with permission.

"A Space to Grow" originally appeared in 1988, *Learning*, November/December, pp. 62–63. Copyright © 1980 by James R. Delisle. Reprinted with permission.

"Letter to a Friend" originally appeared in 1994, *Learning*, September, p. 112. Copyright © 1994 by James R. Delisle. Reprinted with permission.

"Just One Child: A Tribute to Mark" originally appeared in 1996, *Gifted Child Today, 19*(2), pp. 6–7. Copyright © 1996 by Prufrock Press Inc. Reprinted with permission.

"Looking Backward to Learn" originally appeared in 1999, *Gifted Child Today, 22*(2), pp. 32–33. Copyright © 1999 by Prufrock Press Inc. Reprinted with permission.

"First Things First" originally appeared in 1995, *Gifted Child Today, 18*(6), pp. 10–11. Copyright © 1995 by Prufrock Press Inc. Reprinted with permission.

"First, Do No Harm" originally appeared in 1999, *Gifted Child Today, 22*(5), pp. 28–29. Copyright © 1999 by Prufrock Press Inc. Reprinted with permission.

"You Should Go Home Again" originally appeared in 1992, *Understanding Our Gifted, 5*(2), p. 7. Copyright © 1992 by Open Space Communications, (800) 494-6178, http://www.open-spacecomm.com. Reprinted with permission.

"Remembering the Roepers" originally appeared in 1991, *Advanced Development Journal, 3*, pp. 95–98. Copyright © 1991 by the *Advanced Development Journal*. Reprinted with permission.

"'You From Around These Parts?': How an Outside Might View Gifted Child Education" originally appeared in 1998, *Gifted Child Today, 21*(2), pp. 18–19. Copyright © 1998 by Prufrock Press Inc. Reprinted with permission.

"Fourth Grade, Seventh Heaven" originally appeared in 1995, *Roeper Review, 17*(4), pp. 244–245. Copyright © 1995 by The Roeper Institute. Reprinted with permission.

"Turn Left Down The First Paved Road" originally appeared in the 1999, *Ohio Journal of the English Language Arts*, Winter/Spring, pp. 24–29. Copyright © 1999 by *Ohio Journal of the English Language Arts*. Reprinted with permission.

"One Teacher's Credo" originally appeared in 1997, *Gifted Child Today, 20*(6), pp. 30–32, 46. Copyright © 1997 by Prufrock Press Inc. Reprinted with permission.

"Our Students, Ourselves" originally appeared in 1989, *Gifted Child Quarterly, 33*(2), pp. 79–80. Copyright © 1989 by *Gifted Child Quarterly*, a publication of the the National Association for the Gifted (NAGC). 1707 L Street, NW, Ste. 550, Washington, DC 20036, (202) 785-4268. http://www.nagc.org. This material may not be reproduced without permission from NAGC. Reprinted with permission.

Prufrock Press, Inc.
P.O. Box 8813
Waco, Texas 76714-8813
(800) 998-2208
Fax (800) 240-0333
http://www.prufrock.com

To my Uncle John.
I knew him for too short a time before he had to leave.
The gift of his words, though, remains with me forever.

Acknowledgments

Putting together a book is hard enough, but it is darn near impossible without a good editor. In my case, I was doubly blessed with two: Jim and Christy Kendrick. They know how to dig deeper than anyone else I know. I thank them for their dedication, their precision, and their patience.

I also acknowledge the many children whose lives have crossed paths with mine on this exciting journey. From Matthew and Stephanie in Gorham, New Hampshire, to Craig in Stafford Springs, Connecticut, to Sara and Alan in Twinsburg, Ohio—each has taught me that a teacher's best quality is a vision to see beyond (and beneath) the obvious. If I possess any wisdom at all, it is due to the trust placed in me by children like them.

Table of Contents

It is important that students bring a certain ragamuffin, barefoot irreverence to their studies; they are not here to worship what is known, but to question it.

— Jacob Bronowski

Introduction

To me, one of the hardest parts of writing a book is determining its title. I find this a difficult task for several reasons.

To start with, the title is the first thing about your book that readers notice and, despite the timeworn admonition not to judge a book by its cover, many people do. I know *I* do! If a book's title doesn't grab me, there's only half a chance that I'll pick it up and consider it for purchase.

Secondly, the title is supposed to convey, in fewer than 15 words (preferably, *many* fewer than 15 words), the entirety of the book's content and tone. That's why subtitles are so popular: Authors can't make up their minds what their books are really about, so they just throw everything into the title in the hopes that some of it will stick with their potential audiences.

And, lastly, you have to live with that title for the rest of your book's life, so you want it to be something that is either easy to say or a cinch to remember. Frankly, I can't even recall some of my other books' subtitles, which probably means that the titles were selected by some committee of people who thought up what they hoped would be a marketable title.

This time, though, the task was easy; in fact, the title came to me while I was walking along a beach thinking less about my book and more about how much I enjoyed warm waves lapping at my toes. It was one of those "Aha!" moments that creative types often talk about as occurring during the "Incubation" phase of creativity. In other words, while actively thinking about nothing in particular, I got this little nudge of mental adrenaline that shouted, "Hey you, the one without shoes! Here's your next book's title!"

And so it became: *Barefoot Irreverence*.

This title is appropriate for a variety of reasons. First, I love to use quotes with my students. These one- or two-liners are often filled with the wisdom of past ages, and we can spend 30 minutes dissecting a carefully and thoughtfully conceived quotation. That's exactly what happened with the Jacob Bronowski quote that begins this introduction, as I used it to review with my eighth graders their views of the purposes behind education and learning. As I tell them each year, "If you end this year with more questions than answers, I've done my job as your teacher."

The second reason that *Barefoot Irreverence* seems to fit is that many of these articles were written at the beach in South Carolina—thus, the "barefoot" part. My family and I have had the privilege of spending most of our last 12 summers at our home in North Myrtle Beach. This is the time of year that I clear my head of the educational gunk I've collected during the past nine months and reflect on the reasons I entered this field of gifted child education 23 years ago. It also gives me time to reassess why I remain involved in this field despite a continual uphill battle to gain professional acceptance in the eyes of many who see gifted child education as "fluffy" or "elitist." But, when I sit on the beach or the deck with a pen in hand (yes, the old-fashioned way of writing still works for me), what comes out of my thoughts and onto the paper are the lives of gifted kids who have touched my own. And who, as a child, does not want to run around barefoot?

The third reason that the title works—the "Irreverent" part—has to do with the writing style and content of the articles themselves. I'll be the first to admit that I am not an accomplished researcher in the sense of chi squares, analyses of variance, or degrees of freedom. But, what I lack in statistical precision I make up for in observational abilities. I watch kids and colleagues, and I wonder why they do and say what they do. Then, I write about it. To me, there are no sacred cows in this field, and if the emperor really does have no clothes, I'll be among the first to say so. This, of course, has garnered me both criticism and consternation from coworkers and others, many of whom wish I would just keep my mouth shut. Still, I don't know how to stay quiet when I perceive a practice, a principle, a definition, or an ideology hurting the children I have been trying to help for almost 25 years. And I have learned that, although my critics are many, my strongest advocates are classroom teachers, gifted child education specialists, and the children and parents they both serve. They are the people for whom I am writing.

So, there you have it: a too-long, and only slightly irreverent, introduction to the book you are about to read. If you like a particular article or story because it helps you to clarify an issue or identify a child with whom you work or live, please let me know. Even better, write an article of your own and share it with an audience who can benefit from your personal font of wisdom. Enjoy!

Jim Delisle
July 2001
North Myrtle Beach, South Carolina

Part One

The Lives of Gifted Children

t's been more than 20 years—1980—since my first published article, "Roger and Jim," appeared in a magazine called *Media and Methods*. Since that time, I've published more than 200 articles and 10 books, an accomplishment I feel hard-pressed to acknowledge as real. Early on in my career, it had never been a goal of mine to become a writer. Instead, all I wanted to do was be the best special education teacher I knew how to be, and my efforts were focused toward making school livable and curriculum likeable for the more than 20 kids assigned to me in my resource room for children with special needs. But a writer? Never.

Then, I met Roger, who was 12 years old. In the fall of 1975, he became my student, I his teacher (or was it vice versa?). By the next winter, Roger had become my foster son, living with me during the week while returning home with a relative on weekends so that I, a 23-year-old single guy, could have a life apart from parenting.

3

The first story in this anthology is Roger's story. It began as a class assignment in a graduate course called "Writing for Publication," taught by Dr. Vincent Rogers at the University of Connecticut in 1978. Vince told us to write two paragraphs about a child we knew, and the next week, he asked us to share our writing in class. Out of the 12 graduate students there, I read last, embarrassed that my story was so different than theirs, as it focused on a negative event, not a positive one. When I finished reading, though, I heard applause. Then, the questions began: "Who was Roger?" "How long did you know him?" "Why did they allow a teenage boy to live with his 23-year-old teacher?" "Where is Roger now?" My story struck a chord in my classmates, and I felt an obligation to them, to Vince, and to Roger to complete it. Little did I know that it would be the first of many stories about children that I would write and publish.

"Every child has a story to tell, and every child must have someone to hear it," I tell my own graduate students now. My first exposure to this truth was through Roger.

Roger and Jim

Roger's entrance explodes the silence of my small, square classroom: fists bloodied, cheeks streaked with tears, his once-white shirt stained and soaked with sweat. He has had another fight.

This time, Roger knows there is no second chance; he must go away once again. As before, his short fuse was ignited by the comments of other kids who do not understand that just because he lives with his teacher, Roger is not "queer." And, as before, he now regrets having gone out for recess and exposed himself to these taunts.

He is sobbing and breathing, sobbing and breathing, trying to mouth the words "I'm sorry" through his tense, quivering lips. All that comes out is air. As his teacher, as his father, I hold him close. His blood and sweat now stain my clothes, as well.

Roger is 14, but his strong body belies his youth. He struggles to free himself from my tight, containing embrace. I respond by loosening my grasp, but he clings to me all the more. We share closeness, however it was earned.

Roger and I have not always been son and father. Last year, he had another father, and before that still another. Roger is a foster child, a perennial orphan, returning to his natural parents only when we well-intentioned others gives up.

When he is with his parents, Roger usually sits glued to the TV, his lips parted by the butt of a cigarette that they first dared him to try. He cannot go to school in his hometown, having been expelled too many times. That's all right with Roger's parents because it gives him more time to chop wood (the family's only source of heat), fetch water (when the pipe freeze, the backyard spring still gurgles), and be a diversion for those two lonely adults who are tired of having only each other for company. It's all right with Roger, too. At least he doesn't get into fights at home, and he can fulfill the assignments of his parents much more easily than he can those of his teachers.

But, the state said "no," and Roger was placed recently in the care of a couple in a nearby town where he could go to school. They had been his foster parents before I came along, and it was a fight—like today's—that transferred him from their home to mine.

In fact, Roger has had many fathers in his 14 years; many mothers, too. His foster brothers and sisters probably remember him more clearly than he remembers them. Words like *sister* and *father* have no permanence for him; they serve only to identify those people with whom he is currently living and eating.

Roger and I walk up the corridor toward the principal's office. We are met by the startled stares from teachers whose heads turn to watch this wounded pair. They wonder—some out loud—why a 23-year-old teacher takes on the responsibilities of a child who is feared and often hated by his peers.

The principal talks. I try to listen, but attend instead to Roger's quiet sobs and sniffles. Looking downward, I see my hands trembling, so I grab one with the other. Roger hears the principal's words, but understands few—he is retarded, the state said so.

No more chances for Roger. Suspension didn't work, neither did the principal's threats after previous fights. I suspect Roger remembers these threats only when he is calm. When he gets angry, he hits.

We leave the office, then the building. I don't look back—I'll be there again tomorrow. But, Roger gives a parting glance to the art display where his papier-mâché skier smiles back at him. It had earned him third prize and a brief moment of positive attention from a surprised student body. Now, it is just a remnant.

The ride home is quiet. Roger's dried blood flakes on my car's white seats. He pokes the bits of blood, crunching them into still smaller pieces. He looks down at his discolored clothes, plays with the shoelaces of his Keds, and whimpers.

Suddenly, I think that Roger may have been hurt in the fight, that perhaps his tears are caused by a cracked rib or a chipped tooth. I pull the car onto the shoulder of the road. "Nothing hurts," he says. "I'm just sad."

Roger's bedroom is crowded with Kiss posters and homemade cloth-and-paper airplanes. The top of his bureau is cluttered with the latest Matchbox cars. An assortment of his already-worn clothes connects bed and hamper; only a few shirts have made it to the laundry bin. Roger sits, staring outside at the crisp morning with its melting snow—the last time he will see this view.

I call our social worker. Roger overhears and begins to pack his few, small possessions into a musty olive duffel bag. Wood clanks against metal as Tinkertoys strike cars, trucks, and pennies. Then, he returns to his chair, staring outdoors once again.

We have shared so much, Roger and I. The ocean at Hampton Beach, one of my favorite summertime retreats, became Roger's big, salty pool. His first escalator ride, at the National Air and Space Museum, had been a highlight of our trip to Washington, DC. Even a traffic jam on the Capital Beltway had been fun.

It seemed easy for Roger to see me as "Mr. Delisle" at school and "Jim" at home or on vacation. He played his roles well, and, except for being unable to con me into believing that he had no homework, he kept my roles as teacher and father distinct.

I found it more difficult, as I tried to combine teacher and father in both settings. Maybe it would have helped if I'd given him a title like "Mister" for school and kept "Roger" for home. Maybe.

The social worker's car pulls into the driveway. I walk to Roger's room, swallowing a large and sour lump in my throat.

"You take care, Roger, okay?"

"Okay."

Steve, the social worker, enters. No one looks at anyone else. His last visit had been to deliver some of Roger's winter clothes, and he was pleased with my report on how well Roger was doing. Now, the scene is awkward. Steve clears his throat. I manage a handshake. Roger's eyes glisten, and a tear or two plops onto the blue kitchen carpet. He turns to me.

"One last hug."

"Okay."

The car backs out of the driveway and soon disappears down the quiet street. Roger will spend the night with his real parents (it'll be cold; they'll probably need wood).

I climb back up to my second-floor apartment, aware of my failure, aware of my grief. Sorting out what went wrong will have to wait until later. I guess I'll have to clean out Roger's desk at school (damn, he had just begun to feel confident about his reading and math), and his bedroom will probably get used for storage once again.

A tear of my own darkens the kitchen carpet. I am sobbing and breathing, trying to mouth the words "I'm sorry" through tense, quivering lips. All that comes out is air.

Media and Methods
April 1980

Gift Rapping—
Children Speak Out!

Introduction

I never knew it would be so easy to get a book published. While completing my Ph.D. in gifted child education, I came across a book called *On Being Gifted*. Sponsored by New York's American Association for Gifted Children in 1978, this book was a compilation of short essays by gifted teenagers on what it was like to grow up gifted in America. The high points and hurdles were all discussed in the honest detail that adolescents are experts at sharing.

I read the book cover to cover in one night and, shortly thereafter, wrote to the publisher, Walker and Company, telling them in a two-page letter that I liked their book a lot and that it needed a companion volume written by younger gifted children. I sent the letter off, "Sincerely yours" and all, and within two weeks had a return letter and contract, complete with an advance of $1,200! I never thought it would be so easy to get a book published . . . and since then, it has not been!

"Gift Rapping" is an excerpt from my first book, *Gifted Children Speak Out*, in which more than 6,000 gifted children from across the world responded to numerous questionnaires about their experiences growing up gifted. In today's era of e-mail, instant messaging, and the Internet, 6,000 letters may not seem like a lot, but to the poor postal worker who carried each of these letters to my mailbox back in 1982, it was a different story!

Despite our heightened awareness about the needs of bright children, and despite our best intentions and efforts as parents and teachers, gifted children can still lose out on a full education. Perhaps we disregard a strong interest, or maybe we fill their school days and years with items that we, not they, deem important. Instead, the key to success in working with gifted youngsters—or at least one of the keys—might be to ask them what it is they need or want out of school.

Recently, more than 6,000 gifted 5–13-year-olds from all across the country, as well as Canada and Europe, responded to questions about their perceptions of giftedness and the "high points and hassles" of being bright. The collective and typical responses to these questions represent a good cross-section of perceptions and attitudes of gifted children from as diverse geographic regions as British Columbia and Puerto Rico, Kentucky and California. The responses may provide parents of other gifted children—and the children themselves—with some valuable insights. Starting with the obvious:

"Are You Gifted?"

"I think I'm smarter than other kids my age because, when my teacher gives a spelling test and it's time for me to go to my gifted program, she speeds up for me, and the other kids can't keep up." (Girl, 9, Alaska)

"I don't think I'm gifted because I can always learn something from others." (Girl, 10, Connecticut)

"It depends. I am not what you'd call brilliant, but I'm not dumb, either. I do get some nice comments on my reading abilities, though." (Girl, 8, Illinois)

". . . in a sensitive way, yes, I am gifted." (Boy, 12, Georgia)

Children also responded to questions about the definition of giftedness, the pros and cons of special programs, and the term *gifted* itself (most children don't like it; they prefer the word *talented*). In general, a consensus shared these views:

1. *If I'm gifted, tell me in what.* ("Sometimes, I feel pressure into always being better than average." [Girl, 12, Kansas])
2. *Talk to me about my talents.* ("My parents have helped me feel okay about being intelligent. They gave me self-confidence." [Boy, 11, West Germany])
3. *Help me to put my talents into a real-world perspective.* ("I'm just different because I'm a little smarter, but that's not to say I'm better than anyone else." [Boy, 9, Georgia])

Friends and Classmates

Another area of concern to gifted children and their parents involves friendship. Many children report that intellectual differences make no difference in beginning or maintaining friendships: "My friends don't really seem to care, unless they're just keeping it inside them" (Girl, 12, Pennsylvania). Others find that academic talents tend to stifle relationships with anyone except other gifted children, a reaction many bright children attribute to envy from less-able agemates. Still others hide their abilities in the hopes of being accepted as "just another kid." For example:

"Sometimes, we'll do an easy thing, and I'll take my time to look like I'm just as puzzled as everyone else." (Girl, 9, Illinois)

"There are times I try to act dumb so that my friends who aren't so bright won't feel uncomfortable." (Boy, 12, Kentucky)

However, just as many children refuse to "suffer fools gladly," as one comment illustrates:

"I don't think I should ever hide my abilities. You should never hide what you are because then people will never know what you are inside." (Girl, 13, New Jersey)

Overall, gifted children seem content with their talents, despite the occasional hurtful jibes from classmates who don't yet realize that "being bright" is not something done to spite others.

Schools and Programs

Schools help . . . and hurt. To listen to the children tell it, it seems clear that someone is doing something right—and, every so often, it's a teacher.

"Teachers encourage originality and creativity, stimulate your imagination, and care about you personally, as well as schoolwise. They understand you're not perfect, and they make you feel good and happy. Teachers can help." (Boy, 11, Michigan)

The most-often-stated desire of gifted children regarding learning is that they want hands-on activities, applied information. Despite the fact that many gifted children have high verbal skills and can relate their ideas using impressive vocabulary, they want to manipulate objects, as well as ideas.

"I like learning by doing experiments and playing Mrs. Aaron's math and reading games. It's more fun than memorizing and doing workbooks." (Girl, 7, New York)

"I enjoy hands-on activities most of all because they allow you to discover for yourself. Nothing is more strange than finding that all those words and figures in your text actually mean something." (Girl, 12, Connecticut)

If only this one change were made in school curricula, a full one-half of the school-related complaints registered by the children surveyed would be remedied.

Another area where bright children believe that schools are already succeeding is in the establishment of gifted programs.

"Gifted programs help students to learn more and to 'keep up' with their brains." (Girl, 11, Puerto Rico)

"I like to be around children who are as intelligent as I am." (Boy, 11, North Carolina)

"We should learn how many inches from the Earth it is to the moon." (Girl, 7, Maine)

"We should use computers, play advanced games, and learn a lot about ourselves and how to deal with the fact that other people will always expect more out of us." (Girl, 10, Arkansas)

However, not all is well in schools. In fact, the children are quite specific about those aspects of education that, for them, stifle learning. For example:

". . . most of the time it's just review, review, review." (Girl, 10, Maine)

"I sit there pretending to read when I'm really six pages ahead." (Boy, 10, Connecticut)

". . . the teachers often have me do extra things, like move desks or go get their coffee." (Boy, 12, Ohio)

In summary, it appears that gifted children's needs at school will be met if the following points are considered.

1. *Give bright children credit for what they know.* ("If you do something right once, you won't have to do it again." [Boy, 11, Michigan])
2. *Offer bright children the chance for hands-on explorations.* ("I'd like a science lab table, a planetarium, and an invention room." [Boy, 10, Louisiana])
3. *Remember that school is also a place for learning social skills.* ("Teachers should not say, 'There was only one A and so-and-so got it,' because the class snickers." [Girl, 11, Michigan])

4.   *Allow the teacher to humanize the classroom.* ("Once, I told my teacher I was bored, and she even admitted that it was boring. Somehow, that made it more bearable." [Girl, 11, Connecticut])

A Helping Hand From Home

Parents, as well as teachers, receive high grades from their children for the jobs they are doing—which, in this case, is "child rearing." High on the list of children's compliments are those strategies parents use to interest their youngsters in new topics. For example:

"They have challenged me to do things I don't even like to do just to prove that I don't really know the good from the bad . . . and, again, they prove themselves right." (Boy, 8, New York)

"My father teaches me everything in math before I even know what he is talking about. This helps me to get interested in new topics." (Girl, 10, Massachusetts)

Regarding parental "weak spots," it is ironic that the area of greatest concern for gifted children is their perceptions that they are not "good enough" to please Mom or Dad. Such concerns lie in two areas: expectations of parents for their children and comparisons of siblings by parents.

"My mother expects me to be smarter than before I was labeled 'gifted.'" (Girl, 12, California)

"I think my parents want me to do better even at home just because I'm gifted in school. I think they expect too much." (Boy, 10, Kansas)

"I'm compared to my brother and sister by my father. It makes me feel like I have to do everything they did, like winning spelling bees and science awards." (Girl, 12, Kentucky)

Nevertheless, a large number of children reported that home-based expectations are neither too high nor too low and that they are pleased in knowing that their talents are appreciated: "I get a real good feeling inside me when I know I pleased my parents." (Girl, 10, Rhode Island).

Personal Note From the Author

During the past year, I have spent much time talking with gifted children. I have spoken with dozens in person and thousands more in writing. Expecting to find the typical gifted child somewhere among these thousands, I instead realized that there is no such character, that children who share the intellectual signals of giftedness—early reading, advanced vocabulary, varied and intense interests—are a diverse group. I learned, too, that I had to reexamine my own stereotypes about which children are "gifted" and what teachers and parents should offer them. Overall, the children provided me with a reality seldom found in either college courses or at curriculum conferences: The most important part of "gifted child education" is the child.

One final comment that speaks for itself:

Dear Jim Delisle,
Even if you can't use my answers, I'm glad you gave us kids a chance to tell what we feel.
—Julie, 11, Illinois

So am I, Julie . . . and thanks!

Gifted Children Newsletter
October 1983

A Space to Grow

Letter to a Friend

Just One Child
A Tribute to Mark

I have clustered these three articles together because they address a common theme: the need to see gifted children as the unique individuals that they are—warts and all. Each of these three boys—Craig, Jason, and Mark—was a student of mine for more than one year. Each left an impression on me that is as indelible as ink on a blotter and as permanent as eye color.

Craig was in my first gifted class ever, a grade 4–6 pull-out program in rural Connecticut. Craig had trouble completing what he started; he was interested in so many things that focusing on one project for too long seemed to him a pointless endeavor. He wanted to learn what he could about a topic of interest, and then move on. In gifted jargon, "task commitment" was not his forte, but learning about the wide world outside of his little town of 4,000 was. I liked Craig then—I bet I would like him now—because he was the first student to teach me that giftedness is not always about products and projects. Rather, it's about having the space to grow.

Jason, by today's liberal standards of labeling, would definitely have been identified as ADHD. When he was a student in my fourth-grade class, though, I saw him merely as a spunky kid who had all the answers, but simply refused to write them down. In many ways, Jason was a challenge. He tried my patience frequently and was even suspended for some physical outbursts toward others that, while not justified, were certainly understandable if you knew what other kids had said and done to him. When I nominated Jason for our school's gifted program, most everyone laughed, except Jason's mom. She, too, knew Jason was smart, and she thanked me for looking past the negative behaviors and finding in him something worth cherishing: his fine mind. I still keep in touch with Jason, even though he lives almost 2,000 miles away from my Ohio home. A college sophomore and track star (he always *could* run), Jason, his mom, and I get together whenever I do a West Coast swing near their home—about once a year. We reminisce about fourth grade and the antics that, to this day, keep me wondering how each of us made it through that year intact.

Mark, ironically, was a classmate of Jason's, both in my fourth-grade room and in our school's gifted program. More than any other child apart from my own son, Mark affected my life in ways I will never forget. "A Tribute to Mark" ends when Mark is 14, but the pain that Mark felt toward living continued to plague him. He dropped out of high school at age 16 (his grade-point average was 0.90) and found drugs to be a temporary escape from the turmoil he lived every day. He learned on his own how to program computers and, shortly after turning 17, became licensed as a Microsoft systems engineer, pocketing more money annually than the teachers who had ignored him at his high school (Mark was especially proud of this wage disparity). Four times Mark attempted suicide, and four times his mom and I carried him to a local hospital to try to sort out with him the mayhem inflicting his brain and his heart. But then, a turnaround: Mark got accepted to a college based on his GED and his seventh-grade SAT score of 1200 (which he took as part of the Midwest Talent Search). Mark was dating, living in a dorm with a roommate he liked, and acting as do most 19-year-olds: He seemed happy to be alive.

But, we missed something, for in February of 2001, Mark ended his own life with a shotgun. His pain, cleverly disguised, had ended; ours deepened. No note, no explanation, no goodbye.

I haven't told Jason yet about Mark's death. I'll wait until I see him next, probably this summer. It's not something you tell to someone over the phone.

A Space to Grow

raig started school with gusto. In kindergarten, his teacher raved about his limitless potential. In first grade, his proud parents bragged that was the best reader in the class. By fourth grade, his enthusiasm had waned, and his teachers were voicing frustrations: "So many abilities, but he's such a daydreamer." "If he'd buckle down, he'd be a straight-A student."

Starting With an Acorn

When Craig was in sixth grade, I came to his school to start a program for the academically talented (A-T). His test scores made him a shoo-in for the program, but his daily work gave little indication of his abilities.

I asked Craig's two teachers if they thought we should admit him into the A-T program. One teacher said "yes." She thought the program might rekindle Craig's interest in school. The other said "no." "Craig's bright, but he's also lazy. If he has a math page with 30 problems, he'll do half, then mentally wander around the room. I *know* he could finish the whole page in 10 minutes if he wanted to." She argued that getting into A-T should be based on performance, not potential.

After much debate, we agreed to admit Craig into the program, but under one condition: He had to keep up with his regular classwork. When I told Craig about the program and that we'd like him to be in it, he was excited. "Oh, wow!" he shouted. "When do we start?"

"We can start tomorrow. But, there's one catch: You'll have to be on your toes in your regular classes, too," I told him. Smiling broadly, he assured me he'd buckle down.

Our A-T classes began. Without the constraints of the regular classroom, I could plan lessons based entirely on student interest. I challenged Craig with creativity worksheets, science experiments, logic problems, the works. He eagerly did every assignment and asked for more. When not enmeshed in his own work, he'd go around the room, helping his classmates and challenging *them* to think harder. I couldn't believe this was the same boy who'd wool-gathered his way through the last two years. "It's not that regular school is so bad," he explained, "but, in A-T, we have more room—we have space to grow."

Signs of Wilting

At first, Craig was conscientious about his regular classwork. But, after a few weeks, he drifted into complacency. He didn't complete his worksheets, he forgot his homework, he made careless errors on the simplest assignments. I had a few conferences with him. Each time, he promised to do better, but he never did.

With the end of the first marking period just three weeks away, I met with Craig's teachers to review our options. We decided that, unless Craig's performance improved dramatically—and soon—we'd take him out of the A-T program. We practiced our "shape up or ship out" speech, which we planned to deliver to Craig the next day.

An Idea Takes Root

My ride home that afternoon was awash in the autumn splendor of rural Connecticut. Such vibrancy, such splash! It made me think of Craig and the progress he'd made in A-T. I thought, too, of his remarkable sensitivity to his classmates. For example, a few weeks before, as I looked over his shoulder during a chess match, I was surprised to see him lose the game. I know he could have won it hands down. Later, when I asked him about it, he said, "Well, Monica was just learning, and I wanted to give her a chance to be good at something new." Such vibrancy, such splash!

I felt discouraged. I knew reading the academic riot act to Craig would fail. Each year, his teachers had given him similar warnings, and Craig always reacted the same way: He'd make an effort to change, and as soon as the pressure was off, he'd resort to his old habits. Why should this ultimatum work when others hadn't? Sure, Craig would lose something he liked, but he was used to losing privileges.

Craig wouldn't be the only loser if we dropped him from the A-T program. The program would lose, too. The other A-T kids would miss Craig's spirited, incisive comments during class discussions. Also, they'd miss him as a friend. I decided then and there that I'd have to find some way to get Craig interested in *all* of his schoolwork, not just A-T.

I began to reflect on my own school years. I remembered being bored when I had to do assignments I'd already mastered. And I remembered how exhilarated I'd felt when a teacher let me do a project on something *I* chose. Such freedom!

Those thoughts gave me an idea for helping Craig change. Now, all I had to do was convince Craig's teachers to try my plan.

A First Leaf Appears

The next day dawned fresh, crisp, and sunny—the kind of day that makes you smile for no reason. A good omen.

When I got to school, I told Craig's teachers that I'd come up with a new plan I hoped they'd consider. I explained that, although I agreed Craig shouldn't be allowed to slide by in his regular classes, I hated to lose him in A-T. Then, I outlined my plan. Somewhat reluctantly, they agreed to try it for the rest of the marking period. After all, if it failed, we'd have to live with it for only three weeks.

We sat down with Craig to set the plan in action. "Starting today," I told him, "your math assignments are cut in half. If there are 50 problems on the page, you have to do only 25—and *you* get to pick which ones to do. If you have two errors or less, you won't have to complete the remaining problems.

"There'll be a spelling test on Monday. If you get 90% or better, you won't have to write the misspelled words five times each or put them in sentences. Instead, you can use that time to work on other projects of your choice."

Craig's eyes lit up. For the first time, he'd be rewarded for good work instead of being punished for poor work. Rather than having to complete every workbook example *ad nauseum*, he could prove to us what he knew, then get on with his learning.

Craig's teachers started with one subject each—math and spelling. As we began to see Craig's progress and his change of outlook on "the basics," we added other subjects. This time, Craig didn't revert to his bad habits after a few weeks.

A Mighty Oak

Craig continued to excel in A-T, and he improved in his regular classwork, as well. In A-T discussions, he'd bring up such subjects as respect, understanding individual differences, and making exceptions, all topics he'd learned about firsthand. In his regular classes, he did everything expected of him and was able to devote more time to the projects he liked best. As a result, for Craig, *all* of school, not just A-T, had become a space to grow.

Learning
November/December 1988

Letter to a Friend

Dear Jason,

I just heard you'll be moving soon—a big move, 2,000 miles away. When your fifth-grade teacher told me the news, she seemed surprised that I said I'd miss you.

"Jason's such a quiet boy," she said. "He doesn't attract much attention to himself."

If that's the truth, you've changed a lot since I taught you in fourth grade.

If you remember, by this time last year, you and I had already had several conferences. There we'd sit, your face covered with tears and mine looking artificially stern. I'd be asking why you'd called Martina "dog face" or why you'd motioned one finger—your middle one—in my direction.

Remember the time you lost the chess game with Amber? I saw the anger in your eyes, but before I could reach you, you'd already lashed out. Amber ended up against the wall, dazed by your strong push. I still recall your sorrowful words: "I didn't mean it, but she called me stupid. I hate being called that!" Still, a push was a push, and you had no right to hurt Amber physically, even though she'd hurt you verbally. You know that now, and you knew it then—you just forgot for a second too long.

Your punishment was an in-school suspension the next day—the day of our field trip. I knew you hated me for that punishment. It's not that the field trip was that great—you'd been to the museum before—but you'd have had a chance to be with your friends. We were all looking forward to it, especially you. But, instead, off we went and there you stayed. You learned your lesson well, I think.

How often I wanted to be like a friend to you, Jason, but I couldn't. I was your teacher. But, if I were 10 years old, too, I think we'd be buddies. We both like bad jokes (groaners), hate cursive writing, and wish the summer lasted just a little longer. Believe it or not, the field trip punishment was as hard on me as it was on you. I thought of you a lot that day and kept wondering what you were doing. We were both glad when that day was over.

Something else, Jason. I often wondered if you realized that I treated you a little differently than your classmates. Knowing that you cried so easily, I always disciplined you in private. I found out how you felt about that on Parent Conference Night. Your mom and dad entered our classroom cautiously. I think they were prepared to hear the same things they'd heard other years—that you were a troublemaker and that you needed to control yourself and learn to sit at (not under) your desk. Instead, I told them that you were bright and eager to learn and that I was recommending you for the gifted program (which I hear you've really enjoyed). Yes, I told your parents about your fist-fight with David, but I also mentioned that, by recess, you two were teammates again.

That's when the weird thing happened. Your mom cried, just a little, and then she told me something I'll remember forever. She said she'd asked you if you liked your new teacher, and when you said "yes," she asked why. You told her: "Mr. D treats me like a big person, not a kid." Yes, Jason, I saw you as a person to be respected, not a child to be tamed. Thanks for noticing.

We'll miss you here, Jason, but your freckled face will be etched into my memory forever. Thanks to you, I learned that all kids behave better when their minds are challenged, their views are heard, and their emotions are respected. You've been a good teacher for me.

Well, that's about it. I really just wanted to say good bye, good luck, and, most of all, thanks.

Oh, one last thing. Now that you're moving, I can sign off the way I often wanted to last year.

Your FRIEND,
Mr. D

Learning
September 1994

Just One Child: A Tribute to Mark

Dear Mark:

You told me once, as your fourth-grade teacher, that your year's goal was to learn algebra because your "third-grade teacher didn't understand it much." So, I went home that night and dug out my old college algebra texts so that, together, we could learn about equations. It was a skill at which you excelled, at least when the subject was numbers. If only all of life's variables were that predictable, its inequalities that easy to balance!

But, for you, they weren't. As gifted as you were, there were still some areas that were difficult for you. Recess was one. Try as you might to squeeze onto a kickball team, others more athletically inclined purposely kept you from playing. From the sidelines, I watched as you were picked last, if at all. I wanted to intervene, and perhaps I should have, but I thought you'd prefer the integrity of not being picked over the forced camaraderie of being chosen just because your teacher said you had to be. I only wish I'd told you then what I'll tell you now: Kids can be cruel and they were wrong. You could have handled a dodgeball if only they had given you the chance.

By October, you chose to bypass this kickball ritual and just started hanging around with me. On some days, you talked about protons, neutrons, and quarks, while on others, you helped me to understand the relative merits of Sega versus Super Nintendo, helping me to pick the right gift for my son. Three years have passed since you gave me that advice, Mark, and the once-new Nintendo system now gathers dust somewhere in our attic. Still, we stay in touch, you and I, and, instead of electronics, we now talk about deeper issues: philosophy, religion, the meaning or life, and the purpose of death. And, sometimes, we talk about girls or music or food. But, even now, as during your fourth-grade year, I often feel pain for you. All you've ever wanted to do was to fit in with your classmates, but to do so on your terms, not theirs. You said it beautifully to me one day: "Hey, if I accept them for who they are, why can't they do the same for me?" Good question, Mark. I wish I knew the answer.

When you entered fifth grade, I hoped you would have a teacher who savored the type of intellectual discussions we had so enjoyed. Instead, you got a fine teacher, but one whose own life was hectic enough that she didn't have a lot of time for your accelerated diversions into physics. So, you conformed, behaved, and missed 29 days of school that year—the uppermost limit of absences that would still allow you to move on to sixth grade.

Puberty hit you hard, suddenly, and before all the other guys in your sixth-grade class. "How appropriate," I thought. "Mark's body is finally catching up to his mind." But, instead of making you "one of the guys," this premature entrance into the world of adult sensations caused a further rift with your classmates. As envious as some of the other boys probably were, your rapid maturation set you apart from them in yet another way. Who would've thought that your growing up would be so hard?

Today, you're an eighth grader. The physical milestones you hit so early have been matched by your classmates, but, intellectually and socially, you still seek a soulmate. I want so badly for you to fit in, Mark, but, if anything, the rift between you and your classmates is growing exponentially, just like the algebra you have now mastered.

Long ago, you discovered one of life's inequalities: It's not easy to be a lot smarter than everyone else in your class. It's not just that you know lots more about the world than they do, you also know more about yourself. This depth of understanding has affected your relationship with adults, too. For example, you don't tolerate adults who talk to you in a "condescending tone" (your words), and you abhor teachers who think that, by making you afraid of them, they can get you to conform to their standards, their rules. Your picture is often bigger than theirs, your vision more inclusive, your approach more direct: You just want to be able to talk and think and play according to your interests and abilities, even if they aren't typical for a kid your age.

There are those who say that there is no such thing as giftedness, or that everyone is gifted in some way. People who hold those beliefs have never met you. You are different, intellectually and emotionally, and even though we make a big deal in our country that it's okay to be an individual, that generosity seldom applies to kids, especially those who, like you, sometimes challenge adults in uncomfortable ways.

You need something different, Mark, than most 14-year-olds. There's nothing wrong with that. I only hope we can give it to you before you totally lose faith in a society that isn't quite as tolerant of unique human gifts as we'd like to think we are.

You have taught me much, Mark, by simply choosing to be yourself. I take great pride in having known you, and I look forward to walking alongside you as you travel the many paths that lie ahead.

—Mr. Delisle

Gifted Child Today
March/April 1996

Part Two

Gifted Child Education: Past, Present, and Future

I have always been intrigued by the wisdom of George Santayana, whose quote that "those who ignore history are condemned to repeat it" crosses all areas of human endeavor—history, parenting, education, you name it.

When I first became involved in the field of gifted child education, everything I read was new to me. The benefits of enrichment and acceleration, where children were encouraged to explore their interests and talents, made more sense to me than did the lockstep progression through curricula that were already mastered. The belief that being a smart kid didn't necessarily mean you had things easy in a social or emotional sense was a new concept for me to absorb, and so I read the works of Joanne Whitmore and Annemarie Roeper for further elaboration.

Like a kindergarten child discovering the magic of letters and numbers for the first time, everything I explored sounded new and important. I was in an intellectual candy store with an unlimited appetite and new stock arriving each day.

Only later did I realize that there were other places to find the wisdom and insights I sought about understanding gifted children—and those places, those books, those people, were all in the past. Thus began a great adventure, which continues today, into understanding the current state of gifted child education by looking backward to those who built the field and looking forward in a quest to use their collective wisdom to progress with our ideas and our ideals.

A toast, then, to George Santayana!

Looking Backward
to Learn

This brief article could not have been written without serendipity having played a role in its creation. I was in the right place at the right time and, for free, picked up a classic book from a colleague who was retiring from more than 30 years of service to children.

Even though I had now been studying gifted children for more than 20 years, my first exposure to this 1957 book by Norma Cutts and Nicholas Moseley was by accident. But, as I read and reread their ideas, I realized that they were two magnificent, straightforward thinkers who had asked the hard questions that have still not been answered today: "Why don't *all* teachers see themselves as being responsible for teaching gifted children?"; "Why don't *all* teachers become 'talent spotters,' seeking out gifts in children who are smart, but who may not show it through high grades or steady academic progress?" Yes, Cutts and Moseley caused me to think about how much we ignore the past ideas in gifted child education. We ignore ideas that were forged in an era not unlike today, when gifted children are still viewed suspiciously by those who contend that such a concept of giftedness is "elitist" and that the children who are tagged as gifted are, somehow, different from the norm in some unflattering ways—social misfits, academic snobs, spoiled rich kids.

I offer a suggestion and a challenge to each of you: Go to a university library that prizes its old collections and look up this book by Cutts and Moseley. After devouring it, turn to the bibliography (it is extensive) and find one other book whose title intrigues you. Then, locate *this* book and have another intellectual smorgasbord in the land of the past.

Bon appetit!

It was only a discarded book on a tabletop, placed there by a just-retired guidance counselor cleaning off her shelves. "These books have helped me over the years," read an anonymous, hand-lettered sign. "I hope they help you, too."

Intrigued, I looked over this small collection, which had already been picked over by a middle school faculty as quickly and completely as is any food item left in the teachers' lounge. One book's title struck my fancy, *Teaching the Bright and Gifted* by Norma Cutts and Nicholas Moseley, two authors with whom I had never crossed paths in my more than 20-year history in gifted child education. I picked up the yellowed book and found that it was published in 1957, when I was 3 years old. Like me, it showed signs of aging around its edges. The book was dedicated to Lewis Madison Terman—a good sign—and its authors opened their preface with the following sentences:

America's greatest resource is her bright children. The need today is to discover every bright child, challenge him to work to his full capacity, and see that he receives all the education from which he can profit. (p. vii)

I wondered then if the rest of the book's information was as current as the thinking in this opening passage because, except for the sexist language, the appropriateness of its message was as intact now as it was those many years ago. So, I kept reading.

"Calling All Teachers" was the name of Chapter 1, and in it, the authors made it clear that every teacher is a teacher of gifted children. They addressed the acute teacher shortage, especially in math and the sciences, and lamented the fact that "largely because of a lack of teachers, more than half of our high schools [do] not offer either physics or chemistry" (p. 5). No longer true, of course, but just as scary is the fact that, in many schools, teachers of math and science are not certified to teach these subjects. Which is the greater dilemma?

Cutts and Moseley then addressed the finding that some teachers are intimidated by gifted students who may know more than they do about a particular topic. If only these teachers listened to the wisdom of Carolus Linnaeus, one of the world's greatest scientists, who reminded us that "a teacher can never better distinguish himself in his work than by encouraging a clever pupil, for the true discoverers are among them, as comets among the stars" (which appears, by the way, on page 11 of the Cutts and Moseley text).

"Keep going," I told myself, "you're learning from a pair of academic ancestors you didn't even know you had."

The chapters progressed onto familiar topics like identification ("Large classes make sound appraisal difficult . . . when your room is overcrowded, you mainly notice students who compel your attention. Too often, the activator is not good work, but bad work or bad behavior," p. 14) and standardized testing ("A pupil who does well on a modern standardized test is almost surely superior. The tests are so constructed that luck and guessing play little part," p. 30). There was even a section on portfolio assessment, that buzzterm of the '90s, although Cutts and Moseley called it "systematic observation" ("If you have any doubts about how a pupil rates on a trait, think what activities would give him occasion to display it and make a point of watching him the next time one of these activities is under way," p. 17).

Enrichment was defined as "the substitution of beneficial learning for needless repetition or harmful idleness" (p. 37)—as worthwhile a definition as I have ever heard put forth—while acceleration was noted as "any procedure which enables a student to complete his education a year or more earlier than the norm for his age" (p. 103). Both forms of curriculum enhancement were seen as advantageous, as the gifted student "discovers the world of the mind and progresses in knowledge and in skill" (p. 11).

I could go on with additional similarities offered in this undiscovered classic and the thoughts being put forth by our current stock of gifted child education specialists, but by now I would guess you get the gist of my message: that, as George Santayana proclaimed, "those who ignore history are condemned to repeat it."

But, why must it be so? Why does every generation of educators think that its views are unique, new, and vividly original? Instead of coining new terms that cause our colleagues to decipher more jargon—Problem-Based Learning, developmentally appropriate practice, Type III Enrichment—why don't we just come to a common understanding of some basic principles that underlie what we do in our classrooms? Next, perhaps we could adopt a common vocabulary so that, when I talk with teachers about "enrichment" in Ohio, it means the same thing as another educator giving a similar talk in Nevada. I'm not trying to homogenize the field of gifted child education as much as I am asking for some common ground that makes us resemble a cohesive area of study, rather than a disparate set of argumentative individuals. As a start, could we agree that the following set of principles, straightforward and workable, might be the only outline we need to bring to fruition the talents of the children we teach? Consider what would happen if:

- all teachers made a systematic attempt to identify all bright and talented children;
- all teachers used methods that helped all children make the most of their abilities;
- all teachers continued to think, study, and experiment with a view to improving the teaching of the bright and talented;
- all parents and all communities organized all of their resources with a view to providing the best schooling for the bright and talented; and
- all the bright and talented were educated to apply their gifts in the service of humanity?

What a forward-thinking agenda for the future this set of principles would instill in our efforts to help the gifted children in our care!

But, yes, you've guessed it: this set of ideas comes from Cutts and Moseley (p. 238), who close their book with this invitation, still unanswered, to improve the lives of "bright and talented" children. (Another thing that never seems to change: the varied terms we use to describe the gifted child.)

Can we take up the challenge? Can we reflect on our past as we envision our future? Can our "gifted vocabulary" be condensed and consolidated to the point where educators other than ourselves know what in the world we're talking about when we use terms like *enrichment, acceleration,* or that granddaddy of all jargon, *differentiated instruction*? If we can do so, we may learn that those who came before us—the Cutts and Moseleys of the world—offered time-tested suggestions and advice that is still relevant.

Like that generous guidance counselor who shared her dog-eared copy of a long-ago text, let us remember that some of the best lessons for gifted child educators are still being taught by our professional ancestors. It is time to reclaim their bounty.

Gifted Child Today
March/April 1999

First Things First

Some things I write I disagree with not long thereafter. Other pieces I write seem to withstand the test of time in ways that I never could have predicted. In a way, both ideas are true of this 1995 article, "First Things First." In it, I argue that the field of gifted child education has removed itself from the mainstream of educational innovations, slamming such popular concepts as cooperative learning and the so-called "middle school movement" as being detrimental to gifted students. How absurd. No idea, no educational undertaking is inherently good or bad; it is the interpretation or overapplication of the idea that makes it so.

On this point, I still agree with myself. But, immersed within this logic, I can see the inkling of an idea that seemed good then, but now does not. Specifically, I believe that we have made so many efforts to align ourselves as a field with curriculum and instruction that we have neglected the most important part of our field that makes it an entity unto itself: the unique emotional make-up of the children we label as gifted.

"First Things First" should have stressed this more, and it did not. Like many others, I believed that ingratiating ourselves to every educational innovation (that is, "fad"), from inclusion, to Multiple Intelligences, to differentiation for

29

all, would link us with colleagues in other disciplines of education in important and relevant ways. Instead, the closer we get to the likes of Howard Gardner, Jeannie Oakes, and Paul George, the fuzzier gifted child education becomes as a unique entity.

I now feel a certain affinity to separateness from other educational trends, for I understand better now than I did in 1995 that gifted children need advocates who care about them as people, not just as students.

An anachronism is something that exists although it belongs in an earlier time—a remnant, a vestige, a trace—an outdated leftover from a bygone era. If a poll were taken today of some front-line educators, I wonder how many of them would relegate our field, gifted child education, as an anachronistic oddity? My guess is that quite a few would. And, whether or not their views are based on firsthand knowledge of our field's theories and practices, an opinion is still an opinion. The vote of an ill-informed decision maker counts just as much as a vote from a well-educated advocate.

Historically, gifted child education has been a fringe specialty in most educators' eyes. Sure, there is the occasional governor or superintendent who places it in a position of prominence; but, for the most part, our field has stayed alive because of the efforts of people like us, those with a vested interest. Our jobs depend on its survival. Thus biased, gifted child educators fight a continuous uphill battle for acceptance— never more so than now, perhaps, when the trends of many educational reforms bear remarkable similarity to the ideals of gifted child education.

Examining Our Options

At this uncertain time for our field's direction, it seems to me that we have several options. We can go into our state of cyclical hibernation (remember the early '70s?), lying low in hopes of evading the incessant axes of the budget police. Or, we can take on the educational reformers who outnumber us 1,000 to 1, in a David versus Goliath battle of epic proportions (still . . . our slingshots and barbs might miss gifted child education's favorite enemies, Jeannie Oakes and Robert Slavin). Or, we can backpedal a bit, admitting our mistakes, giving back to general education that which is rightfully theirs—curriculum and instruction—and reemerge as a more focused field intent on assuring that gifted children are cared for in areas that have been too-long neglected: the social and emotional arenas and the many issues of guidance and counseling that fall under this umbrella.

So, first things first: We must own up to a situation that we have too long ignored, namely that gifted child educators are responsible for creating their own "quiet crisis."

Recognizing Our Mistakes

For being as smart as we are, we've really made some foolish mistakes. Case in point: When cooperative learning came along, we manufactured all types of evidence that this practice was detrimental to "our" kids. Of course, there are instances of abysmal things happening in the name of cooperative learning—gifted students being forced to teach others, group grades being given when only one or two students do all the work—but chalk these anomalies up to poor practice and misinterpretation of cooperative learning's basic principles. Instead, though, many gifted child educators and "experts" have discounted the whole idea of cooperative learning as rubbish, the education Edsel in our gifted garage of well-tuned Cadillacs. In doing so, we have lost the chance to work *with* our classroom-based colleagues, choosing instead to work *against* them.

Unfortunately, we have taken the same self-serving approach in dismissing the middle school movement as "anti" gifted education. How absurd! The ideas of interdisciplinary teaching, student advisory groups, and multiage teaching teams should have been embraced by gifted education experts. Instead, we were so afraid of losing our resource rooms and honors classes that we failed to see the benefits of inclusionary practices for kids who are at an age—11 through 14—when the last thing they want is to be different than, and separated from, their friends. And don't even get me started on the National Center for the Gifted and Talented's sponsored "research" that shows that classroom teachers almost never differentiate curricula for their most able students. Suffice it to say that researchers can get any results they want if they skew their questions just so.

Hopefully, our admission of our own shortsightedness will be applauded by colleagues who seem to know better than we that gifted child education does hold a place in educational reform. It's just in a different place than most gifted education specialists have spent much time recently: the general education classroom.

Better At vs. Better Than

In addition to reexamining the benefits that accrue from working with classroom colleagues, we must also reassert a basic principle that we seem to have ignored: We need to explain—and re-explain—the distinction between "better at" and "better than."

Twenty years after it should have become a nonissue, the connection with gifted child education and elitism is still alive and well. Spawned in part by our field's preference for separation over inclusion (both pragmatically and philosophically), the gifted equals elitist equation is also a by-product of our culture's discomfort with the obvious fact that children *do* differ intellectually, even if that seems to run against the "pull yourself up by your bootstraps" ideal of Western democracies. Time and again we must raise the distinction between "better at" and "better than." Specifically, even though a gifted 9-year-old is better at math or reading or whatever than most other third graders, in no way is that gifted child "better than" anyone else intrinsically. The hue and cry that "everyone is gifted in some way" comes from our deep-seated wish to equate unequals. So, rather than denying or arguing the point, a more rational approach might be to acknowledge that, although difference *do* exist in individuals' abilities to think, reason, and create, the intrinsic worth of each person is sacrosanct.

Beginning with our reason for existence in the first place—that is, that gifted children exist in our schools just as surely as gifted musicians inhabit our concert halls and gifted athletes compete in our stadiums—may seem to some to be a giant step backward in our field's evolution. On the contrary, it brings us back to our philosophical foundation, a place that holds securely both our past and our future.

Perhaps you think I'm being too pessimistic or caustic. If so, I'd take exception to the former and umbrage in the latter. Indeed, I am *most* optimistic about our field's future—but, we cannot continue operating by the same set of exclusionary practices that have relegated us to a brackish backwater, far from the mainstream of educational reform. Before others take us and our work seriously, the gifted child education field must first take an honest inventory of its own attempts to see the views from the other side.

The sole difference between a rut and a grave is the depth. Let us reawaken our passion for improving our field from the inside out, before our diagnosis by other educational reformers is DOA.

Gifted Child Today
November/December 1995

First, Do No Harm

I f there is a more difficult and imprecise area of giftedness than student identification, I don't know what it is. With so many ways to show you are
smart—test scores, teacher and parent observations, internal intensities that
far surpass the typical—you would think that school personnel would
embrace these multiple methods of locating intellectual and emotional strengths.
Sorry . . . that's too messy.

In this article, I review the absurdity of an out-of-whack identification system
that says, in effect, "IQs of 135 make you gifted; 134s need not apply." Of
course, there is nothing *wrong* with using an IQ of 135 to identify giftedness—
the child certainly didn't get that high a score by accident—but, if that is the
only way to locate giftedness, then something *is* very wrong.

I could name names, but I won't. However, the school district in question in
this article is one in which I worked for several years. It is an upper-middle-class
community that prides itself on offering a good education to all students. The
problem is, if they followed through on teacher recommendations for which students are gifted (and they collect this information each year), there would be too
many gifted children found. Heaven forbid! So, to cut down on the numbers,
the teacher recommendation forms are only considered if the IQ of 135 is first

achieved. And if the teacher recommendation is weak, but the IQ is over 135? The child is identified as gifted. However, if the IQ is 131 and the teacher recommendation is glowing, no identification is made. Go figure. My guess—actually, it's not a guess at all—is that this school district is not alone in being so incorrectly selective in identifying its gifted children.

"First, Do No Harm" is a reminder that there are real children behind these IQ numbers and teacher nominations. Once we forget that—and some school personnel do—we become myopic and cruel.

Medical doctors hang it on their walls as an oak-framed reminder of the first tenet of their profession: The Hippocratic Oath—a promise, first and foremost, to do no harm to their patients. If only the education profession had such a universal guardian for its patrons, the students we serve in our roles as teachers, counselors, and administrators. But, by not having such an overarching ethic by which we treat our students, each of us is left to determine what we believe and espouse about children—who they are, what they need, how they should be treated.

A few of us—probably too few—articulate this vision vividly, hanging it with pride for all to see our dedication and our passion. My guess, though, is that most educators would find it difficult to put into just a few words the essence of their most fundamental professional beliefs. Let me suggest a beginning: "First, do no harm."

Yes, this same Hippocratic Oath is as meaningful and powerful an opening statement for educators as it is for physicians. It means that we look first for ways to help a child's development rather than hinder it. It means leaving open the possibility that human frailties—theirs or ours—can have a profound effect on how we interpret what we see. It means seeking out the good instead of accentuating the bad.

Too often, though, I've seen instances where such a basic understanding of the human condition has been lacking. In the name of consistency or complying with state standards, some gifted children have been more maligned than assisted.

This is a most common occurrence in one of our initial activities involving highly able children: identification of giftedness. An example should illustrate my point: As a prelude to a meeting where classroom teachers were asked to nominate fifth-grade children who appeared to be gifted, a group of experienced educators caucused and came up with a list of children who manifested giftedness in their words, deeds, or thoughts. Reaching consensus (not an easy task!) resulted in the names of several students who each teacher could justify as being gifted. However, the gifted program coordinator, concerned that the teachers had used personal judgments, rather than test scores, as the basis of their decisions, informed the teachers that their choices were invalid.

"We need students who will get high scores on the WISC-3," she chided. "We need something more substantial than your opinions."

Her reasoning? Consistency. How else could she justify to parents that a child with an IQ of 135 is equally as deserving of gifted program services as a child with a 122 IQ and a rash of exemplary teacher nominations? Unable to see the forest for the trees, this coordinator harmed two constituencies: the children she was supposed to be serving and the teachers whose careful efforts were regarded as frivolous. Could this coordinator not fathom the possibility that individual children both above and below a particular IQ score might still require gifted child education services? Shame on this gatekeeper!

Similar bizarre and harmful practices occur when an underachieving child is not selected for gifted program inclusion because his or her classroom grades are low; or when a child from an ethnic or racial group apart from the majority culture is excluded due to factors that have little to do with innate intellect; or when a gifted child with a specific learning disability is bypassed for gifted program participation summarily because of the presumption that "she probably couldn't keep up with the workload."

Have we arrived at a point where we have forgotten that our mission is to promote giftedness, rather than suppress it? In the lives of too many gifted children who do not fit the "WISC-3 ideal" or who do not go to school as successfully as some of their classmates, I'm afraid the answer is "yes."

So what is the solution? One of them—easy to state, but hard for some to implement—is flexibility in our thoughts and actions. Whether it is a gifted coordinator who sees the benefits of multiple methods of student identification, or a classroom teacher who notices positive sparks in an otherwise lackluster student who has finally been allowed to pursue an area of passionate interest, flexibility is a key that unlocks unused potential. Another choice solution is humility—the ability to recognize that one's individual belief or action might not be the most appropriate. For instance, the all-knowing coordinator in chase of a 135 WISC could learn a valuable lesson in noting her own biases.

As a final example and following the medical model of the Hippocratic Oath, perhaps any educator so sure of his or her opinion about a child should get a second opinion, another view from a fresh set of eyes. For when our personal view is the only vision we can see, myopia is more common than not.

So, if our first tenet of gifted child education is "First, do no harm," then what is our second belief? Perhaps something as simple as "Find the good in each individual student" would be a natural complement to the Hippocratic Oath. But, I'm open to your personal suggestions. After all, it is your promise; they are your students.

Gifted Child Today
September/October 1999

You Should
Go Home Again

Introduction

A short article deserves just a brief overview. This piece served as the introduction to a special issue of *Understanding Our Gifted* that focused on "promising practices" in gifted child education. The curmudgeon in me (he comes out frequently) wondered which *old* practices would have to be discarded to make way for these new ones.

The primary reason I include this article is to reveal the names of some of our field's most important contributors you may not know well—Ruth Strang, Virgil Ward, Abraham Tannenbaum—and encourage you to seek out the wisdom with which they wrote about gifted children 20–50 years ago.

Your quest will be worth the effort.

"Promising Practices"—the theme of this issue of *Understanding Our Gifted*—is intriguing for several reasons. First, it implies that our knowledge of gifted and talented children is transitory, ever-changing, as we learn how better to locate and serve high-ability students. Second, "Promising Practices" also hints at the possibility that what we knew in the past, what we *did* in the past, was somehow wrong or incomplete. Lastly, "Promising Practices," as a theme, suggests forward motion and momentum—new trends that develop due to groundbreaking research by eminent scholars at esteemed universities.

So, why does the idea of promising practices leave me cold and oddly disenchanted with the field of education to which I have devoted my career these past 15 years? I'm not against progress—faster jets, medical breakthroughs, and microwave ovens are wonderful by-products of this modern age. So, what is it about the search for "new and improved" solutions to our educational dilemmas that makes me want to shout "*Stop!*" to my colleagues?

I think I know, really, but the reason sounds so . . . well, so *conservative*. (Seldom an adjective used to describe me!) So, at the risk of sounding like a charter member of the Flat Earth Society, let me reveal my secret apprehension: I am afraid that the search for promising practices will leave in the dust some *past* innovations that have been so useful. For it seems to me that our field can embrace only so many paradigms and strategies simultaneously, and, if new ones are to be included, then several old ones will have to go.

Thus, in an effort to simplify this weeding process, let me leave it up to you, my readers, to decide which of these past innovations have worn out their welcomes. And, remember, the more *old* ideas you toss out, the more room you make for new and exciting promising practices!

- Lewis Terman's idea that intelligence can be measured by an individual test and that educational adaptations can be suggested on the basis of the test results.
- Leta Hollingworth's demonstration that the gifted can learn the basic curriculum in half the day and should spend the other half on group projects and biographical study.
- Annemarie Roeper's notion that education is only complete when one considers the emotional and social needs of gifted children, not just their intellectual development.
- Ruth Strang's opinion that a parent's eyes and ears are at least as reliable and valid as objective test scores in determining a young child's special talents.
- Virgil Ward's assertion that gifted students must be presented rigorous and challenging academic options, not merely "fun and games" enrichment.
- Abraham Tannenbaum's belief that prescriptions to solve problems of "underachievement" will not work as long as the term itself is so loosely defined.

I do hope you have selected carefully, for there are many promising practices waiting in the wings.

The point, of course, is obvious: In our perpetual search for the educational equivalent of the Holy Grail, we *may* end up overlooking the fact that the answers to our questions live over our shoulder, not beyond the horizon.

Let us move forward, by all means, but let us also look back at the lives and works of our field's founders to find answers that benefit the gifted and talented children about whom we care so deeply.

Understanding Our Gifted
November/December 1992

Remembering
the Roepers

Introduction

I never had the privilege of sharing in the lives of my grandparents. My paternal "grand pere" had died before I was born, and "grand mere" lived only until I was about 7—and she lived in a town far away (about 20 miles!) so I never even spent a night in her house. My maternal grandparents had grown to hate each other and, even though they stayed together as the good Catholics they were, we never really had time to get to know each other. Pepe died early on, and Nana got "hardening of the arteries," the precursor to what we now call Alzheimer's Disease, so my mom never trusted her to stay alone with my brother and me to baby-sit.

How wonderful for me, then, that I got to "adopt" a set of grandparents when I found the field of gifted child education! George and Annemarie Roeper came into my life when I was in my 20s and they were in their 60s. "Remembering the Roepers" will detail the way we shared our lives, personally and professionally, so I won't repeat those incidents here. Instead, let me detail a time I will never forget: the night I stayed overnight at their home in northern California.

Having retired as Heads of the Roeper School in the early 1980s George and Annemarie bought a wonderful home in Oakland, California, that looked out directly onto the bay. They had invited me to speak to a local parent group and, to save money, asked if I wouldn't mind staying at their house instead of a hotel. How glad I was to do so, and we had many good talks, they brought me out for my first sushi dinner, and we got home and shared some good red wine and coffee.

The next morning—it was early—I arose and was going to have some quiet time alone on their porch, thinking that inspiration for my thank-you note would come naturally, considering the view. But, George beat me to it. He was out there, alone, sketching or writing or just thinking—I can't remember which. But, when I arrived, he stopped what he was doing and we just talked. And talked. And talked. It was then that I realized how unfortunate I was to have missed the life opportunity of sharing in the life of grand pere or Pepe.

About two years later, George and Annemarie lost that house and all their possessions in a fire that destroyed the tangible assets they had accumulated through the years. Not too long thereafter, George's health declined. He died surrounded by his children and wife; I was there only in spirit.

In reading "Remembering the Roepers," I hope you come to understand the beauty they have brought into my life—and continue to, in many ways. I served on the Roeper School's Board of Trustees for seven years and continue to chat with Annemarie about gifted children and the lives they lead.

Thanks, George and Annemarie, for raising me right!

I t is difficult to appreciate fully the significance of life's coincidences until they are seen from a distance, over time. Such was the case in my own life and career as they relate to my introduction to the Roepers, their school, their work, and the journal that bears their name.

It was in 1978. I was just beginning my graduate study of gifted child education, having spent the previous few years teaching in a program for children with learning and behavior problems. During my teaching career, there was one young boy, Matt, who used to toss his desk regularly—but I had been trained to handle such outbursts. What I was perplexed by, though, was how to handle Matt's intellect; for every day, Matt would complete, flawlessly, several papers and projects that he found interesting, and shoot the other papers back to my desk in the shape of paper planes—Matt's form of personal air mail. Usually in red crayon, Matt would have written the word *irrelevant* on top of the page. Generally, he was right—they were.

So, for me, it was time to learn more about children like Matt. Thus, I began my doctoral program at the University of Connecticut. While there, I ran across a journal—*Roeper Review*—that had begun publication within months of the start of my Ph.D. program—coincidence. For me, always enamored by the beauty of words, it was love at first sight. For as I read about the journal's mission and its humble beginnings as a parent newspaper for a school of which I had never heard—Roeper City and

County School—I began to see Matt's image reflected in the pages. Connecting intellect with emotion and placing the goal of "caring to learn" on an equal basis with "learning to care," the articles and editorials taught me much about this field of study that was eventually to become my career.

"Imagine," I wondered, "what a wonderful place that school must be. Perhaps some day I'll visit it." The very next year—coincidence again—my doctoral advisor, Joe Renzulli, was unable to attend a conference at which he was to present—a conference to be held at the Roeper School. In his place, scared stiff yet eager to try, I presented my first large-group presentation on a panel that included Dorothy Sisk, Harry Passow, and John Feldhusen. In the audience were the Roepers, listening intently, smiling and guiding me with an unspoken message of assurance—something, I came to learn later, that they had done for students for more than a generation at the school that bears their name. Later, at dinner and through a tour of their school on a crisp, October morning, I came to know better the two people who have meant so much to so many—George and Annemarie Roeper.

A history of their backgrounds. Having escaped from the terrors of World War II Nazi Germany, the Roepers came to the U.S. to operate the Editha Sterba Nursery School and to integrate the Roeper Grade School, both located in a rented house in Highland Park, Michigan. That was in 1941. Ten children enrolled the first year. With borrowed money and more than a little help from their friends, the Roepers purchased land and an old house—the Stephen's mansion—that today is still part of the Roeper School's Bloomfield Hills Campus. That was 1946; 90 students were now attending the school.

In 1956, the Gifted Child Institute was held at the Roeper School, chaired by Dr. Harry Passow. From that institute, a decision was made to focus the Roeper School expressly on the needs of gifted children, up through sixth grade. Within the next decade, junior high and high school grades were added, and enrollment blossomed into the hundreds. Today—bigger, stronger, better—the Roeper School includes two campuses and enrolls children from nursery school through 12th grade.

The importance of the Roeper philosophy, the Roeper difference, can probably best be expressed by children who attended that school and their parents. Some sample comments:

"I have been going to Roeper for five years and it is special to me because it is noncompetitive, and that affects me because it makes it so I can mess up and always try again."

"It makes me feel like I'm not just a little kid. When I was 7, I thought the only way to solve a problem was to fight it out. I now know that isn't a good way."

"In the future, I may put my children in Roeper, or, if I build a school, I may make it like Roeper."

"My son can write a paper with 35 footnotes, and he also knows that everybody deserves his respect."

"There's no division between jocks and intellectuals. It's assumed everybody has a body and a mind."

More than any other testimonials, these comments give firm evidence of how a philosophy of education can be the same as a philosophy of life. *Educare*, the Latin root of our word *education*, means "to lead to" or "to bring forth," not "to fill up." And *teacher*, from the Germanic word *taikjam*, means "to show." How beautifully and effectively the Roepers have exemplified those ideas, both in their school and in their daily lives.

Now residing in Oakland, California, the Roepers continue to enhance our world in so many visible ways. For example:

- They remain as executive editors of our field's most complete and respected journal, *Roeper Review*.
- Annemarie and George have been actively involved in the nuclear disarmament movement, and they have been involved for decades in the now-trendy topic of global and intercultural education, which has always been a component of their school's curriculum—even for nursery school students.
- Annemarie has written what is, to me, the most comprehensive and common-sense definition of giftedness in our literature: "Giftedness is a greater awareness, a greater sensitivity, and a greater ability to understand and transform perceptions into intellectual and emotional experiences." She gives our society the real-life perception that gifted children must be seen as "average with gifts," not "superior with faults"; that underlying each gift or talent is a child who needs, and wants, to simply belong and to be perceived as being as human as the next person.
- Annemarie's newest book, *Educating Children for Life: The Modern Learning Community*, recently released just this year, explains beautifully and completely how she and George perceive the lifelong process of education. In the book's acknowledgements, Annemarie writes, "This book is the result of living my life."

And that life, that vision, that dream shared by George and Annemarie Roeper are as alive today as they were in 1941, when 10 lucky, lucky children were entrusted to the care of the Roepers and their school.

Ethologist Jane Goodall, another individual with a vision of the world as it could and should be, once wrote:

The way in which my own life touches those of so many others, those I know and thousands of those I don't, has strengthened my belief that each human has his or her own unique place in the ocean of existence.

George and Annemarie Roeper, having long ago crossed an ocean to attain the freedom that they know all the world's people—children, too—deserve, are visionaries who have made our field of study—indeed, our world—a more beautiful place where everyone—everyone—is of consequence.

Remember Matt? The paper-airplane-throwing kid whom I taught so long ago? I lost touch with him, yet I hope and, indeed, I believe that he is doing well.

Thanks to George and Annemarie Roeper, I have learned (this is no coincidence) that underlying all our goals and objectives is the need to provide respect—to Matt, as an individual, and to our global neighbors, most of whom we shall never meet. From this base, everything else that our field of gifted child education espouses will flow naturally. Or, as George Roeper wrote back in 1966, for the children of Roeper, "You have learned a great deal in our school academically, as well as personally. Your strength is thinking . . ."

To George and Annemarie Roeper, our heartfelt gratitude for sharing your vision, your philosophy, and your love with the imperfect world that we all inhabit.

Advanced Development Journal
January 1991

"You From Around These Parts?"

How an Outsider Might View Gifted Child Education

I tend to use life circumstances to prime the pump for my writing ideas. This article emanated out of envy: My college-age son, Matt, was doing a semester of his schooling in Europe, and he detailed his adventures there in such ways that I grew envious. Matt wrote home frequently via e-mail, letting us in on at least *some* of the experiences he was enjoying (my bet is there are also many untold stories to this day!).

I hadn't read this article since it was published in 1998, probably because I was never keen on its title—even though I'm the one who came up with it. But, as I read it again for this compilation, I was surprised how much I liked it. It brings up issues and concerns familiar to those of us for whom gifted child education is an obsession, not just a career choice—identification of minority students, appropriate programming in the regular classroom, early childhood giftedness—and it was designed to make the reader—you—just a little bit uncomfortable with the status quo in our schools. It made *me* uncomfortable just rereading it!

Chew on the content and see if you come up with the same conclusion that I have: that, for my son, his school years were filled with part-time excellence. We can do better, can we not?

My son Matt, a college junior, recently landed in Amsterdam. He is embarking on a four-month adventure of foreign study and travel, with emphasis on the latter. He sent me an e-mail just last week stating that he was going to Switzerland for a few days. When I asked why he was traveling there on his first weekend in Europe, he responded with terse clarity: "Because I can."

Matt's semester abroad got me to thinking about my own journeys and the learning that always occurred when I was a stranger in a strange place. Whether it was a barrier of language or a foreign currency that looked like "funny money" from a board game, each day brought new experiences that linger on even today as cherished memories.

My mind then wandered from these literal journeys across the globe to the ones I have taken as a professional—the highways and backroads of a career that began in 1975 as a teacher of mentally retarded children and that have led to the jobs I enjoy today as a university professor and a teacher of gifted students. It got me to thinking: How would a visitor who knew nothing about the way we educate gifted children in our nation interpret this field of study we call our own? What would make sense? What would cause questions or concerns? If you weren't from around these parts, this enterprise of gifted child education might appear very foreign.

Educating Terry

Lesson #1—Identification

"It's good to see you, Ms. Terry. Have you had a chance to walk around our schools?"

"Oh yes, Ms. Contrary. I especially enjoyed the openness of the children—particularly the young ones. They were very willing to talk to me about their work."

"And our gifted programs—Have you had a chance to observe them?"

"Indeed I have!"

"So, I'm sure you must have some questions."

"Actually, I'll have questions later. Right now, though, I just have some observations. Perhaps you can clarify how to interpret them for me."

Ms. Contrary nods willingly, ready to help her visitor understand the benefits of the gifted program for the children it serves.

"My first observation, Ms. Contrary, is that while everyone in your school looks very diverse, your gifted classes look very . . . White."

"Well, not for lack of trying, Ms. Terry. We seek diversity in our gifted programs, but we only admit children who meet certain criteria—who reach particular 'cut-offs' on the tests that we administer."

"So, children are gifted only when they perform well on tests with paper and pencil? What about your young artists or the creative children who think in many directions at once? What about children who come from backgrounds that are very different from those who develop the tests? What about—"

"Let me stop you there, Ms. Terry. But I assure you we always look for ways to admit children from various backgrounds. But, we *must* maintain standards, you know, for everyone's sake."

Lesson #2—The Curriculum

Now that Ms. Terry understands that gifted programs would never be discriminatory toward children whose abilities can be compromised by life circumstances or learning barriers like dyslexia, she has some observations about the connection between the gifted program and the rest of the school's curriculum.

"I've enjoyed watching the children learn in their gifted classes. So many projects and good ideas! Children were working independently on topics of interest to them. Their teacher acted more like a facilitator than a lecturer, and almost all the children responded positively to the intellectual freedom they were given."

"Yes, we're very proud of that. Our resource room program has always been strong."

"And when the children go back to their classrooms, they can continue to work on these projects?"

"Well, not exactly. You see, they have a regular curriculum they must follow in each grade level."

"Are they not already capable of that work?"

"Well, yes, in some cases. But, it is so difficult for our gifted specialists to communicate with classroom teachers. There's so little time."

"This is curious. It seems to me that, if these gifted children are so engaged in their learning, they could bring this enthusiasm back to their other classrooms. Also, it would seem that many more children could benefit from these creative lessons going on in the resource room. Too, if children are gifted all week, why do they only spend an hour a day with a gifted education teacher? And the classroom teachers, shouldn't they be working with the gifted teacher so that—"

"There you go again, Ms. Terry! You just don't understand the constraints of teaching in today's schools. We have standards to meet, state tests to pass, and parents to please. What you're talking about would take more time, more money, and many more people."

"But, wouldn't the children be better served?"

Lesson #3—The Outlying Years

It appears obvious that Ms. Terry has some pretty naïve ideas about the realities of public education in America. Instead of praising us for what we do well, she criticizes us for things we neglect to address.

"How is it, Ms. Contrary, that children come to be gifted in fourth grade and they stop being gifted once they enter your high school?"

"That's absurd, Ms. Terry. Children are gifted throughout their lives, not just for one small portion of their schooling."

"It's interesting, then, that special services for gifted children do not begin until they are 9 years old. Cannot parents see high abilities in their children before then? And teachers?"

"We prefer to *not* label and identify children at too young an age. The stigma of labels and all that."

"But, don't young gifted children often identify *themselves*? By their vocabularies, their intricate thought processes, their heightened emotions and sensitivities?"

"Well, yes, but . . ."

"And what about students in high school?"

"We offer Advanced Placement classes and an honors curriculum."

"Do you offer creative options or advanced options for leadership or community service? Do you have any programs for smart students who do not like school and are failing? So many questions I have!"

"It sounds like your visit has left you frustrated, Ms. Terry."

"Funny, that's exactly the thought I had about the children in your programs."

Bon Voyage

When traveling, it is always important to remember that you are a guest in another person's home. It is essential to observe customs different from your own with an open mind and an obliging attitude. It does a traveler good to consider that what works well in one place may not be important in another.

But, the traveler, the outsider, often has a vision of the possible that should cause the folks at home to be a little less comfortable with whatever status quo they are maintaining. In gifted child education, this status quo has lingered on for a generation, my son's generation. And, as he enjoys the freshness and wonder that are sure to accompany his adventures in Switzerland, Poland (his next weekend trip), and beyond, I can only hope that he is equipped with the tools that part-time excellence in schooling have afforded him.

We can do more and we can do better for our gifted children, and it doesn't take an outsider to tell us so.

Gifted Child Today
March/April 1998

Part Three

Reflections From a Recycled Teacher

W hen I was 6 years old, I declared to anyone who was within earshot that, when I grew up, I wanted to be a teacher. People just kind of smiled and nodded, knowing that someone with "my potential" would never choose to go into such a low-status field. They were polite enough not to say anything out loud, but it was their quiet discomfort that came through most vividly.

I didn't state my career objectives to most people much beyond that, and I did pretend to listen when relatives and well-meaning others informed me that "with my brains, I should be a doctor."

So, I did become a doctor. A Ph.D. Unfortunately, this was *not* the kind of doctor Aunt Peggy (among others) had in mind.

"I'm a *teaching* doctor, Aunt Peggy," I remember telling her.

"We are proud of you, Jim," she shot back. "It's just that we wanted you to be the kind of doctor who really helps people."

That was the last conversation that Aunt Peggy and I have ever had, back in 1981.

But, by 1990, I began to wonder if, maybe, Aunt Peggy was right after all. I had been teaching at the university level for more than a decade, and I felt that I was affecting no one. I was becoming both bored and boring, and I could not imagine fumbling my way through a career, a profession, that I had cherished since I was 6 years old.

"I could sell shoes . . . or insurance," I told myself. "But, teaching for 15 more years . . . ?"

So, I went to the dean of my college with a proposition: I wished to leave my tenured university position for one year and re-enter the world of public schools as a teacher. Maybe, I thought, that would revitalize my energy and recharge my intellectual battery. I did not have any jobs lined up, but I would start applying for them as soon as she gave me the go-ahead to proceed with my *paid* leave of absence.

"You can have a leave of absence," the dean said, "but they are always unpaid. Good luck in finding a job."

The specifics are spelled out in some of the following articles, so I won't repeat them here. Suffice it to say I did secure a teaching job as a fourth-grade teacher for 1991–1992 and another one in 1997–1998. In the intervening years, I have worked one day a week as a teacher of gifted children in grades 4–8, a position I continue to enjoy today.

Thanks to the kids and my many fine K–12 teaching colleagues, I feel I am a better professor of education than I have ever been. And, if the cards and notes I get from my students—in college and eighth grade—are accurate indicators, I am even meeting Aunt Peggy's standard of being the kind of doctor who really helps people. At least I'm trying!

Fourth Grade,
Seventh Heaven

Introduction

I had sent out over 40 requests for teaching applications and received back only about 7 in the mail. I had four job interviews scheduled and was not called back for second interviews by the first three. It was crunch time: Either the last interview would go well, or I would probably be looking strangers straight in the eye, asking them if they wanted fries with their burger.

Luckily for me, the fourth time was a charm: I was hired to teach 26 fourth graders of all abilities in a "self-contained mobile unit" (a trailer) in a suburb of Cleveland. The following story relates what I learned about children, curriculum, and teaching gifted children in the regular classroom by sharing 185 magical days with the class of 2000.

Some History

When I was completing my master's degree in teaching emotionally disturbed children, my practicum supervisor demanded that I meet him at the school's entrance and usher him to my classroom. I thought this a bit odd and formal, yet, since there is no one more vulnerable than a graduate student attempting to pass a course, I complied.

Once in my classroom, he just sat there silently—a stark contrast to the noise and occasional mayhem that permeated my children's behaviors. My supervisor seldom stayed more than 30 minutes; his suggestions for improvement were few. At the lesson's conclusion, he insisted that I accompany him to the exit. Again, I complied.

It was only after discussing this situation with some seasoned doctoral students that I learned the reason for this supervisor's behavior: He had never taught emotionally disturbed children and was afraid of the prospect of doing so. From that day on, any shreds of professional respect I had for that man were gone. How could he help me be a good teacher when he had never stood in my shoes in an effort to do the same?

Sixteen years later, Ph.D. firmly in hand and a tenured professorship at a fine university, I felt I was becoming a clone of that supervisor who had taught me so little. Who was I to tell my graduate students that many strategies used in gifted child education (GCE) could be applied in regular class settings? I'd never done it! How could I know the complexities of infusing creative and critical thinking into basic skill subjects? I was never responsible for doing so myself!

With each passing year, I grew more aware that I was becoming a professional anachronism; a guy steeped in the educational theories and practices of a bygone era who wouldn't know a fifth-grade curriculum if it slapped him in the face. I needed a change, both for inner credibility and for the sake of my students' own growth.

The Searches

So, with a sense of hopeful risk, I took an unpaid leave of absence from Kent State for the 1991–92 school year and went searching for a job—a "real" job, a teaching job. In my first three interviews (I sent out about 40 applications), I explained that I was hoping to take the best of what I'd learned in GCE and apply it in an elementary classroom, any grade between 3 and 8.

I got very nice rejection letters from these three school districts. Still, no job. I was losing hope and, considering the omen of an unpaid mortgage, I was also losing sleep. In a valiant effort to ward off discouragement, my wife assured me of two things: First, I was doing the right thing in looking for a return to classroom teaching. Secondly, she told me that, if I found myself in an employment pinch, Burger King always needed closers. (Humor *does* help!)

But, then, thanks to a long-ago contact in a town 20 miles from home, I had another interview and, this time, a job offer! I'd be a fourth-grade teacher at Orchard

Middle School in Solon, Ohio. My classroom would be imported from Indiana—a modular unit (i.e., a trailer) attached, like an appendix, to our school of 900 students. I couldn't wait to start!

Some Questions

There were some general concerns I shared, I'm sure, with every teacher who anxiously awaits the opening day of classes: Will my students like and respect me? Will I be able to meet their individual needs? Will parents and colleagues support my efforts? Will I really have recess duty every day?

But, in my case, there were some additional concerns. I had made this decision to return to the classroom for three main reasons: I missed teaching children, I needed professional renewal, and I needed to discover how much of GCE applied with 26 children of varied abilities and talents.

Specifically, these were the questions I hoped to answer:

- Could I teach without textbooks, substituting in their place the many resources available from the publishers of "enrichment" materials that I'd often touted in my in-service workshops?
- Would I be able to "compact" the curriculum without all the piles of paperwork that often seem to accompany this process?
- Would I be able to combine affective learning into my content-based lessons?
- Could independent study and theme-based units become an everyday occurrence in my classroom?

Maybe it should have been obvious to me from the start that these questions did not have definitive, "one-size-fits-all" answers. But, to a recycled teacher like me, whose base of reality was teaching graduate courses twice a week, common sense was not so common. Indeed, I discovered within the first week of classroom teaching that, if it were clear-cut solutions I sought, I'd not find them in classroom teaching. For like a raw onion, wherein each thin layer reveals yet another one just beneath it, I found that my questions far outnumbered my answers. Within days of the school year's onset, I realized, anew and first-hand, just how amazingly complex is the art of good teaching.

Some Answers

As a professor, I had always prided myself on keeping my finger on the pulse of classroom teaching by observing student teachers and visiting classrooms as a guest speaker. Now, in retrospect, I see just how effectively I had pulled the wool over my own eyes for far too many years. For there is no way to understand the complexities of the classroom teacher's role other than by doing what they do each year: teach very diverse students for 185 days.

So, as my year in the classroom ended, I had some answers (tentative, to be sure) to the self-imposed questions with which I had entered my trailer on that hot, hot day in August. Here is some of what I learned:

1. Teaching without textbooks is not only possible, it is preferable—and not just for gifted students. We are all aware of how mediocre most textbooks are for highly able children, but we must also be aware that students with less aptitude are equally as turned off to them. Face it: Texts are dull, programmed, lifeless. Melissa is a case in point. When she used her math text to try to understand a new concept, her eyes glazed over and her mind clamped shut. ("I hate math!" was her daily reaction.) But, when actively engaged in math explorations ("How many giant steps would it take to circle our school? How many baby steps?"), even Melissa acknowledged the fun of numbers.

Admittedly, most of my weekends were tied up in planning original lessons that used resources such as films, magazines, hands-on experiences, and guest speakers. But, when the week was through and my assessment of my students' progress showed that, indeed, they did learn some of the things I'd hoped they would, the effort seemed worth it.

Was it tiring? You bet. Did some of my lessons flop? Of course! Still, when I considered the alternative—page by page, chapter by chapter—I realized that my students deserved more than the predigested curriculum brought forth in textbooks.

2. Compacting the curriculum is less a procedure than it is a mindset. When I first learned about curriculum compacting, the procedure was tied into all manner of color-coded forms. I was supposed to document every step of the process, assuring both consistency and accountability. In my graduate courses, I emphasized the importance of this ritualistic paper chase, yet, when I visited by students' classrooms, I saw no evidence of their use.

Now I know why.

Compacting has very little to do with forms and very much to do with philosophy. All I needed to do was listen to David describe photosynthesis to know that it was okay for him to move on to a different topic. Too, if I gave Letitia permission to write her own book of poetry and short stories, I was pretty much assured that she was also refining her spelling and syntax skills.

Informally, without a lot of hubbub or hassle, I just let compacting occur naturally, which is what good teachers have done for generations. At times I felt a twinge of guilt that I should be more concerned about precision and documentation; but, during the year, there was very little need for such attention to detail. Throughout the school, I saw my colleagues doing the same thing, day in and day out. They didn't call it "compacting"; in fact, they didn't call is anything. What they did was merely adjust the curriculum in a manner that took advantage of the individual and collective talents possessed by their students.

The mark of a true professional is knowing when to act like one; to follow one's instincts about what works best for individuals students. More teachers than not do this, I believe. It's time they got some credit for their actions—and some support. Indeed, education professors like me need to allow ourselves to do something in our graduate courses that we too seldom do: listen instead of lecture; seek answers from students, rather than dictating to them how they can improve their classroom practices. In fact, if I were in charge of the world of higher education, I'd require education professors to return to classroom teaching at least once every 10 years in order to retain their university tenure. In their place, excellent classroom teachers would teach university "methods" courses now in such need of a practical, hands-on treatment.

3. Any division between cognitive and affective learning is artificial. I'd been introduced to Bloom's Taxonomy in 1973 during an undergraduate course on social studies instruction. Krathwohl's Affective Taxonomy came years later, somewhere in a graduate counseling course. I wish that someone had pointed out to me how similar the taxonomies were and how it is impossible to teach or construct a lesson that does not involve both types of learning.

Going into fourth grade, I realized that I was teaching in (to use Leta Hollingworth's term) "the golden age of the intellect," a time in children's lives when everything is an adventure. I introduced my students to the ideas of Bloom and Krathwohl. I told them that my lessons with them were going to require use of both their minds and their hearts. No one was going to get away with thinking without feeling, or vice versa. So, in social studies, we eschewed the use of texts and devised "Project Person to Person," a yearlong study of people and the lives they led.

Our first major project began when we found a local man who had become paralyzed when someone hit him in the head with a brick that had been thrown through a car window. We "adopted" this man and his family, who visited our class throughout the year to thank us for the cards, letters, flowers, and fundraising donations. Also, we sent stuffed animals to a family shelter in Cleveland in February, a time when, according to Billy, "nobody thinks of poor people, 'cause the holidays are over." In science, we designed ecological calendars and distributed them to second graders, telling the importance of preserving the Earth. In math, we wrote fairy tales using geometric shapes as the main characters, producing one-act skits that introduced kindergarten children to the magic of both math and monsters. In writing, we traded poems and stories with another fourth-grade class in Australia for editing and comments. Both here and "Down Under" some of the students' work was published in national magazines.

In each of these instances, I tried to remind my students that the greatest measure of success was not the grade they earned on their projects, but the personal satisfaction they derived from them. I told them that, if they fell in love with "learning" instead of "earning," there was no way possible that they couldn't succeed in school and in life. I mentioned to them that they'd run into teachers and classmates who thought that school was something you had to do to help you when you got older, but that they should always remember that today is the most important day of all.

Each student—gifted or not—has a personal investment in being a little better, a little smarter, today than yesterday. By combining affective and cognitive growth within the curriculum, children begin to see their places in the vast ocean of existence.

And something else happened. In watching young children change for the better the world that they shall someday inherit, I, too, found a chance to grow and learn. Within myself, I found a renewed willingness to look at the world through the eyes of children—through a lens that was neither tinted with pessimism nor stained with complexity. Hope and simplicity replaced the cynicism that is so easy to adopt once one leaves the innocence of childhood. Thanks to them, I wallowed in a world where everything is possible. (I'd like to think a part of that lesson still remains in me.)

Tentative Conclusions

I learned more about teaching gifted children in one year as a "retrofitted" fourth-grade teacher than I did in all my college courses combined. I learned that there is really no such thing as a "gifted curriculum" and that higher level thinking benefits both the ablest students and those who struggle academically. I learned that interdisciplinary teaching allows each student to shine in his or her own light without falling under the shadow of someone who is a quicker thinker. I learned that classroom teachers frequently use the methods and materials of gifted education without ever having taken a graduate course on how to do so—they just call it "good teaching." I learned that my initial instincts were right: Gifted children can be taught in a regular classroom setting and, in fact, most teachers prefer this venue over resource or pull-out programs.

Most importantly, I learned that the surest way to become stale as an educator is to cloister myself away in the ivory tower of higher education, pretending I know how difficult a job educators have because "I used to be a teacher myself." Get real.

My job as a fourth-grade teacher ended the day that all my kids got promoted to fifth grade. It was one of the happiest, and saddest, days of my life. Experiment over, it was time to return to Kent State.

However, thanks to a bit of finagling and flexible scheduling, I have been able to maintain my contact at Orchard School, teaching fifth and sixth graders every Wednesday for the past three years. My students, now seventh graders, have grown taller in more ways than one. I'd like to think the same is true for their used-to-be teacher-in-a-trailer who realized that fourth grade can, indeed, be seventh heaven.

Roeper Review
May/June 1995

Turn Left Down
the First Paved Road

Introduction

About five years after my adventure as a fourth-grade teacher in suburban Cleveland, I was eligible for one of higher education's greatest perks: a sabbatical. Like other faculty before me, I would be given the chance to have a full semester off from my university responsibilities, with pay, in order to explore my field and refresh my energies.

The trick was this: If I took a sabbatical in the spring semester, I would actually have off from mid-December through mid-August, thanks to the quirkiness of university calendars. I pondered the possibilities: I could travel overseas under the guise of investigating international approaches to serving gifted children (it is *always* important to manufacture a legitimate-sounding reason for international travel). Or, I could plan out and write a book about what we could learn from the Bahamian approaches to teaching (from my field-based site in Nassau, of course). Or, I could do something real, like teaching in a situation unlike any I had taught in before. I chose this last option, landing in a small town in rural South Carolina in January 1997.

The first thing I noticed was me: I was the only White adult male in this building of 800 kindergarten through fifth-grade students. My necktie was so foreign a piece of cloth that three timid fourth-grade boys asked if they could come up and touch it, since they had never felt one before.

"It's soft," they said, "but does it hurt to be so tight around your neck?"

I lied and said, "No."

That was only one of many adventures I had during my seven-month stay in this year-round school in the middle of cornfields and tobacco barns. I hope you enjoy some of the scenery, both educational and visual, on this first paved road.

I n February 1997, while on sabbatical from Kent State University, I returned to my roots as a classroom teacher. For seven months, I volunteered in a fourth- and fifth-grade classroom in a year-round school in South Carolina. I had never worked in a town so rural and so Southern. Little did I realize in February that the life lessons I would learn in that magical school would teach me so much about both the beauty and pangs of childhood.

What follows are excerpts from my journal, which I have titled "Turn Left Down the First Paved Road," which was the final travel direction given to me by the school's principal. Included are stories of children, tales of teachers, visions of life. Indeed, as I reflect back on my time in this small Southern town, I realize now that I learned much more than I taught, and I thank the children, parents, and educators who shared pieces of their lives with me.

I am now back at Kent State University as a professor of education, but in my continuing commitment to learn all I can from children, I teach one day per week at Dodge Middle School in Twinsburg, Ohio. If I have anything to say about it, I will never again be more than a week away from the realities of classroom teaching.

I hope you enjoy these excerpts and, further, that you travel down some new roads of your own.

Turn Left Down the First Paved Road

When I called to get directions to the school, I knew I was in for a rural experience when the principal told me to "turn left down the first paved road" once I had already traveled down three other roads without names. A mile later, past tobacco farms and an ancient cemetery, I noticed a sign for a school crossing, the first sign that, indeed, I was not lost. Pulling into the circular driveway, I was anxious: Would I fit in? Would the teachers accept me? Would the kids like me? Even though I've taught for 20 years, these questions were as important for me as they would be for a first-time teacher. I took a deep breath and walked into what would be my school home for the next four months.

I asked for the principal, Catherine Chester, a Black woman with a voice that far outbeamed my own.

"She'll be a few minutes," I was told. "She's busy doing a teacher observation."

So, I settled comfortably into the living room furniture that comprised the front office. There was a blonde-haired boy, a third grader, sitting uncomfortably in a comfortable chair outside of the assistant principal's office. He was in trouble for some 8-year-old form of indiscretion, but, to Monroe (that was his name), it didn't matter much. As he told the school secretary, "I stayed up 'till midnight watching a movie and I'm moving away tomorrow, anyway." Still, he was as nervous as an Amish woman at an Avon convention. So was I, if for different reasons.

When the secretary went back to her desk, Monroe looked toward me. I looked back. Our eyes met in mutual stares of curiosity, and, when I gave a half wave to acknowledge our silent relationship, he waved back and smiled. I would never see him again, yet we both shared our sense of nervousness. I was beginning a school he was leaving, yet we both felt a bit of unease as we waited for the school's leaders.

Mrs. Chester's voice arrived way before she did. Dressed all in green, she looked up like a ripe olive. She shook my hand as hard as any man ever has. Her office, as gentle as was her smile, invited me to relax. I took a seat in a rocking chair opposite her desk, and we began to talk. Within two minutes, we were interrupted by an assistant of hers who needed signatures and information, "Otherwise, we won't get that grant!" Mrs. Chester signed without reading. Then, just as we began to talk again, a second-grade girl ran into the office.

"Miss Chester! Miss Chester! I not be getting in trouble on the bus anymore!" She beamed with pride and wrapped her arms around the principal's neck.

"That's great news, Miwanda. I'm so proud of you."

"And I not be cussin', too," Miwanda continued. "I be good."

Another quick hug, a glance toward me, and then Miwanda scurried out of the room. She'd made her point, and she was proud.

"That's who we've got," Mrs. Chester said, "kids who don't know any better than to interrupt two adults who aren't yelling at each other."

Mrs. Chester and I talked about the kids in her school. There were 800 of them, and 90% received both free breakfast and lunch. They came from homes that were a mixture of yesterday and today: dirt floors with VCRs; empty refrigerators and cellular phones; tar-paper roofs protecting used Cadillacs. If these kids were confused about what should be of value to them, it was easy to see why.

When I walked into my first class, a fourth grade of 21 kids, I stood out in so many ways. I was tall, White, and male, a triad of characteristics that described no one else at Dodge. Also, I was from the North, a place as foreign as another country to kids who had not even seen an ocean that existed only 18 miles away. I told them I was from Ohio—I might as well have said Mars. In the minds of these kids, the two were equidistant.

The teacher, Mrs. Jones, continued teaching about parts of speech and correct sentence structure. As her students struggled to figure out why the name of a magazine had to be underlined in a sentence, I thought to myself how unimportant this skill was in a school where few of the students had ever seen or read a magazine outside of school. Still, Mrs. Jones was kind and patient and encouraging. Students would remember her for her qualities, not her instruction. And that was okay.

Students gawked and giggled as they looked my way. I'm sure they were asking themselves why this pale guy wearing a tie was spending time in their classroom. (The tie, by the way, was intentional. I wanted students to see that dressing up was a form of respect for them. Funny, three of the boys touched the tie—they'd never done that before—and asked if it hurt to be around my neck.)

Minutes later, I was working with students. First, I met with Jerome, a 10-year-old who had read for the first time last week. As he read again the book whose words, by now, he had memorized, he smiled with unmistaken pride. He closed the soft cover of the thin book, and I asked for a favor: "Gimme a high five, Jerome. You did a great job!" His small, black hand brushed against mine, and our eyes met with a smile. Jerome was a success, and he was happy.

Then, I spoke with Stephanie, who told me how honored she was to be in the Explorers Program (the school's small gifted program). Then there was James, who thought I must be some kind of professional athlete "because I looked rich and tall." Bryan was next, a cartoonist whose father had died when he was 2 and whose illustrations always had a reference to a far-away dad. Each child had a story to tell, and, over these next few months, I expected to hear them all.

Then, fifth grade and a teacher who was as loosely structured as Mrs. Jones was sequential. Her class of 24 was rowdy and tall—they seemed as if they should be in junior high school. Nine of the students, I was told, had been recommended in earlier grades for classes for emotionally disturbed children, yet none had left the regular class setting. This year, today, they were all with Mrs. Ward . . . and me. We're talking a true test of skills and patience!

I was introduced as a visitor who would be spending the rest of the year in a class, and I noticed a swell of verbal activity among many of the students. They were asking each other questions their polite Southern heritage would not allow them to ask me directly: "Who was I?" "Why their class?" "Was I fun?" "Was I strict?"

In their math lesson on symmetry, I produced a figure that required producing a mirror image. Most tried, some succeeded. Then, I roamed the room checking on the autobiographies that each child was writing. Ashley shared with me his skills in sports; Kristen wrote about her father who had died when she was 3 (he had hanged himself in his prison cell); Martin wrote about his love of sports cars and his hatred for school (already he had been suspended for 25 days this year); Ralph wouldn't talk to me, suspicious as he was, I'd guess, of any stranger who had questions about his life.

When it was time for gym class, kids asked me if I'd join in (which I will next week) and if I'd stay to share lunch with them. I felt honored, and I told them so. They just smiled and said they'd see me next week.

To tell you the truth, I can't wait.

What did I learn in this one day in the classroom? First, I learned that it is a place I need to be on a regular basis to keep in touch with the realities of life and childhood. Second, I learned that children want to succeed in any way they can—and, with your help, they will. Third, I learned that, despite all the negative press about teachers getting physical with their students, there is still a place for a high five, a hug, and a warm handshake between two people who share the common bonds of humanity.

Dividing Fractions

The last time I struggled to divide fractions, I was in fifth grade as a student, not a teacher. But, yesterday, Mrs. Ward rekindled my aversion to this archaic process as I watched her attempt the impossible: trying to teach this skill on a warm, spring afternoon to learners even more reluctant than I was at age 11.

In reviewing the complicated process of reconfiguring a mixed numeral into an improper fraction while also reminding students to "turn upside down" the other fraction after having, of course, changed the division into a multiplication operation, Mrs. Ward lost at least half the class. Many just looked up and said, "Huh?"

While I sat wondering why it was still necessary to perform this mathematical problem that had no need beyond fifth grade, Ralph approached me quietly: "Mr. D, I don't understand this."

I looked up at Ralph, a young man whose interest in matters academic was generally low. Preferring the anonymity of doing no work to the recognition of being wrong too often when he tried it, Ralph surprised me with his statement.

"I wanna know how to do these," he said, pointing at page 354 of his math text. His dark eyes connected with my own. "I gotta know how to do this."

Grabbing a pencil and a few sheafs of blank paper, Ralph and I left the classroom and retreated to an unused corner of the school library. As the classroom door clicked behind us, Ralph ran ahead to get a table, "a good one in the back." I wondered, did he want quiet for us or privacy for himself?

I began my one-on-one instruction by telling Ralph I was going to talk through the problem while he watched and listened. I told him I was going to do the first two problems right, but I would make a mistake on the third problem.

"I want you to be a detective, Ralph. Tell me when I mess up."

This intrigued Ralph. "You want me to tell you when you mess up?"

"Yup. You better watch me carefully."

"But you a teacher . . ."

"So?"

". . . And I can tell you when you mess up and not get into trouble?"

"I'm counting on that, Ralph."

He grinned with both his mouth and his eyes. "This all right," he said, nodding his head approvingly.

I began reviewing the problem, instructing Ralph to stop me as soon as he saw my mistake. While I correctly changed the mixed numeral and converted the division sign to an x, Ralph observed carefully, saying nothing. When I did not invert the second divisor, Ralph stopped me.

"Hold it right there!" he warned.

"What'd I do?" I tried to feign surprise.

"You messed up. You didn't turn that number upside down."

"Show me."

Ralph continued the operation correctly, telling me that I should have known better. "Who your teacher?" he asked. "She should be fired." Ralph, obviously enjoying this role reversal, had admonished my math skills while displaying his own.

"Might as well just finish the problem, Ralph. You're doing a better job than I."

This give-and-take and the casual banter that crossed between us continued on for another 10 problems. We corrected each other with exaggerated word jousts.

"My, my . . . and they call you a fifth grader," I'd say.

"I can't believe you a teacher," Ralph would volley back, savoring this chance to equate our skills, to indulge our humor.

We returned to class just in time to receive the night's homework assignment: 10 more problems with mixed numbers and fractions. Ralph took one gladly, immediately beginning the first problem when he returned to his seat. Several minutes later, Ralph interrupted another lesson I was leading with a small group of students with similar concerns to his.

"Please check these, sir," he requested. "Just to make sure."

"You must've had a very good teacher," I winked. "These are all correct."

Smiling, confident, and anxious to complete the remaining problems, Ralph strutted back to his seat, the proud owner of a skill that he had mastered more quickly that he thought he could. Seconds later, a shoulder tap interrupted me again. It was Ralph.

"This is for you, Mr. D."

I looked down. Ralph had handed me a blank copy of the night's math homework.

"What's this for?" I asked.

"You need the practice," he told me.

So what if the skill Ralph so needed to learn was obsolete except for carpet layers and fifth-grade math teachers? So what if it would have mattered more for Ralph to have learned some of math's life skills—decimals, money, distance? For now, at least, little else mattered because today Ralph had learned two things: that he could divide fractions and, more importantly, that he was capable of working with a teacher who needed a little more practice.

The Rhythm of Life

My teaching continues to be wondrous. Each day, I drive home with a mélange of emotions that causes me to have a smile on my face and a tear in my eye. These kids have suffered so many losses in their young lives that I see one black-and-blue hardship after another. Yesterday, I found out that Martin, the young boy whose dad had killed himself and who saw in me (or in any male adult) a father he had never been allowed to know, was sent to another school. He'd now be in a class for emotionally disturbed children, with Martin being the youngest. I'm afraid for him. I'm afraid that he'll learn specific ways to be bad that he never before considered. The lessons mastered will leave permanent scars on his fragile soul, all because he told a teacher who was berating him to "F— off."

Why is it that some adults always assume a child is the rightful owner of his or her worst emotions? Martin may have sworn, but he also smiled and he wanted to please people who cared about him. Some call Martin's move to this new class a "second chance"; I think of it as a way for adults to assuage their guilt that they could not reach inside a boy and pull out the good that was inherently there. Indeed, Martin does deserve a second chance, but I'm afraid that he won't get it in a classroom where everyone strives to become not first best, but first worst.

Also, yesterday was a joyous celebration of the end of Black History Month. Picture this: 800 kids, age 5–12 (and my one 14-year-old fifth grader) sitting on the floor of a carpeted auditorium waiting for people they knew to celebrate the songs and lives of Black entertainers. Act 1 was a class of second graders enacting the West African legend "Why Mosquitoes Buzz in People's Ears." I'm afraid that I can't answer why mosquitoes do this annoying practice, as the cute kids, dressed in construction-paper costumes and dad's (or someone's) oversized shirts, performed a free-form, inaudible interpretation of this legend. To the adults present, interpreting what the kids were doing was like trying to understand a mime show while wearing a blindfold. Of course, the second graders were a huge hit with their classroom colleagues, who clapped the clap of childhood—an uneven pattern of joy understood only by innocents.

Next, there were various renditions of songs by the Four Tops, Tina Turner, and other Motown heroes, all performed by blonde, White teachers trying desperately to find some rhythm. Their hearts were into it, but the hips just didn't follow. There were some exceptions, though: Mrs. Chester, our principal, a perfect replica of Aretha Franklin in body, if not in voice, who got the kids and teachers to their feet as, together, we all spelled out and learned the meaning of R-E-S-P-E-C-T. And Mr. Watson, the custodian, who bravely came on stage to tell us of his own African roots and theirs: "Your ancestry didn't start where you live on Freemont Road. No, sir, your roots go back before Jesus, to a place across the sea." He then went on to tell the children, and me, that he had lost his brother, mother, and sister in the past years and that they were all embalmed, as dead people are, before the funeral. "Embalming was invented by a Black man to preserve the beauty of the human being." His story, graphic and sad, shared the spirit of pride he felt for his race, a quality appreciated by his wildly supportive audience of 800.

Other memorable acts included six kindergarten teachers, dressed as nuns by using black garbage bags draped over their backs as habits, performing a rousing version of "I Will Follow Him" from *Sister Act*. The highlight was the lead nun, who oozed herself over, under, next to, and on the piano keyboard, causing peals of laughter and joy from a grateful collection of kids. Finally . . . rhythm!

But, most special for me was a little moment, a smidgen of time during a chorus of The Temptations' song "My Girl," a tune whose lyrics, surprisingly, were known by most every student. When the classic chorus began—"I guess, you'd say, what can make me feel this way . . ."—800 pairs of hands flew heavenward and bodies weaved back and forth in a subtle, silent wave of togetherness. At that moment, I looked around this sweaty, swaying crowd and realized that we were all one, we were all equal, we were all smiling. How desperately I wished that sitting next to me, or behind me, or anywhere else in the room was Martin. He deserved the joy that will now never be a part of his repertoire of happy times, where berating wasn't allowing and swearing wasn't necessary.

Filing out of the auditorium, dripping with sweat and hunger, we were greeted with a selection of soul food, cooked and presented by parents and grandmothers. I feasted on food that had graphic names of perfect description: fat back, chicken bog, butter beans, collard greens with gristle, and red velvet cake. Whatever inherent nutrients may have existed in the raw version of these foods had long given way to excess cholesterol and heavy doses of frying. I ate and ate and ate.

A day of song and food. A day of departure for Martin. Would I ever see him again? Doubtful. A day of wonder for me. Like no other time since I had arrived, I felt a closeness to this community called Dodge Elementary School. Family they were, family we are.

Proficient at What?

I wondered if my students were in as much pain as I was for them. It was time for the BSAPs, the Basic Skills Assessment Program tests used throughout South Carolina to show how much students have grown academically from one year to the next. For 90 minutes each morning for five days, students in grades 2–5 stopped learning and began bubbling in circles, an arduous task in itself for some, whose chubby, short fingers tried mightily to color within the lines, a task not yet mastered even with big-page coloring books.

I saw chagrin in my students' faces as they entered our classroom. Their desks, usually clustered in small groups, were isolated into rows, reminiscent of bleak, washed out photos from "the good ol' days" when the teacher was a schoolmarm, a wood stove provided heat, and bolts and screws kept the desks immobile. Newspapers covered the alphabet charts and word walls, textbooks were marooned into a far corner instead of beneath each owner's chair, and all indications of the children's talents—their creative writing, their maps of their favorite imaginary places, even their drawings—were removed or blanketed from view. Our room, usually vibrant and full of color and life, looked to be preparing for a whitewash. Indeed, perhaps it was.

Before testing began, we met in the "community circle," a daily reintroduction to one another where we share our hopes, our fears, our hands. I looked around at the tired, Monday-morning eyes of my 25 students. All indications were that many had ignored my suggestion to get a good night's sleep and eat well to prepare for the tests. The open-ended phrase of the day was "I know this will be a good day because . . ." As we went around the circle, several mentioned after-school sports, a few looked forward to the afternoon assembly, one stated that the day's end would mean one less day of BSAPs (lots of sympathetic groans of agreement), but most took the option that they always have, but seldom choose: "Pass." This no-comment said more than the other responses combined. It's hard to hush up a fifth grader's mind and mouth, but BSAPs do it well.

We did a few calisthenics, stretching to the sky and reaching for our toes. The grunts and moans sounded like so many reluctant lawnmowers struggling to kick over after a restful winter slumber. They, like we, needed to be oiled, and these simple physical movements seemed to do the trick. When we closed our circle, eyes looked brighter, banter was common, and giggles about something humorous only to fifth graders were making their ways around this arc of bodies.

Then, it was time. Thick, anonymous test booklets were distributed, and children were given the standardized welcome provided by designers: DO NOT open your test booklet. DO NOT begin until you are told to do so. DO NOT look at anyone else's answer sheet.

Once the cover was allowed to be unsealed, the children again were reminded of the rules. They could not work ahead, nor were they allowed to look at a book or anything else if they happened to finish early. They were to answer as best they could, although they were not expected to know how to do some of the problems. They were to keep an eye on the clock and the number of test questions they had remaining, in hopes that they would reach simultaneous closure. So, under these "ideal" conditions, the opening volley was heard: "You may begin."

For 15 minutes or so, there was little more to see than children hunched over their desks. The only sounds were occasional sniffles and coughs and the near-silent rubbing of an eraser to correct something wrong. But, then, after the first few easy questions were completed and the children were hooked into believing these tests weren't really as bad they thought, a sneak attack of those questions "you weren't expected to know" appeared.

Brandon called me to his desk. "What's this word, Mr. D? I've never seen it before!"

"I can't tell you, Brandon. I can only tell you to try your best."

He looked angry. "If you tell me the word, maybe I've heard it and I can figure out what it means."

I looked at the word and wondered if I'd ever used it myself in fifth grade. I gave him an illegal hint: "Use context clues, Brandon. Maybe then you'll be able to at least eliminate one or two choices that they gave you."

Brandon looked resigned to getting the answer wrong. Our class's brightest child, Brandon had most likely used that method already. His calling me to his desk was a sign of desperation; I was his last resort before he made a mistake in an area where he had previously felt confident and successful: vocabulary.

"Maybe this is one of those questions you're not supposed to know, Brandon."

Unconvinced, he shrugged his shoulders and carelessly circled in "D" (a wrong choice). Then, he moved on without looking up at me. As I walked away, I heard him mutter to himself, "And I thought teachers were supposed to help you learn stuff."

After that, there were few other questions asked, although there were many obvious in the motions of my students. I watched Jesse, a bright boy with some reading problems, as he bit his pencil end and twisted his long blonde hair with a finger of frustration. He had wanted to do well, I knew, but his body language indicated that he didn't think that was going to happen. Shatiqua, a perfectionist who took every task seriously, rushed to the end of the first test and then went back to change more than half of her answers. Her motions were frenetic; I'd assume her thinking was, too. Carter's pencil sat alongside his elbow, still as sharp as new, 15 minutes after the test began. He had correctly answered three or four questions, leaving the rest blank.

"You've still got time to finish some questions," I reminded him.

He told me he knew that, but he didn't care to because the stories were too boring. "Can't they give us something fun to read? I could answer lots of questions about a *Goosebumps* book."

Caryn, a sad, lost soul on the best of days, whose academic struggles were accompanied by a pitiful home life, followed Carter's lead. Perhaps, in her eyes, it was easier to do no work than to prove to others by your wrong answers that you really aren't very smart. And Reggie, always jolly and rambunctious, said the test was "real, real easy," and he completed it in 10 minutes. If only he had read the questions before he answered them, I'm sure his score might be higher.

For 90 minutes, with occasional breaks to stop one portion of the test and begin another, the students did what was uncommon and unnatural: They sat quiet and motionless in desks that were never designed for such extended stays. They squirmed as if they were sitting in a mixture of Jell-O and rocks. When the microphone call finally came—"That concludes today's testing"—the children rushed, madly and with absolutely no decorum, to a restroom that many had probably needed to use two subtests ago.

I'm not sure what the students learned that day. Neither are they. But, I do know what I learned: I learned that my students' varied ways of learning were not respected by a test that demanded only one type of response. I learned that the work my students had done up until March had to be covered up with newspapers so they did not "cheat" by referring to a word or concept they had learned previously. I learned that my students were expected to do their best even when they were deprived of the guidance and assistance of a teacher they had previously looked toward to give both. I learned that physical needs had to wait until all the test bubbles were filled in throughout the school. I learned that my students were expected to give their best under these worst of conditions.

Perhaps at the next session of the South Carolina General Assembly, where politicians discuss the sad state of affairs in our public schools, we should give each legislator a couple of No. 2 pencils, a booklet of meaningless stories and questions, sit them at small tables with chairs that do not move, refuse to allow in any coffee and refuse to permit any restroom breaks, and then ask these men and women to "show us their best thinking" from the multiple choices given in their test booklets. And, just to keep things fair, we'll ask them to do this for five mornings in a row.

We can do the same in Illinois for the IGAPs; in Texas for the TAAS; or in any of the many other states that try to probe something as complex as learning through a device as simplistic as an acronym-laden test of basic skills.

If this is not appropriate for intelligent lawmakers and governors—and it is not—then neither is it beneficial for Jesse or Shatiqua or Carter or Brandon, my students, each of whom is trying to be smart and all of whom deserve the right to show what they know in ways that are personally meaningful, legitimate, and humane.

Ohio Journal of the English Language Arts
Winter/Spring 1999

One Teacher's Credo

Introduction

I will be the first to admit that some people see my writing as "schmaltzy." It is filled with stories that are designed to make you laugh or cry; stories of children both similar to you and me and from backgrounds that are as different and difficult as any that can be imagined.

I don't apologize for this schmaltz, as all the children I've ever met have stories to tell and they all deserve someone to share their stories, if they cannot or will not do so themselves. As long as their lives are respected as their stories are told, there are no losers.

In writing "One Teacher's Credo," I wished to send a collective "thank you" to the children I have met along this magical path called teaching. I have not left a positive mark on every student I have taught, and I didn't even like some of the kids I was assigned to teach; but, whether the student in front of me was someone I loved or loathed, I did manage to learn from each of them. The 10 promises that I cite in my credo are dedicated to the children who have entered my life . . . and never left. I hope they know, in some way, that I am a richer man because of them.

As an opening assignment in one of my undergraduate education classes, I ask my students to write down 5–10 things they will promise their students—in other words, to compose their own credo of teaching. At the end of their semester-long field experiences in classrooms, I ask them to revise their credos. Always, the second list is longer and more detailed than the first, as the kids my undergraduates meet, even briefly, add texture and depth to this process we call education. Indeed, it is a *great* assignment. And it is filled with schmaltz.

Recently, while enjoying a timely and necessary sabbatical from my university, I returned to my professional roots in a classroom. Volunteering as a fourth- and fifth-grade teacher in a rural Southern school surrounded by acres of tobacco fields and Baptist churches as small as dollhouses, I learned anew about the trials and triumphs of teaching. Whether it was Brian, a gifted boy who blurted out answers before many of his classmates even had time to process the questions, or Chantelle, who uttered Monday-morning hopes that the man who had spent the weekend with her momma would become her next daddy, each child's face is etched into my memory.

In time, some of their names will be forgotten—the plight of all teachers, I suppose—but, in honor of these children who, collectively, gave so much to me, I'd like to give them something in return: one teacher's credo that guarantees their impact on my life will remain intact, even if their now-sharp names are dulled by the erosion brought on by time and distances.

For my students, to each of you I promise these things:

1. I will always remember the every day you enter my classroom, a part of you wants to succeed.

Even if your behaviors show otherwise, I will remember that no one wakes up hoping to have a bad day. So, each morning as you first enter my classroom, I will remind myself that you and I were both given a special gift: another day together in which to learn.

2. I will always remember that you have multiple ways to show me what you know.

Some students like to dance or sing or act, while others prefer the quieter forms of self-expression that come from writing or drawing. Still more prefer the verbal route: talking, telling stories, sharing legends. However you learn best, I will nurture and respect this element of individuality that sustains you and helps you grow.

3. I will always remember that your life is filled with passions.

One cannot be alive without being passionate. As a toddler, your passion might have been things like dinosaurs or a special stuffed animal. As you grew, your passions matured and broadened into new realms of pleasure: football, guitar, cooking, chess, reading. Whatever your passions, I want you to know that they have a place in my heart and in my classroom. Share them with me so that we may both learn more.

4. I will always remember that, although you may appear as strong as timber, parts of you are as fragile as glass.

No one's life is free from grief or worry, and even children are not immune from the dangers and illnesses that accompany being human. With me, you may feel the need to be strong, to prove what a big boy or girl you are. But, I want you to know that, in my classroom, tears are as much a sign of strength as muscles, for tears show that you care enough about yourself and those around you to show it in nature's most natural form: crying.

5. I will always remember that you may not be the sole owner of your strongest emotions.

If someone teases you on the bus, you might be angry when you enter my classroom. Similar strong emotions might be there if you can't find anyone to play with at recess, or if you hear your mom and dad fight before breakfast, or if your older sister called you "stupid" because you got a C on that math quiz you forgot about. I will always try to remember that, if you are acting in ways that make me upset or frustrated with you, there is a reason behind your actions. I may not excuse your behaviors, but, with your help, I will try to understand them. Only then will we both feel satisfied.

6. I will always remember that your life experiences might be different than mine, but they are just as valuable.

We come from different generations and different families. I have traveled to places you've never seen, and you have crossed paths with people I shall never know. But, the tie that unites us is stronger than any differences that may seem to divide us. I will always remember that every event and person in your life had an impact on you, and I will value the learning of these unique adventures. In one way or another, each has caused you to grow.

7. I will always remember that success cannot be measured in numbers.

In schools, we teachers spend a lot of time comparing you to other students, and we usually use numbers to do it: test scores, IQ points, report card grades. I promise to look beyond these numbers, be they very high or very low, to seek out something that is otherwise hidden: you. I will always remember to measure you by the size of your heart more than by the weight of your achievements.

8. I will always remember that success requires discipline—from both of us.

I've always been taught that "good things take time" and that success is "1% inspiration and 99% perspiration." And, yes, it's true that honest success in life is not achieved without effort. But, effort doesn't have to hurt, and learning need not be painful. I promise to find safe ways for you to feel successful, and I vow never to offer you a challenge unless I honestly believe you can meet it.

9. I will always remember that teaching and learning are issues of trust.

If you don't believe I have your best interest at heart, we will struggle through our times together. If I don't believe you are capable and responsible, then I won't notice it when you are. Before we can teach each other anything at all worth learning, we must first share a basic human trait: trust. I promise to be honest with you, for honesty is the foundation of trust, and trust is the bedrock of learning.

10. I will always remember to listen.

Perhaps you got a new kitten last night, or maybe your parents got a letter inviting you into a new school program for smart kids. Maybe Grandpa sent you $5 for no reason at all, or maybe something bad happened that makes you feel sad or afraid or confused. Whenever your heart rejoices, please share that with me. And, if your burden seems heavy, I want you to ask me for some help in carrying it with you. My shoulders are bigger than yours for a reason. This is your personal invitation to use them.

In my more than 20 years as an educator, I'd like to think that I've learned at least as many lessons as I have taught. I want to believe that my career has made a difference in the life of at least one child, making it possible for even a single boy or girl to succeed more fully because, together, we practiced the art of mutual respect. By writing down my credo, I have come to appreciate the emergence of the guiding percepts that I hope have influenced my career to date and that I know will do so from this time on.

I invite you to do the same, to share your own One Teacher's Credo with those to whom it will mean the most: your students. Perhaps if all teachers made conscious choices to articulate their teaching/learning beliefs, some of the most profound school reforms would occur exactly as they should: one classroom at a time.

Gifted Child Today
November/December 1997

Our Students, Ourselves

Appreciating the Significance of Common Bonds

When John Feldhusen was editor of *Gifted Child Quarterly*, he contacted me about writing a short—and I do mean *short*—article where I would be "speaking" to teachers about some aspect of teaching gifted children that I found important. That was the only guideline he gave to me. John wanted to have the *Quarterly* seen as a more "teacher-friendly" journal than it had been in the past, and this attempt to do so was one I applauded then and I respect today.

So . . . what to write? After mulling over several options, I chose to write about the seldom-discussed topic of the common bonds that unite gifted teachers with gifted students. Certainly, we are all aware that some teachers are just better at working with and understanding gifted children than are others. Where ineffective teachers are intimidated by students who may know more than they do about particular topics, excellent teachers of the gifted cherish the new learning they will pick up from their gifted kids. While some teachers believe that "gifted kids can make it on their own," wise teachers know that gifted students need as much guidance as other pupils because having unlimited choices means that you have more ways to fail than other kids your age. The list of qualities of effective teachers of the gifted could go on and on.

In this brief article, I relate several truths about how gifted students and those who teach them effectively and passionately do so because of the similar traits they share, both intellectual and emotional.

Does a teacher of the gifted have to be gifted him- or herself? Let's just say it doesn't hurt.

When Dorothy returned from Oz, she was struck by a reality that, in retrospect, seemed obvious: Her search for happiness need go no further than her own backyard. Likewise, in our own lives—as teachers, parents, or counselors—the grand revelations we achieve are often grounded in simple truths, truths so blatant that we often discard them for fear that our colleagues will consider us naïve, silly, or (horror of horrors) "unprofessional."

Yet, in my own career, I have found that fool's gold shines as brilliantly as does the real thing and that my search for exotic answers rather than simple truths has often led me down dead-end paths. It was only when I took time to examine the close-at-hand, the obvious, that my "a-ha" was reached. And, generally, the children I have taught provided all the guidance I needed for a workable solution or a fresh insight.

My latest "a-ha" came recently and at an inopportune time: during the middle of a presentation to a group of gifted child educators. As I was reviewing some of the social and emotional aspects of giftedness, I realized that the issues I was addressing were equally relevant to gifted students *and* their teachers. Here's what I learned:

1. *Our students, like ourselves, are often stifled by the misperceptions people have about giftedness.*

Ask a gifted student to define giftedness, and you will likely hear a series of "nots": "It's *not* being a straight-A student"; "It does *not* mean that you are perfect"; "It doesn't mean you hate sports"; and so forth. Likewise, gifted child educators often feel the pressure to be perfect. Teacher lounge comments like "Do you have to *be* gifted to *teach* the gifted?" or "I found a spelling error in your newsletter" may be said in jest, but there is such a thing as carrying a joke—even a good one—too far.

2. *Our students, like ourselves, spend more time considering future efforts than they do reflecting on current achievements.*

To a gifted child, "what will be" often seems more important, more special, than "what is." In a constant search for higher goals and greater achievements, gifted students often downplay the merits of their most recent accomplishments. The independent study project that just took second place in the science fair was "Okay, but wait 'til next year." Educators of gifted students also share this fascination with the future and often neglect what is right in front of them: the curriculum just completed, the identification plan just revised, a successful evening session for parents of their students.

Instead, they look for ways to fill in gaps that the most recent accomplishments failed to address. There is nothing wrong, of course, with looking ahead, but there are merits, too, in enjoying the fruits of one's present efforts.

3. *Our students, like ourselves, feel awkward about using the term* gifted *in relation to self.*

Our society prizes the accomplishments of people—the curative drug discovered, the invention of a timesaving appliance, the passage of a law to reduce taxes. Yet, ironically, if the same people who achieve these goals take (or get) too much attention for their efforts, our egalitarian society gives these individuals a collective slap on the wrist. After all, "we don't want them to get big heads or an inflated view of their own importance."

Gifted students, and those who educate them, struggle constantly with this fine-line distinction between "better at" and "better than." Typically, a gifted student will tell anyone who cares to listen that heightened academic ability, for example, is no predictor of empathy, compassion, or tolerance of others' ideas. (History has proven too often that smart people are capable of evil deeds.) Unfortunately, though, few people take the time to listen to—or even ask about—this distinction, so a myth is created, a myth that equates "betterness" at school subjects with "betterness" as an individual. The result can be a misunderstanding between those individuals identified as gifted and those who do not wear this label. Likewise, teaching colleagues may be less than accommodating if they perceive the "gifted teacher" as someone whose personal qualities and worth surpass their own in importance.

There are other ways in which educators of gifted children are like the students they teach, and if one believes that childhood is the most sublime time of life, then the more similarities the better. In fact, our research on teacher effectiveness shows clearly that educators judged to be most influential in students' development are those who have an affiliation with their pupils' needs and characteristics; they are teachers who know their students' special needs from the inside out and are willing to work with them to answer questions and address issues in which the students have a personal stake.

Back to Dorothy: When she returned from Oz and described to those around her the wonders she had seen, the adventures she had had, the insights she had gained, everyone laughed. "It's your imagination, dear; it was just a dream." But, Dorothy knew better. She knew the truth behind the growth she had made, and, due to her journeys—both on the yellow brick road and inwardly—she would never again look at those around her from quite the same perspective.

I invite you, and your students, to share with each other the many pieces of knowledge you own as a result of the insights gained from working together. You will see, I believe, that there are more similarities than differences and that individual growth is achieved by an appreciation of the significance of common bonds.

Gifted Child Quarterly
Spring 1989

Too Smart to Teach

Introduction

I n an earlier introduction in this section, I mentioned my Aunt Peggy, a sweet (but misguided) relative who thought she knew what was best for me, her nephew, when it came to choosing a career. Aunt Peggy is married to someone very much like herself, Uncle Ray, who has the same way of making me feel bad when giving me a compliment.

It was eighth grade: my graduation party. All the relatives were assembled for free food and cheap wine, and Uncle Ray cornered me in the kitchen. He wanted to tell me how proud he was that I had graduated first in my class (there were only 13 of us in the graduating class, though), and he wanted to know what "a smart boy like me" wanted to be when I grew up. When I stated proudly that I wanted to be a special education teacher, Uncle Ray looked puzzled.

"Jim, you don't want to be a teacher!"

"I don't?"

"No!"

"Why not, Uncle Ray?"

He took a too-big sip of his Chablis. "Three reasons," he began. "First, there's no money in teaching. You'll struggle financially for your whole life. Second,"— he took another gulp—"boys aren't teachers—especially elementary teachers.

74

That's weird that you'd want to be in a woman's profession." He looked askew at me, silently questioning my motives . . . and more. "And, third, Jim, you are *too smart* to become a teacher—what a waste of a good mind."

It was then I knew why God had granted me two ears: Words could enter one and immediately go out the other.

"Thanks for coming to my party, Uncle Ray."

"A pleasure, a pleasure." He then reached in his pocket and pulled out a $5 bill. "We've already given you a gift, Jim, but here's an extra $5. You'll need it if you're going to be a teacher."

He laughed and laughed at a joke that was not funny. I just smiled and walked away, not even taking the $5 that he offered.

Years later, I thought of this incident as I sat around a teachers' lounge and listened to seasoned teachers talk about how they would discourage their own sons and daughters from entering the teaching profession. They'd also discourage their most able students, for many of the same reasons that Uncle Ray gave to me a generation before. This time, I couldn't just let the "two ear thing" work for me; I had to say something. So, I did, in writing. The following article, "Too Smart to Teach," has been reproduced in numerous magazines over the years and has garnered more thank-you letters from educators than any article I've ever written.

If we, as educators, cannot take pride in our own profession, then how can we expect others to respect the career of teaching? This vital and sensitive issue is addressed in "Too Smart to Teach."

I couldn't state it then, but I will say it now: "Uncle Ray, you were wrong on all three counts."

When I was 5 years old and in the first grade, Sister Patricia Ann asked me to help her teach my 36 classmates their consonants. Later in the year, while we were learning to tell time, Sister asked me once again to help out. I could count to 60 by both ones and fives, a skill especially useful in that earlier era when clocks had hands and faces, not digital readouts.

At the end of first grade, I announced to my parents that I wanted to become a teacher. They didn't say much. I said the same thing again in second grade, and fourth grade, and especially eighth grade (when Mr. Sheppard, my first guy teacher, was my hero). It was then, at my eighth-grade graduation party, that Uncle Ray took me aside to offer some of the advice he was so prone to give.

"Jim," he said, "you don't really want to be a teacher. There's no money in it."

"Besides," he added, "boys don't become teachers, girls do."

"But, Uncle Ray, I had a man teacher this year!"

He just sighed, shook his head, and, laying his hand on my right shoulder, added his final comment. "Jim, you're too smart to be a teacher."

Today I am what Uncle Ray admonished me not to become—a teacher. Albeit a heavily credentialed one—B.S., M.Ed., Ph.D.—but a teacher nonetheless. Working in both a college of education and a suburban middle school, I attempted to do what Sister Patricia told me I could do so well: teach others without making them feel bad that I knew some things they didn't.

I enjoy my jobs immensely, as do most of my colleagues, which is why it bothers me so much that the same advice I received from Uncle Ray more than 30 years ago is still being given to wannabe teachers today. The difference is, the people who now most often say "You're too smart to be a teacher" are not well-intentioned but out-of-touch relatives, but rather educators themselves, who want to take away from others the dream that they themselves had sought: to become a teacher.

Why is this? Why do so many individuals who work daily with young people discourage the most capable ones from entering the field of education? I can't imagine it's the low pay—except in South Dakota, salaries are pretty decent and on the rise. It can't be the feeling that one cannot make a difference—every teacher has virtually dozens of stories of student success. And it can't be a lack of camaraderie—teachers' lounges are hotbeds of lives in motion.

Perhaps this aversion to recommending a career in education is due to a perception that educators aren't as respected as they once were, by either students or the public. Maybe it's because teachers' unions have become so powerful that the personal voice of one teacher is stifled by the din of the many, leaving individual accomplishments secondary in importance to collective bargaining. Or, maybe it's the restrictions placed upon the art of teaching by the too-numerous proficiency tests and reforms mandated by out-of-touch legislators and "experts" who dictate from afar how we should do our jobs.

Even though I don't know all the causes of dissatisfaction, I do know this: In both my university and in many K–12 schools, a career in education is considered the lowest of the low in terms of professions that matter. And the people one would assume to be most enthusiastic about what they do—educators themselves—are often the field's most vocal opponents. In the now-familiar words of Pogo, "We have met the enemy, and he is us."

To be sure, educating today's youths in our virtual-reality culture is a tough task. We compete with Big Bird (at least until the Contract With America makes him extinct) and Power Rangers. We vie for the attention of kids raised on Nintendo and Prodigy. We try to teach 30 students at a time as the individuals they are, knowing full well that those at the extremes, the very brightest and the educationally neediest, are somehow missing out on the full measure of what they need to succeed.

Yet, these realities are little different from the interferences that plagued past generations, when the introduction of rock 'n' roll, radio, TV, even the backyard swimming hole all provided new nirvanas for students to explore. Though more complex in nature, today's distractions to academics still share some common ground: Each appeals to children who are active, friend-conscious, and more interested in having fun than in learning math facts. Times may change, and the kids may become more superficially sophisticated, but a deeper look reveals what should be obvious: Students need caring and intelligent adults to teach them as much as they ever did.

I'm sure some readers will find me naïve, perhaps believing that those bifocals I've just begun wearing were fitted with rose-colored lenses. They may even tell me Uncle Ray was right—that a real professional would look for a higher status job than classroom teaching; or that teaching at any level is a career relegated to those who choose to settle for something less than they are capable of doing (the "Those who can, do; those who can't, teach" syndrome). They'll suggest that teaching should be just a stepping-stone to something more meaningful—like administration or personnel management.

In small but gnawing ways, comments like these send two messages to prospective teachers: first, that the further removed from children they become, the more important their job in education is; and second, that becoming a career teacher is professionally stifling. Both messages are wrong, for to assert that teachers must remove themselves from the classroom to feel professionally fulfilled is akin to asking Whoopi Goldberg to direct *Oklahoma!* in order to round out her resume.

To the many naysayers in our profession, I kindly ask a favor: Resign or retire or retrain or do whatever it takes to reignite the idealism that brought you into the field in the first place. Leave education until such time that you once again believe anything is possible in the life of a child—drugs, poverty, or emotional bankruptcy notwithstanding. If educators do not see their ability to make a meaningful difference for a child who believes in the inevitability of his or her own defeat, they are taking up valuable space in front of a classroom—space that can and should be occupied by an optimist who takes the role of teacher seriously—and assumes it with pride.

And while they're at it, these same teachers who complain that education is not a worthwhile career should realize that, by discouraging able young people from becoming teachers, they not only downplay dreams, but demean themselves and a noble profession. It's easy to bemoan one's lot in life, but guess what? No one is forcing teachers to remain as teachers against their will. In the words of former Chrysler Corporation chairman Lee Iacocca, "You've got to lead, follow, or get out of the way." So, if education is as bad as some teachers say it is, then those unhappy pessimists should stop frustrating themselves and exit the corps.

The longer I teach—it's been 18 years, now—the more firmly I believe that the finest teachers are born, not made, that all of the teacher education courses and national accreditation standards in the world can't create an educator out of someone who just doesn't wholeheartedly want to be working with children's minds, hopes, and dreams. I also believe that many prospective teachers knew when they were 6, just as I did in Sister Patricia's class, that teaching was the only job worth having. To those bright young people who want to enter the profession that has been so good to many of us— education—I say "good choice!" My advice to them is not "You're too smart to be a teacher," but rather, "You're too smart not to be one."

That single affirmation, if made by every educator alive who believes in its truth, could be the greatest impetus ever in our collective move to reform the profession.

Teacher Magazine
November/December 1995

Why is the Next Grade Level Always the "Serious" One?

Introduction

With children at home and students at school, we're not allowed to pick favorites. We are supposed to treat everyone with equal degrees of kindness, respect, and attention.

In a perfect world, this would happen; in reality, it does not. Human nature being what it is, we do treat differently people who show us the same types and degrees of kindness, respect, and attention that we give to them. Is this fair? Perhaps not, but it is fact.

So, what does this have to do with the following article? Well, if truth be told, this is one of my favorite pieces of writing, so much so that I even read it, verbatim, as part of a keynote address I often give at those first-day-of-school in-service workshops that teachers loathe because they just want to work in their classrooms. Even then, though, teachers sit up and listen because they see themselves within the context of this piece.

Each of us, as a teacher, plays a vital role in the lives of the students we teach. Indeed, in today's too-busy world, we often see and talk with our students more frequently than the kids interact with their parents. Sad, but true.

What this article does, and why I enjoy it so much, is this: It causes us to reflect on the fact that the only element we have guaranteed is today. The students in front of us may not be there tomorrow, or the day after that, and so the threats or admonitions to always look toward the future instead of the present may put both learning and enjoyment on hold. School is not a dress rehearsal for life; it is life itself. We forget this at our peril.

If you find yourself giggling because you have said more than once the quotes within this article, join the club. If you can shout "Guilty as charged!" because you have once (or more) said to a student, "If you don't learn this now, you will be behind next year," then I think you will understand the underlying reason why I enjoy this article so much: It speaks to a truth that is universal among teachers: the desire for our students to excel.

I t happened again this week. Twice. I was visiting two of my student-teachers who were just weeks away from becoming certified in their respective grade levels. The cooperating teachers with whom my students had worked these past 10 weeks were full of compliments about both the personal and professional qualities our wannabe teachers possessed.

And then it happened again. Twice. The conversations went something like this:

"Stella will be a fine teacher once she gets her own classroom. She's very creative and the children love her. My only concern is that she needs to focus more on 'the basics'— you know, getting the kids ready for the next grade level. It gets tougher next year and the kids need to be prepared for it."

I heard the same thing from Todd's cooperating teacher and, in years past, I'd heard the same from Julie's, Sam's, Rita's, and countless others'. It doesn't seem to matter what grade level I observe—Stella was in a kindergarten class; Todd in sixth grade—the comments and the concerns are the same and they boil down to this: The previous grade level may have been fun, but now it's time to get serious about learning. Whether it's 12th-grade English ("College is tough, you know") or 5th-grade fractions ("If you don't learn them now, you'll be behind next year"), teachers lead students to believe that the worst is yet to come.

In doing so, we take away some of the joy and wonder of learning, for instead of exploring a new concept with the unabashed excitement that often accompanies new adventures, students may undertake school tasks out of fear that, if they don't, it'll catch up with them in first grade or fourth grade or graduate school. In preparing our students for the future, we often forget that the only thing that both they and we have control over is the present.

Perhaps I'm overreacting. Maybe it's appropriate for us, as teachers, to justify what we do by what someone else—the next grade's teacher, the principal, the state department of education, a parent—expects us to cover. But, taken to the extreme, as it often is, education becomes a constant dress rehearsal; the play itself, the real performance, lying elsewhere, in another grade, with another teacher. Trouble is, the next grade level brings yet more practice, leaving students to wonder if they'll ever get a chance to shine. Too often, they don't.

But, in reflecting on those teachers who left the greatest impacts on me, I recall the ones who cared more for today than tomorrow. For example, there was Mrs. Bradley, who made second grade special because we got to sing each day for no reason at all. In sixth grade, there was Mr. Bennett, my first male teacher, who extended our recess on warm fall days so he could teach both the boys and the girls how to throw a spiral and fake a pass. In 11th-grade American government class, Mr. Maloney played the Beatles' song "Hey, Jude" and informed us, a group of horny and vulnerable 16-year-old Catholic boys, that the song wasn't about sex or drugs, as we all assumed, but dealt instead with something called "angst . . . a quality, gentlemen, from which you shall all someday suffer." I wrote *angst* down so I could recognize it when it appeared in my life. Trust me, it helped.

What each of these teachers shared was an abiding trust in themselves. A self-assured confidence that it was their job, not the next year's teacher's, to instill in me a love of learning. I was never afraid to sing with Mrs. Bradley, and I don't recall her ever telling me that if I didn't learn "My Country Tis of Thee," I'd be banished from third grade. And, at the time, I might have liked Mr. Bennett because extra recess meant less time for spelling, but I recall him now because he realized the importance of football and crisp, autumn days to a boy whose own dad was often too busy to toss a few laterals in the backyard.

By concentrating on the present, these teachers took charge of my education. They knew that other grade levels lay ahead, and that more difficult challenges than I could now even imagine were just across the threshold in another teacher's class. But, they didn't worry about future events over which they had little control. Rather, they focused their attention on the me that existed today instead of the person I would be later on. In doing so, they gave me the confidence to play around with this serious business of education.

Now, as a teacher myself, I realize that Mrs. Bradley, Mr. Maloney, and Mr. Bennett also gave themselves something: permission to teach a new set of basics, one of which was making students like me believe that 2nd grade (or 4th, or 11th) was the most special one of all.

Back to Stella and Todd. Next week, when I observe them both for the last time in their roles as student-teachers, I'll take them aside and ask them to talk about their most memorable moments during these past 12 weeks. If they mention a lesson so good that the students didn't want it to end, or a poignant one-on-one when a child needed a caring adult with shoulders big enough to lean on, then I'll ask them to write down these memories and laminate them on Day-Glo paper. This'll preserve them forever. I'll tell them to keep these papers in their desk drawers and to reread them frequently when they become real teachers. Finally, I'll ask Stella and Todd to give copies of these memories to their cooperating teachers as permanent reminders that we get only 180 days to convince our students that, whatever the future holds, today is the most important day of all in which to learn.

Education Week
December 1, 1993

Part Four

Testing!
One . . . Two . . .
Three! Testing!

There have been many challenges placed on teachers during the past 20 years. The inclusion of special education students in regular classrooms, sex and drug education programs, and assuming the role of social worker for students in dire need of adult companionship and supervision are but three responsibilities that teachers have taken on over time. And, even though most teachers would agree that these new endeavors are time-consuming, most would probably also agree that they are worthwhile and in the best interests of the majority of students.

But, there is one "innovation" that is almost universally noted by teachers as a gross intrusion on their time and their professionalism: the growth of state assessments that are given annually to every child, regardless of ability or level of achievement. In Texas they are called the TAAS, in Ohio the OPT, and in Illinois the tests are called, appropriately, the ISATs (. . . and sat, and sat!).

The tests sprang up like dandelions on a spring lawn because politicians (not educators) decided a one-size-fits-all accountability plan would serve the needs of voters who want to know which schools are succeeding and which ones are not. So now, instead of spending money on new textbooks, staff development, or supplemental curriculum materials, billions upon billions of dollars are spent annually on testing materials. The only winners are the companies who publish the tests who, ironically, are not even held accountable to prove their tests are valid and reliable—a double standard that has thusfar eluded notice by the politicians who mandate these silly tests.

Okay . . . so I'm not a fan of minimal skills assessments, especially not for gifted students, who must sit through weeks of "drill and kill" exercises to assure they do well on tests they could have aced on day one, if anyone had given them the chance to do so.

The following articles present my views on this continuing trend in education, a trend toward mediocrity and homogeneity that is causing some of our nation's best teachers to throw in the towel on the profession they love dearly.

A word to the politicos who are sponsoring legislation that promotes these tests: Just because you went to school at one time does not mean you know how to run them. Leave these decisions to those educators who know far better than you that student assessments done over 185 school days are much more relevant than are the results of high-stakes test that promote little more than anxiety among students.

What is It
We're Searching for,
Anyway?

Introduction

This short article was published just as the high-stakes testing movement was getting its full head of steam. In it, I question why we provide public accolades for kids who do well on tests, but do not provide any such forum for kids who have clothed the naked, fed the hungry, or otherwise made the world a kinder place. Don't get me wrong: I'm not against acknowledging kids who perform well on standardized assessments—some of my best friends are good test takers. All I'm asking for is balance.

A "Talent Search" for empathy—now there's a novel idea!

The month of May is usually a very busy one for me. It is the month that I am popular on the "sixth-grade circuit," speaking to hundreds of children who have recently taken the SAT as part of one of our country's "talent search" programs. These freshly scrubbed kids (and their equally clean parents) sit in an auditorium where they are being recognized for their fluent abilities in mathematical or verbal skills. They range in age from 10–13 (the kids, not the parents!), and, as I wait to be introduced as the guest speaker, I sit in awe at the accomplishments of these boys and girls, many of whom scored better on the SAT at age 12 that I did at 17, and *definitely* higher than I would score now at 40. They are the academic cream of the crop of their generation, proof positive that intelligence is as varied among children as are shoe size, hair color, and personality type.

As I move toward the podium, the applause I receive is less in recognition of my academic credentials than it is for the fact that I once appeared with Oprah Winfrey on TV. That's okay. Kids, like adults, often acknowledge that which is most familiar to them. My talk begins with a cartoon about a kid doing so well in school that even the teachers don't know how to help—a situation that is far more humorous on the funny pages that it is in real life. I move quickly into a reminder that gifted students don't always have to get straight A's—"less than perfection is more than acceptable"—and then tell them that is common for gifted kids to have friends who are chronologically younger or older than they. I make each of these points with a combination of bad jokes, solid research, and personal examples, hoping beyond hope to keep the attention of my audience, which ranges in age from 6-year-old siblings to 70-year-old grandmas.

Throughout my talk, I find myself telling these extremely capable children a lot of "okay" things: *"It's okay to act silly"; "It's okay to know (or to not know) what you want to be when you grow up"; "It's okay to ask deep questions that have no firm answers"; "It's okay to be you, whoever that happens to be."*

My 45 minutes evaporate quickly, and I finish my talk with a reminder to parents that the greatest gift they can give their kids is the gift of their own time; too, I remind the students to be patient with their moms and dads—after all, they're still learning how to be parents.

Applause, applause. I retake my seat. If I'm lucky, some people will come up and talk to me privately. If I'm real lucky, it'll be some kids.

I return to my hotel or the airport, and it's usually in those transient places that I recognize anew that the most important talents these children possess are not—indeed, cannot be—measured by the SAT or any other test. Though important, all these high scores tell me is that the kids are quick, sharp, and academically capable; but, a 720 SAT math tells me little about the nature or depth of their true talents, such as how much they like and respect themselves and in what ways they want their lives to matter, now and in the minutes, months, and years that lie ahead.

Perhaps in some future year, some yet-to-be-seen month of May, I'll be asked to talk to a group of freshly scrubbed kids and parents in celebration of a talent search devoted to empathy or human relations or how enthusiastically kids have tried to make their world a better place to live. If this were to happen, I would see it as the most significant speech I ever gave. In fact, I think I would even invite Oprah Winfrey.

Understanding Our Gifted
March/April 1994

How Proficiency Tests Fall Short

Introduction

This article was my "coming out" against high-stakes, low-value testing, and it was reprinted in at least three magazines. In it, I relate how my fourth-grade teacher, Mrs. Voyer, knew I was smart enough to sit in the classroom's middle row, the row right next to where the fifth graders sat in our combined-grade-level classroom.

"Then," Mrs. Voyer said, "you can listen to the lessons that I teach them."

The article asks, in a circumspect way, why we can no longer rely on such informal (but accurate) measures of achievement. Mrs. Voyer knew who I was and how well I could do because she saw me every day of the school year—in this case, over two years. Would a state-issued test score have changed her impression of me? I certainly hope not, as I am much more comfortable putting my trust in a teacher who knows me than I am a test company that does not.

My hunch is that each of you had a Mrs. Voyer somewhere in your educational journey—a teacher who believed in both your promise and your dreams and who let you know that she (or he) was there to support the person you were becoming.

Thanks, Mrs. Voyer. I needed you!

Fourth grade with Mrs. Voyer: I was one of her 48 students in a combined fourth/fifth-grade class. An ambidextrous teacher, Mrs. Voyer taught one grade aloud while the rest of us were working on seatwork that kept both our minds and fingers occupied.

One day, during indoor recess, Mrs. Voyer called me to her desk. Without fanfare or accolades, she told me something in a voice as soft as a pillow.

"James," she said, "I'm changing your seat to the middle row. That way, you'll be able to hear the lessons that I'm teaching the fifth graders. I think you'll understand everything just fine."

That was it. No meeting with parents, no forms to sign, no rationales to document. Mrs. Voyer just did what made sense to her as a professional. In doing so, she gave me the confidence to pursue an education that was beyond my years.

At the awarding of my Ph.D. at age 28, I said a silent thank you to Mrs. Voyer, for she was the first teacher who told me that I was more capable than I thought I was. She gave me confidence, but, even more, she inspired me to see learning as an adventure without boundaries. Also, she showed me that teachers are imbued with a keen ability to know what is best for the children in their care, a trait I have tried to emulate since I entered the education profession 20 years ago.

And now, just as I enter the prime of my teaching career, I am hit face-front with a state-sanctioned rebuke of my ability to teach: a proficiency test that will measure my worth as a teacher and my students' success as learners.

If my home state of Ohio were alone in mandating these tests, I could pass the whole thing off as an overzealous attempt by an "education governor" to score political points with bureaucrats and business leaders who believe that our schools are academic wastelands. But, since more than half of our states require some type of test-based evidence that students are learning, it's obvious that a trend is under way. Proficiency tests, this decade's panacea for all of education's ills, are the latest vehicle for removing from teachers their right to be professional. These paper-and-pencil tests, given at intervals of one to three years, have limited the authority of teachers to do what Mrs. Voyer knew well how to do: determine whether or not I was learning the "stuff" that fourth grade was supposed to teach me. This one-time test score has replaced a full year of teacher observations about students. Numbers have replaced knowledge; statistics have supplanted the professional opinion of teachers who know kids better than any test can ever show. It's all so sad—and so unnecessary.

Especially hard hit are gifted children and academic achievers. Since proficiency tests, by design, are meant to determine who has mastered the lowest acceptable levels of competency, the tests themselves do little more than document what we already know: that highly able students do just fine in basic skill acquisition. And, if the proficiency tests were nothing more than a one-day annoyance for teachers and students to endure, then I could chalk up this exercise as merely one more hoop to jump through to prove that I am, as a teacher, doing my job.

But, the test itself is just a formality, an endpoint to months of preparation for the test. It is the hours spent practicing types of questions that might appear on the tests and the days denying students enrichment options that are truly meaningful that make proficiency tests so harmful and invasive. For our brightest students, this quest for proving excellence has taken a dramatic turn toward mediocrity. By being asked to show only a little, gifted students have been quietly rebuffed for knowing a lot.

Another distinct and troubling aspect of these acronym-laden proficiency tests (in Texas, they're called the TAAS; in South Carolina, the BSAP, and so on) is that there are few incentives for districts that prove they already do a good job of teaching their students. For example, the district in which I have taught for the past five years has more than 85% of fourth-, sixth-, and ninth-grade students proving themselves competent by Ohio standards. Not bad. Still, every year students must take several days to prove once again they are competent. How much more sense it would make for our district to be given a waiver from these tests for three years. Then, based on our solid past performance, we could continue to provide sound educational experiences to all of our students. Who knows? With the added days of teaching time this waiver would allow, we might even have a chance to explore more educational options that would increase our passing percentage to an even higher level. Everyone would benefit: the students who already did well on the tests; students who needed extra attention to their learning needs; and the teachers who would be allowed to teach to the students, not to a test, which is the job they were hired to do.

Yet another disturbing aspect of most proficiency tests is the absolute secrecy surrounding them. Picture this: I am a sixth-grade teacher who has learned that 30% of my class is not proficient (according to test scores) in reading and writing. "Fine," I say to myself, "when I get their tests back, I'll examine what they don't know, and I'll focus some additional time in those areas."

Sorry—not allowed. The tests themselves are not returned, just the scores and a general summary of deficiencies—for example, "low scores in reading comprehension" or "weak expository writing sample." Such general comments can't help me plan compensatory lessons for individual students. It's like riding in a foggy sea in a rudderless boat: If I end up in the right place, it'll be only by instinct or accident.

Lastly, and especially important for gifted and creative students, is the fact that some of our most able children are penalized for thinking too hard or too imaginatively. There are countless cases of magnificent student writers whose work was labeled as "not proficient" because it did not follow the step-by-step sequence of what the test scorers (many of whom are not educators, by the way) think good expository writing should look like. And, with many of the multiple-choice questions having several "correct" options in the eyes of creative thinkers, scores get depressed for children who see possibilities that are only visible to those with open minds.

Perhaps I'm being too harsh and accusatory about the purposes behind proficiency tests. After all, what's the harm in getting a rough gauge of the level of academic competency among a school district's students? The harm, as I see it, is this: We get a false sense of security that the greatest good is being served by universal testing. But, a generic score tells me nothing about the merits of one teacher's instruction, or a teacher's goals for an individual student. A proficiency ranking tells me nothing about how high a child can soar, merely whether he or she can get off the ground.

A proficiency score satisfies only those who look for simple solutions to complex issues. Unless and until state departments of education, politicians, superintendents, and others "in charge" take the responsibility to say "enough is enough," our schools will be mandated to accept adequacy over excellence, and our nation's most able children will be prevented from reaching new horizons in learning, horizons that Mrs. Voyer saw in me, and that today's teachers can see in our students, if only we give them the freedom to do so.

Education Week
April 2, 1997

One Master Too Many

T his article is about child abuse, not the type of abuse that results in visible scars, but the type that is obvious only to the trained eye: the abuse perpetrated by high-stakes tests that are designed less to tell us what a child knows and more to tell us how he or she has failed.

The article is similar in theme to others in this section, but in this closing piece, let me offer a suggestion: If these tests are so good and so indicative of excellence, then why not have those who mandate their administration take the test and post their test scores in the local paper—just as it is done now with public schools? Then, we would be assured that the politicians we are voting for have the mind power to make such bold decisions as the universal testing of young children.

Just as politicians tell school personnel that we should not be afraid of accountability if we are doing our jobs, I would posit the same idea to them. So, State Senator Gray, are you up for it? Can we count on you to do the right thing and put your abilities on public display, as you are asking children one-fifth your age to do?

It's a modest proposal, but one that I hope you will consider adopting.

All this week at school, the children in my fifth-grade class were abused. No one hit them or tormented them physically; no one swore at them or berated them. Instead, the abuse was much more insidious and long lasting. This week, for 90 minutes each day, my students took state-mandated proficiency tests. A crueler form of torture for fragile, young minds has yet to be devised.

I watched Jessie, a bright boy with some reading problems, as he bit his pencil end and twisted his long, blonde hair with a finger of frustration. He wanted to do well, to show us what he knew, but his body language indicated that he didn't think that was going to happen. Shenaya, a perfectionist who takes every task seriously, broke down in tears after the first day's ordeal was over. She'd not had enough time to answer every question, she said, because she was careful to reread her earlier answers for accuracy. Now, due to her careful attention to detail, her score would be lower. Looking toward Carter, I noticed his eyes were elsewhere, his pencil sitting perfectly sharpened alongside his elbow. He had correctly bubbled in three or four responses, but the "stories on the test are boring," he complained. "Why don't they give us something fun to read?" In protest of the test's design, he just stopped trying; he just stopped caring.

In more than 40 states, this scenario will be repeated many times each year, with children as young as 7 and others who are one year away from college taking tests in the core subjects of reading, writing, math, and more. The results of each school's scores will be tabulated and printed for all to see in local newspapers. In some states, teachers whose students do well on the proficiency test will be rewarded while those whose students do not will be chastised in the court of public opinion or in the principal's office and urged to "try harder" next time. Indeed, their jobs may soon depend on the level of their students' test scores.

How did we go so wrong so fast? Who cajoled us into believing that our public education system was so bad that we need to test children *ad nauseum*? (Study after study shows that most Americans are pleased with their local schools.) Worse, who convinced us that a grueling series of standardized tests would provide any answers to whatever problems we might seek to correct? My guess is this: Teachers are afraid to speak out against proficiency tests because such protests will sound self-serving and might intimate that they have something to hide about the jobs they are doing in their classrooms. Parents are cautious in their complaints because it might appear they are speaking against high standards for all students. Don't get me wrong. As both a parent and an educator, I am all for high standards. I just don't believe that we're going to get them by constant testing of basic skills. Someone somehow convinced us otherwise. It's time to admit that they—and we—were wrong.

There are so many problems with proficiency tests that it is hard to document them all without sounding reactionary. Here are just a few.

1. *The tests are boring.* As Carter noticed, they are often filled with stories and problems that have little interest for the children taking them.

2. *The tests are designed to measure competency*—the lowest level of skill acquisition—something that the vast majority of gifted students learn readily.

3. *The tests stifle creativity*, asking students to always select the "one best answer." For the child with a vivid imagination and an eye for the unusual, there is nowhere to go but down.

4. *The tests prevent teachers from teaching.* In every school, teachers take time out of an already-overloaded teaching day to "teach the test," either by reviewing basic concepts that might be on it or by teaching test-taking methods and tricks. In doing so, how much time for advanced content or enrichment is lost?

5. *The tests tell us nothing we can't learn in other ways.* For generations, teachers have been the final arbiters of knowing their students—what they have learned and what they still need to master. Proficiency tests pull the rug out from teachers by saying that this one-time test can tell us more than a year's worth of valuable teacher observations of a student's abilities.

6. *The test results are kept secret.* In most states, the test booklets and answer sheets are not returned to teachers. Rather, they receive a summary statement of their class as a whole accompanied by vague, individual student profiles. Wouldn't it make more sense to review the actual tests to see where the biggest problems occurred? Sorry . . . not allowed.

7. *The tests are more political than educational in nature.* It was state legislatures and testing companies, not educators, who provided the impetus behind this incessant testing. The stakes are high—huge profits for test companies and re-election for politicians who campaign for better schools—but these stakes omit any mention of how our children benefit.

8. *Sadly, I see our situation with tests getting worse before it gets better.* President Clinton recently advocated mandatory national tests for every fourth grader, as if this indiscriminate testing will improve even one classroom teacher's ability to teach every child. Other politicians (and some errant educators) pledge that our test scores will be No. 1 in international competitions of science and mathematics, even though the world's playing field is artificially unbalanced by the fact that we test all of our students, not just the select few who make us look good. It seems to me that this obsession with proficiency and being No. 1 on test scores is the educational equivalent of a schoolyard spitting contest, with the victor getting both bragging rights and a lot of attention. The problem is, next year, when another study shows us doing poorly by comparison with, say, children in Australia or the town next door, the contest takes place again. And the next year, again. We will never truly "win," and the biggest losers are the students and teachers who could be spending their time in much more valuable endeavors than taking tests that serve the wrong master: a political agenda of people whose own lives are far, far removed from the realities of classroom teaching.

Proficiency tests will not improve education any more than a bandage will fix a broken leg or a crumb will satisfy a hungry child's appetite. Proficiency tests will not tell me if Jessie comprehends the meaning of literature or appreciates its nuances. Proficiency tests will not help Shenaya to accept that less than perfection can still be okay and, in fact, that checking one's work for accuracy is a good thing. Proficiency tests will not tell me if Carter will read on his own if given the opportunity to choose some meaningful prose. What proficiency tests will do is this: They will force educators to postpone or eliminate relevant curricula so they can prepare their students for "the tests," and proficiency tests will force children to participate in someone else's game for stakes that have little personal meaning and even less importance.

Yes, my school's fifth graders were abused last week, as were their counterparts in grades 2, 3, and 4. If the psychological scars that I see in these youngsters as they take these tests were immediately visible, perhaps parents and politicians would reconsider the benefits of this frenzied rush to become No. 1. The price our children are paying— in emotional health and increasingly fractured curricula—is not worth that artificial badge of honor.

Gifted Child Today
July/August 1997

Part Five

Underachievement: A Matter of Perspective

U nderachievement is a myth.

That seems like a ludicrous statement to some, I'm sure, as almost every reader will be able to point out a gifted child who "is not working up to his potential." Still, I propose that underachievement is a myth.

How is this so? How can I call such a well-documented and well-researched phenomenon a myth? Easy. Here are just a few reasons:

- Extensive research *has* been done in the area of underachievement, but virtually no two authors use the same definition of underachievement, making generalizations about successful treatment nearly impossible.
- Virtually every study done on underachievement fails to take into account the students' views of their own abilities and achievements. It's as if we assume that their views toward their personal accomplishments mirror our own negative evaluations.

- Treatment for so-called underachievers assumes that the children being "helped" do not have the intellectual power to realize that they are being duped and coerced to change. However, smart kids know when they are not being respected, and few studies or interventions with underachievers even consider respect as part of the treatment equation.

I could go on with additional problems with this misunderstood construct of underachievement, but I would rather let the following articles speak for themselves. Perhaps, collectively, they will put a new enough slant on underachievement that we will begin to call these students what they really are: "selective consumers of education."

The Nonproductive Gifted Child

A Contradiction of Terms?

Introduction

This article was a harbinger of things to come in my life as a writer—that is, someone who often disagrees with the status quo and is not afraid to say so. When this piece first appeared in the *Roeper Review*, I was still a doctoral student at the University of Connecticut. My advisor, Joseph Renzulli, had recently published his interpretation of giftedness as a conflux of ability, creativity, and task commitment, which are then brought to bear on a specific topic or project. In effect, this definition of giftedness downplayed the term *gifted child* and substituted the term *gifted behavior*. Therefore, according to this definition, there was no such person as a *gifted underachiever* because the term itself was contradictory.

When Joe read my article, he was not happy—and I have a two-page letter from him to prove it! But, this was my epiphany, I believe. This article was my first venture into the world of autonomous, independent thinking that is too seldom a component of doctoral study. In this piece, I postulate that gifted children are gifted whether or not they choose to produce a product for the world to see and evaluate. One does not have to "act gifted" to be gifted, because giftedness is not something you do, it is someone you are. I believed that then, and today I believe it even more strongly.

95

I'm not sure if there was one line or thought more than another that caused Joe to dislike my article so intensely. My guess, though, is that this one did not help our professional relationship: "Excluding a highly able child from a gifted program because of the inability to adequately focus and attack an interest may create an artificial comfort that the greatest good is being served."

As I said, I believed it then, and I believe it now.

In his gifted class, Craig sits, bright, but idle. "It's mid-February," Craig's teacher reminds him, "six months into the school year. Can't you think of any project that appeals to you?"

In fact, Craig has had many topics, all aborted or quietly dissolved after preliminary investigations: October was UFOs; December brought comparative anatomy; January was the month for solar energy. None lasted; all went stale.

To some teachers, Craig proves why gifted programs provide an unnecessary frill for school districts concerned with dwindling budgets and enrollments. In some cases, Craig is even the subject of frivolous, teacher-lounge banter:

"Imagine, an IQ of 140 and he can't even decide what his interests are!"

Meanwhile, down the hall, Craig still sits, idle. Snuggling in a corner with a pen and paper, he scribbles and thinks, looking still for that elusive "a-ha." But, today, it evades him again.

As he leaves for his afternoon class, promising to keep looking for possible investigative topics, Craig casually remarks to his teacher, "You know, this gifted program is the best thing that's ever happened to me in school. Will I be in it again next year?"

Is Craig Gifted?

Of course, Craig is not unique, nor are the frustrations felt by the teachers of this bright but targetless boy. Craig is not underachieving—indeed, he *wants* a topic. Yet, something is missing as he ambles through ideas, interested in everything and nothing.

By a popular definition, it is a child's *behavior* that makes giftedness, not a particular score on a selected test (Renzulli, 1978). By this criterion, children who score within the top ranges of selected identification tools (e.g., IQ and achievement measures, creativity scales, teacher nominations) are predisposed to manifesting gifted behaviors.

This predisposition, though, according to the above definition, does not *prove* giftedness anymore than a thorough knowledge of writing styles procures literary merit. The giftedness emerges once particular talents are brought to bear upon specific topic areas and a *product* (e.g., a classic novel) is available for public scrutiny. Gifted behavior, then, is classified as such by the societal standards under which the product is considered.

Let us assume that the above definition of giftedness as behavior is an appropriate, sensible base upon which to design school programs for the child with high potential.

It follows that the focus of such programs should be the establishment of situations that provide the opportunity to *spark* student interest and the availability of time and resources to monopolize on these interests. The literature is not lacking for methods of accomplishing just this (Feldhusen, 1978; Renzulli, 1977; Roberts & Wallace, 1980), but what the literature *does not* tell us is what to do in the most frustrating situation of all: the case of Craig (among thousands of others).

For the high-ability child who sits, considering all options but choosing none, what are the alternatives? For one, we can drop those children from the gifted class, telling them to return only when a project is in mind. Or, we can allow the child the opportunity to continue wandering through a maze of ideas and half-baked projects in the hope that the abilities that we know are present will emerge.

The questions raised by these options are as complex and potentially controversial as are their possible answers: Is there one definition of giftedness that is applicable in all situations? With only scattered funds available, do we make inclusion in gifted programs dependent on student production? Keeping in mind Hollingworth's (1942) contention that, in an ordinary elementary school situation, children of 140 IQ waste half their time, the decision we make—for humanistic and educational reasons—had best be determined individually for each child.

As both a science and an art, education provides few absolutes. The definition of giftedness, once thought adequate when expressed in terms of a particular IQ score, became clouded by the psychological and emotional nuances not recorded by even the most reliable aptitude measure.

The federal government has tried, as have various states and textbook authors, to devise a definition of giftedness acceptable to all. The underlying rationale for locating an unarguable definition is intrinsically tied to a pragmatic purpose: If, for once, we can all agree on who the gifted children are, then selection of and programming for these children will, likewise, be uniform.

The danger, of course, with accepting any *one* definition of giftedness is that, no matter how precise or operational it seems, it still contains the author's biases. Indeed, any definition is arbitrary if it precludes all others as being inconsequential. Therefore, the realization that "the term *giftedness* is a rubric for several populations of children for an increasing body of scientific knowledge about them" (Povey, 1980, p. 9) must be recognized for its merit.

It makes little theoretical or practical sense to disagree actively about the selection and implementation of programs for gifted children if our basic definitions of who they are presume different (even opposing) preconditions or states of being. Instead, a preferable approach is careful enunciation of which segment of gifted children will be served by particular programs. Will you deal with high-achieving gifted children? Define them as such, and identify and program for this subgroup.

The vital point is that, in defining, selecting, and programming for groups of identified gifted children, we are, by our definition, excluding certain other high-ability children who do not meet our standards or criteria.

Production: The Gifted Child on Display

Whatever our definition of giftedness, it seems easier, somehow, to recognize that mentally handicapped children, more so than high-ability children, lose out when not provided supplemental education services. Perhaps, in a society geared to emergencies, education of the gifted is a passionless issue (Gowan, 1972). With increasing frequency, though, provisions for the highly able child are being made in the public schools. Most often, the administrative design is that of a resource room or person whose program includes enrichment and, as a natural extension, some degree of acceleration.

The emphasis on product development within these programs is of ever-increasing concern to educators who are aware of the needs to *prove* the merits of differentiated programming. Children are expected to show off the acquisition of higher level thinking skills through the books they author, surveys their conduct, or city ordinances they help defeat.

And this is all well and good; indeed, it is overdue. For, in the real work of professional adults, it is those who produce the novels, construct the strategies, and provide the cures who are the most effective societal members, responsible for enhancing our collective lifestyles.

There are few arguments, then, to this pragmatic approach to educating the ablest. The resource room alive with the buzz of exploring young minds concentrating on topics of genuine interest is *gifted education* at its best.

And then there is Craig, leafing the card catalog or rambling through library stacks, ever searching (often futilely) for a topic to study. A casual observer would probably surmise that Craig's time is being wasted, that he is taking up space that could be used productively by a more *serious* student who was denied entrance due to space constrictions of the resource room or teacher's time.

But, such may not be the case. The benefits of inclusion into a gifted program for some children need to be measured in terms of more than on-the-spot, short-term projects or interests. For example, research has frequently shown the centrality of one's own perceptions of worth (self-esteem) in bringing forth behaviors that lead to success (Whitmore, 1980). Denying high-ability pupils the freedom to just sit and contemplate potential topics of interest may lead children to the perception that, unless they are always producing, their talents are being wasted. Accordingly, their self-esteem may be altered, beginning a downward spiral of "I can't do it."[1]

The processes of inventing, writing, and creating are often long-term and elusive goals for even the most experienced professionals. Excluding a highly able child from a gifted program because of the inability to focus adequately and attack an interest may create an artificial comfort that the greatest good is being served.

In our current emphasis on providing programs for the gifted that can be evaluated in terms of students' completed products, let us not forget that this need not be the *only*

---

1. It may be that no one ever *asked* the child to develop a product or that interests, though strong, are encumbered by an inability to focus in on a problem of small enough a scale so as to be manageable.

measure of success by which to determine pupil progress. Accountability, if seen solely within such narrow parameters, may be an artificial barometer of student success, especially for the pupil who learns early on that pumping out products, despite their quality, ensures resource room inclusion.

A Moral Mandate[2]

Despite more than a thousand words of advice and admonition, I have yet to answer what, to some, is the central issue of this paper: Is Craig gifted?

It seems to me that, except for isolated instances when such a distinction is needed for public laws or funding allocations, the point is moot. The real issue is Craig's intellectual and affective needs, not his label, and the degree to which his needs are being met by his school programs.

To state that Craig should be eliminated from a resource program because of an inadequately focused research topic is to deny the fact that he is already achieving adequately in his regular classroom curriculum. Craig's problem is *not* one of underachievement, but rather one of nonproduction. This is an important distinction, for the types of resource help Craig requires do not involve remedial help in mastering basic skills; instead, they mandate educational provisions that will acquaint Craig with the purposes for independent production of ideas and projects and the methods of inquiry involved with such production.

Let me put Craig in a resource program and let me keep him there, whether or not he spontaneously writes a book, cures cancer, or, in some other way, produces to my satisfaction. Perhaps with the resource assistance he needs in particular areas of problem focusing and development, his newfound skills will someday enable him to do so.

Roeper Review
May 1983

2. Term borrowed from Whitmore, 1980, p. 201.

Learning
to Underachieve

This article was my initial, naïve attempt to fix the problem of under-achievement by proposing that we look at it from a different perspective: the child's. My intentions were good, but I now find the article a bit lacking in specifics. That's not atypical, by the way, in the underachievement literature; I just thought I was better than that!

If I could pull anything from this 20-year-old article and make use of it today, it is the dualities I present, especially push vs. pull and risk taking vs. risk making. I'll explain both through a story.

I met Aaron three years ago. He was a loud, overweight bully who was smart—and he knew it. If things were going his way, Aaron was a charmer to have in class; but, if there were the least amount of criticism given to him about his work or his effort, Aaron would explode into anger. Some of this anger was genuine—he really was mad about any public declaration of his flaws or limitations—but some of the anger was contrived, a gesture to intimidate both classmates and teachers.

We began meeting weekly, two strangers on opposing missions: I, to get Aaron to open up and discuss his feelings, and Aaron, to circumvent any honest sharing by using big words and strong accusations.

Perhaps it was my opening line to him that first week that caught his attention. "Aaron, your teachers and the school counselor have asked me to meet with you once a week. They said they thought I could help you. That's funny, really, because I really can't help someone I do not know. So, the first thing I want you to know is that I am here to get to know you, not to fix you."

I believe Aaron liked that I was not going to reach for my psychological repair kit during our limited time together. And, to the best of my knowledge, I never did. Instead, we would discuss his friends, family, and his love of anything British. Occasionally, we would discuss school and, if he wanted to work on something but didn't quite know how to go about asking a teacher to let him do it, I served as his go-between, with Aaron at my side. As time went on, he needed me in this role less and less.

Ask anyone who knew him: Aaron had the signs of a "classic underachiever" (I hate that term . . .): high intelligence, low work output, belligerence, haughtiness, and selected skill deficits that made him look "dumb." But, if you looked deeper, if you got to know Aaron better, you would have found, as I did, that he was very interested in learning about lots and lots of things, as long as they sparked his interest (push vs. pull). Also, Aaron was very willing to share his academic and social vulnerabilities if, in doing so, he got to learn more about something that tweaked his many interests (risk taking vs. risk making).

Aaron and I still see each other, but not in the same capacity as before. Instead, I teach him now in my gifted program, and I cheer him on as he plays the lead in virtually every one of our class plays. An underachiever no more—never was, really—Aaron just needed someone he trusted who was there to listen, not lecture.

Tugs of war pitched over mud have observable winners and losers. Caked in layers of wet and brown: the defeated. Dry, but for sweat: the victors. Yet, other tugs occur in both backyard and classroom contexts, where victory is less obvious than that expressed through muddied jeans. Underachievement and its concomitant problems of academic and social discomfort: a tug of war between school and child, between child and parent, between child and friends. A battle in which opposing forces often team to direct blame onto a common recipient—the child—underachievement is a complex web of learned behaviors.

Learning to Underachieve

The word itself—*underachievement*—connotes a level of performance. Though accomplishing less than expected, the child (or adult) who *underachieves* nonetheless produces a measurable amount of work. It is the discrepancy between what is *accomplished* and what is *expected* that defines the term. Underachievement, then, is a behavior. And, as any behavior, it may be modified.

The issue arises, though, (or should) as to the etiology of underachievement. Is it based internally, emanating from an individual's personal choice, laziness, or inability to achieve? Or, is underachievement more of a perception others share about an individual? Authors (Raph, Goldberg, & Passow, 1966; Whitmore, 1980) agree that underachievement is a problem for children because it is recognizable as such by adults. Likewise, underachieving children suffer the pangs of knowing they are disappointing teachers and parents. Thus burdened, children learn to assess their abilities in relation to what they have not done, instead of what they do or are capable of doing (Bloom, 1977). Similar to the frustration of attempting to deepen a hole in wet sand, the underachieving child sees each victory squelched by the collapse of peripheral, unmet goals. For example, one student recounted,

> (My parents) hindered me at times by often expecting too much of me. By being perfectionists, my parents made me feel inadequate and frustrated if I was not constantly performing at my best. (American Association for Gifted Children, 1978, p. 49)

One positive aspect of underachievement is that it is situation- or content-specific. Thus, the child who performs below expectations in school may be a fine accountant on dad's home computer; the teen who puts forth meager efforts in developing friendships with peers may be a strong support in times of family crises. However, the overemphasis on underachievement leaves those strength areas seldom noticed. Instead, we as teachers and parents concentrate on the blatant gaps between potential and performance. There *are* strategies for improving a child's self-worth and awareness correlates of academic and social growth (Colangelo & Pfegler, 1979; Delisle & Renzulli, 1982). However, unless these methods are enmeshed with the following attitudinal shifts, time will be lost and the student's abilities insulted.

Behavioral Dualities: A Matter of Perspective

Education and its antecedent, life, are often examined in a series of dualities: teach vs. learn, right vs. wrong, sensitive vs. harsh. Though artificial and extreme parameters, the duality continua encircle most human behaviors and attitudes.

Underachievement, too, involves such linkages. However, it is the *lack* of distinction between the terms that accounts for misunderstanding of underachievement. Likewise, it is overemphasis on *remediation*, rather than *prevention*, of behaviors that interferes with a child's social and academic growth (Delisle, 1980). A closer examination of these dualities should accentuate causes of underachievement and suggest interventions for limiting the child's ability to learn to underachieve.

Push vs. Pull

> Being gifted, I have a strong sense of future, because people are always telling me how well I will do when I grow up. . . . My feelings fluctuate from a sense of

responsibility for everything to a kind of "leave me alone—quit pushing." (American Association for Gifted Children, 1978, p. 7)

The child who underachieves relies daily on a sense that *I should be doing more.* Whether expressed externally or shrouded in quiet tones of internal conflict, the outcome is the same: guilt and a lowered self-concept (Whitmore, 1979). As a tactic of social influence, guilt reduces effectively one's ability to accomplish preset goals, for the fear remains that disappointment will be the accompaniment of any failed attempt (Mehrabian, 1970).

Underlying underachievement, from this perspective, is the duality of *push vs. pull.* No better example of pushing exists than that of the parent who, in school and at summer camp, rewards only the child's bests. In such an environment, underachieved ambitions become the rule, not the exception, leading one student to ask, "Just how good am I? Just how smart is smart? . . . How do I become better than the bestest best?" (American Association for Gifted Children, 1978, p. 13). Perfectionism, ironically coupled with the knowledge that its attainment is impossible, pushes the child beyond the point of allowing for personal, intellectual defeats.

Instead, the pull side of this duality allows for a child's pursuit of excellence (or otherwise) without correlating one's self-worth with preset standards of academic acumen. Thus, the pull allows for acceleration, should the student so choose, or relaxation, should the mood seem right.

Pushing: an external pressure to perform more, implying that now you're not doing enough. Pulling: an active choice to pursue a course due to a personal dissatisfaction with current levels of work. The former, based on guilt; the latter, based on initiative.

Risk Taking vs. Risk Making

> Teachers told me I was rude,
> Bumptious, overbearing, shrewd.
> Some of the things they said were crude,
> I couldn't understand.
> And so built myself a wall,
> Strong, solid, ten feet tall
> With bricks you couldn't see at all,
> So I couldn't understand.
> (Anonymous, age 11, Sts. Philip and James School, Oxford, England)

Bright children have been accused of fearing to take risks (Fisher, 1981); the uncertainty of outcomes and, again, the fear of attaining less than perfection are given as reasons. However, consider the derivation of risks and the distinction between *risk taking* and *risk making*. For a risk to be taken, its source is some outside agent—a teacher or parent—who wishes to initiate action in someone else (in this cases, the underachieving child). So, the child who refuses to try long division or who neglects the chance to work on an independent project is said to fear risks. Once again, the onus is on the child, not the instigator of the activity, and we continue to concoct new ideas that may stimulate only more apathy.

Risk making, though, utilizes the teacher or parent in a role as spectator as the child pursues an activity that, to him or her, is of genuine interest. With only cursory guidance, but blatant encouragement, the adult *in charge* remains peripheral to the project and its outcome. With this lowered degree of supervision, the child's sole competitor is internal, with disappointment minimized to an audience of one.

The effectiveness of computers with underachieving students (Doorly, 1980) illustrates the noncombatant milieu in which success—achievement—occurs. Risk making, as an alternative attitude and strategy to risk taking, supplies the underachiever with a needed boost in esteem.

Encouragement vs. Praise

Dear Jim,

. . . I have discovered that Craig has been interested in recycling since he was 4 years old. His mom said that he pulled his wagon all around the neighborhood collecting any bit of junk so that he could recycle it!

I still feel a great deal of frustration in trying to get Craig to complete a task of follow through on an idea, but I know . . . learning must come from the student as much as teaching comes from the teacher.

Sincerely,
Nancy

In a less-than-classic phenomenological experiment, a teacher awarded stickers and stars for 100% on any homework or test. Content with such praise, children collected their rewards. The defeated, those scoring 99% or below, sat quietly or begrudged the Hallmark goodies, competing actively then for the classroom's lowest grade. Those who achieved the perfection of 100% pouted (and two cried) when errors dropped their own scores to 94%. The external praise withheld, the teacher's encouraging "Try again tomorrow" provided all the solace of an odorless scratch-and-sniff decal.

Praise, and its subsequent absence, isolates children from their work, making individual self-worth dependent upon a superfluous reward instead of the task itself (Rowe, 1969). Encouragement, though, is a sequential approval of an ongoing project or thought. Praise connotes expectations for more of the same; encouragement imbues the child with a sense of purpose and camaraderie with his or her work's processes and product.

Of course, praise is necessary and can be used effectively. (Few of us, for example, would work for encouragement alone, as devoid of dollars.) However, motivation researchers (Blaine & McArthur, 1971; Glaser, 1971) agree on the purposefulness of intermittent reinforcement over that scheduled on a regular basis.

For the underachiever, or the child wise to the game of praise qua self-worth, encouragement is a greater reward than a reward by itself will ever be.

First Best vs. First Worst

November 5, 1980. Quincy, MA (AP): Two 17-year-old high school boys, labeled by police as "brilliant but immature," were blamed Tuesday for eight bombings that allegedly began with chemistry experiments. "These two are not criminals," said (police). "Unfortunately, they were immature enough not to realize the danger in what they were doing."

In peer and school settings, what the underachiever does best is often different than that which is recognized as being socially or academically acceptable. But, for the child in quest of perfection, most any situation will suffice if it affords positive or negative attention. Vying for the *top spot*, though, is difficult for a pupil who must compete with high-achieving agemates. As an alternative to becoming *first best*, underachievers may instead strive to become *first worst* (LaRusso, 1980).

First worst status is earned—and learned. The child who competes for such a distinction does so out of a sense, and a need, to belong: "Companionship and peer stimulation, those mundane necessities, are just that, necessities" (American Association for Gifted Children, 1978, p. 114). First worst competitors select from among a variety of strategies in a dual effort to gain peer attention while alienating adult authority:

- refuses to comply with rules and requests;
- instead of working, moves about, disrupting others;
- rejects assignments as *silly* or *boring*; and
- exploits any freedom (Whitmore, 1979).

Such overt aggression, executed successfully, is a fine method for achieving the recognition usually reserved for sports stars and scholars. Also, first worst status provides an effective screen behind which underachievers can disguise their discomfort with academic imperfections.

Less obvious, but perhaps more startling, is the youngster whose response to underachievement is social and academic withdrawal. Cloistered in a physical or psychological corner, the child chips away at an already pocked self-image, hoping to reveal evidence that will make less-than-perfect okay.

Ironically, both the disrupter and the isolate share similar pools of social isolation from peers and academic banishment from parents and teachers. The student's freedom to enjoy success is hampered by the knowledge that each new achievement carries the *baggage* of previous failures.

Summary—and a Final Duality

90% of life is just showing up.
—Woody Allen

It is easy to learn to underachieve. In schools where 60% of the 4th and 10th graders know 80% of their math, science, and social studies texts *before* they use them for the school year (EPIE, 1981); in a time when "parents . . . are more concerned with their children's success in the marketplace than with their creative ideas" (Heckinger, 1981); in a context where two-thirds of our country's most talented youth report being confused or misled as to educational and occupational goals while in school (Holtzman, 1960), it seems a feat, indeed, that success and happiness are not underachieved more often.

Which leads to a final duality: *prevention vs. remediation.*

Gifted education's historical link to special education has been fiscally beneficial. Also, the need for individualized learning for both the handicapped and the gifted child has been reinforced via this association. However, unlike the handicapped child, the bright student has a variety of blatant strength areas upon which teachers can capitalize. Yet, curricula continue to be designed and strategies developed that assume that all children need to pursue the same core courses of study. "The boredom that results from discrepancies between the child's knowledge and the school's offerings leads to underachievement and behavior disorders affecting self and others" (Marland, 1972).

In the ultimate irony, the gifted child has become handicapped, emotionally incapable of performing to the potential that exists. We call this syndrome *underachievement,* and we look for causes within the child instead of within ourselves and the curricula we teach.

Perhaps, in the final analysis, underachievement is learned because it is taught.

There is no panacea for dealing with underachieving students. No text, no simulation game, no lockstep motion through creative problem solving will guarantee the reversal of a downward trend in academic or social performance. The key (or one of them) lies not in remediation, but in prevention. Underachievement seldom occurs overnight, but rather manifests itself in cumulative clues obvious to astute peers, parents, and teachers. Underachievement begins with *I don't think I can do its,* and papers crumpled in frustration, and quiet sobs that result from not being chosen for a recess kickball tourney. Mental health and a classroom climate that transcends the intellectual are safeguards against the onset of underachievement.

Finally, let us base some of our curricula on the individual interests of students, while deleting those components that the student has already mastered. More than a frill, such preventative interventions are both the student's right and the teacher's responsibility.

Underachievement is never a goal, but a situation accepted as being less than desirable. Through the recognition of behavioral dualities that may precede low performance and the introduction of preventative strategies at home and in school, learning to underachieve may become a task seldom accomplished.

Roeper Review
April 1982

Dealing With
the Stereotype
of Underachievement

Introduction

This brief article is but one more of my attempts to dislodge the field of underachievement from its foundation of sand. I pick on something called the underachievement syndrome (small letters), but, if I were braver then, I would have used the capital letters in dismissing the Underachievement Syndrome as proposed by Sylvia Rimm. To my view, it is unfortunate that this book became so popular because many of the suggestions it makes, if applied liberally, will chip away at a gifted child's self-concept until he or she relents out of mental exhaustion. I dare say that, if any adult were subjected to the same disrespectful suggestions for change proposed by Rimm (and the dire consequences if change is not forthcoming), we would rebel against our oppressors.

Underachievement does not have to become a win-lose situation, but it often is dealt with as such. The child is not taken seriously, his or her views of school situations are neither believed nor respected, and any change that results is often temporary and due to external pressures, rather than an internal desire to improve.

We can do better by our children, and this short article addresses how that might happen.

T he best description I ever heard of the word *lazy* is "people who are not motivated in ways you want them to be." This same description could also be given to the word *underachievement*, one of the most overused and misapplied terms used in our field.

Reams of articles and books have been written on the "problem" of underachievement and its resolution. But, with one notable exception—Joanne Rand Whitmore's *Giftedness, Conflict, and Underachievement* (1980), now, sadly, out of print—most of the work on this topic is vapid, void of either substance or respect, and filled with techniques to coerce "underachieving" students into performing at levels that cause adults to smile. While pretending to have the best interests of underachievers at heart, authors on this topic do their best to zap out of these often creative children the very essence of what has kept them alive, intellectually speaking: their nonconformity and their refusal to accept mediocrity in their education.

Why am I so against the idea of underachievement and the subsequent plans given to ameliorate it? First, because much of the research is based on an erroneous (or at least suspect) assumption: the presumption of guilt. If a teacher or parent or national expert so much as hints at the possibility that a particular student is an underachiever, then that's as far as it goes—he or she is labeled. No counter claims or trials—nothing. Just a sentence. Next, a whole army of strategies is employed, most involving contracts, verbal agreements, and subsequent losses of privileges to the offending underachiever for promises unkept. "Solutions" surround the underachieving student, becoming the educational equivalent of white blood cells amassing around an open sore to prevent infection. "Catch it quick," we're told. "Keep underachievement from spreading!"

Solace is offered the underachieving student via suggestions for change:

"You're a smart kid if only you'd apply yourself."

"I don't care if the homework is boring—an assignment is an assignment."

"If you'd argue less about your work and just plain do it, you wouldn't be having these problems."

These statements and others like them tell the student that his or her opinion doesn't matter or that his or her perceptions are inaccurate. Now, not only is the student guilty of academic neglect, he (it is mostly males who are labeled underachievers) is often told that change is up to him—his responsibility, his burden. So much for education being a positive partnership involving school, home, and students!

Standardizing Definitions

Another reason I protest the term *underachievement* and its application to children is that no two people really define the term the same way, nor do they document when underachievement turns that magical corner and is transformed into "achievement." Is it an improvement in grades that prompts us to pronounce the child cured? If so, which grades are high enough? Or, is it a shift in attitude that causes us to claim victory? And is this attitude a general mood swing or just related to academic affairs?

That's the funny thing about underachievement: It has no statute of limitations. Once applied, the label is seldom revoked.

I would suggest another look, a different look, at this so-called "underachievement syndrome." First, I would suggest that we treat individuals who are not doing as well in school as their aptitude indicates they can as just that: individuals. We need to ask these able students if they can pinpoint any reasons for their disinterest in or distrust of school. Perhaps there are specific forces operating against a child's own best self-interests that are prompting his negative responses. If so, could it be that the situation, not the child, is what should change?

Secondly, we can locate areas of intense interests—or, as George Betts calls them, "passions"—that even the most dyed-in-the-wool "underachiever" enjoys. That passion could be anything from rock climbing to rock music, but, whatever it is, that passion must be acknowledged and nurtured. If it is taken away as a "consequence" (i.e., punishment), then we are kicking a child who is already down. How immature, how hurtful.

Third, have we ever considered the effect the label of underachiever has on the child who wears it? It implies nothing but negatives—bad student, lazy kid, lost potential—that are all pretty heavy burdens to bear when you already know that you've been disappointing people whom you have grown to like, love, or respect, at least to a degree.

Assigning Labels

Underachievement is an adult term used to describe a set of troublesome child behaviors that don't match some preconceived notions of just how high a gifted child is supposed to perform. *Underachievement* is a hurtful and disrespectful term that is defined differently by every person who uses it. Underachievement is a myth, existing in the eye of the beholder who deems it to be there.

There is no argument that some very capable children are not performing as well in school tasks as they could. It is equally true that some individual schools and teachers provide very little intellectual sustenance for gifted students, Still, to label any of the parties to this problem as an "underachiever" does little more than assign blame to some unwitting victim, usually the child.

Before we can alter any behaviors in children about whom we are concerned, we must first change two things: our vocabulary and our attitudes abut this misnomer labeled "underachievement." Only then will students gain both the inner desires and strength to perform well in school.

Gifted Child Today
November/December 1994

"Who Am I, Anyway?"

*Self-Concepts
and Sibling Comparisons*

Introduction

This is a brief article that needs just a quick overview. Directed toward parents of gifted children, this article discusses how seemingly harmless parental comments and comparisons made to siblings can cause each child to think that he or she has to be more like the other! Of course, some sibling comparisons are natural and healthy, as they help children distinguish each other, one from the next. Gifted children, though, have a tendency to take away from the comparisons only the negatives and the areas needed to improve, foregoing the positive comments parents make on their behalf.

Like most articles on parenting, this one contains more ideas related to common sense than research findings. Its intent is to show parents that even their best of intentions might be misinterpreted by their gifted child as an urge to do better. If this happens, it's time for another honest talk.

t has always seemed ironic to me that children begin to develop *self-concepts* only after they see themselves in relation to *others*. For only when children become aware that other people differ from them—in appearances, abilities, and so forth—do they begin to get a sense of who *they* are as individuals. Inevitably, comparisons then begin, and sometimes children see themselves as less able than they really are.

Many parents feel an unfocused sense of guilt when this occurs. "What did I do wrong?" they ask. Or, "I never compare my children with one another," they state. And, quite often, the parents are right—they did nothing to promote the negative self-image that their son or daughter has developed. Instead, the comparisons are often more subtle, and they take root quietly within the child's own mind, as he or she begins to "rate" him- or herself to other children—often, siblings.

For example: Anna is the younger of two daughters, ages 6 and 9, and, recently, has enjoyed her "career" in preschool and kindergarten. She was already reading by age 4 and has always seemed to enjoy the company of her big sister, Leslie. Now, though, Anna has started coming home from school and reporting that she is stupid. She hates school, she says, and she doesn't like reading anymore, either. Of course, Anna's parents are concerned for her—she *is* a bright child, and they don't want to see her develop a negative attitude toward school or learning.

What should or shouldn't Anna's parents do? The first thing to avoid is a verbal assault on Anna's beliefs. Statements such as, "But, you *are* a smart girl, just look how well you do in school," or "Don't be silly—you *love* reading," do not register with Anna because she is not yet ready to accept them. In a sense, she *can't* hear them because those statements go against everything Anna is saying about herself to her parents. If Anna were to say, "Okay, I guess you're right," that could mean (to her) that she *is* stupid, as she doesn't even know what she readily likes and is good at.

Instead, it would be better if Anna's parents took their daughter's statements as seriously as Anna does. Statements and follow-ups like, "It must be awful to have to sit in school all day if you hate it so much," or "When do you hate reading the most?," will enable Anna to continue the conversation to get more specific about her likes, dislikes, fears, and joys.

More than likely, Anna knows that she is not as stupid as she says, and if you were to observe her in school, you would probably find her enjoying her time there quite a bit. What Anna is doing, then, is sending out messages that may be saying any of the following: "I'm not my sister, so don't expect me to be," "Just because I'm smart doesn't mean I'm perfect," or "If I tell you now that I'm dumb, then you won't be surprised later if I get a bad grade." In her own way, Anna (and others like her) is trying to preserve the fragile concept of herself as a student. Earlier, when was 3 or 4, it was only her parents' reactions and approval that mattered—Anna became whole if she knew she was pleasing Mom and Dad. Now, in the wider world of school, there are more people to answer to: parents, teachers, classmates, siblings. So many people to please for a 6-year-old! Now, to forestall disappointing others and to hold onto the still-emerging self-concept that she has, Anna will keep expectations "in check" by keeping them low.

Most likely, this reaction is more a "holding pattern" than an impression that is set in stone. Eventually, as children match and exceed the somewhat low standards they talk about publicly, and if they begin to see that others appreciate them for who they are as individuals, *not* just as scholars, their self-concepts and expectations will rise. Of course, parents and teachers can help this process along by doing the following:

- not overreacting to or negating what a child says;
- acknowledging that each of us is better at some things than others;
- encouraging children to try now topics or activities "just for the fun of it," with no mention of grades or other evaluation;
- helping children to notice their own successes—even small ones—with comments like, "What was your favorite part of this project?" and "Can you notice any change between your first and your latest attempts?"; and
- relating their own embarrassing moments or mistakes and talking about how silly they made them feel.

Sibling rivalry and comparisons are unavoidable, a natural part of growing up. In only-child families, comparisons still crop up, with friends, relatives, or classmates used as a child's reference points. Often, though, these comparisons are part of a bigger picture, as the child is trying to link a developing self-concept to something real, like the performance of an older brother, sister, or cousin. Understanding the importance of these comparisons will help parents see the bigger picture as it relates to the growth and development of self-concept in their children.

Understanding Our Gifted
May 1990

Part Six

So . . . You Want
to Be the Parent
of a Gifted Child?

I n a wonderful video series called *Young and Special* that was produced in the early 1980s, the segment on gifted children includes an interview with one of gifted child education's most renowned experts, Dr. James Gallagher. When asked the question, "How do parents react when they first learn they have a gifted child?," Jim gives a two-part response. Paraphrasing his remarks here, I recall Jim saying the first response from parents is "Oh, Wow!," while a few seconds later comes the reality: "What are we supposed to do now?"

When Dr. Spock wrote his baby books, he seemed to leave out one vital area: advanced development. The milestones in a baby's life (and a child's life) might be similar in content, but when the events occur way in advance of when they are "supposed to," what's a parent to think? To do?

Since entering this field more than 20 years ago, I have found an amazing increase in the number of resource books, organizations, and (recently) Web sites that help parents understand that, although their gifted child may not develop in a *typical* way, he or she is still developing in ways that are *normal.* This boom in available material has been a real boon for the millions of parents who sometimes question if giftedness is so fragile that they will surely ruin it if they make a wrong decision.

The following articles show my own growth, both as a gifted child educator and the dad of a gifted son, in my thinking about ways to demystify the phenomenon of giftedness for parents who sometimes question why it isn't easy to raise a gifted child.

Too Young
to Be Taken Seriously

Introduction

I sometimes wonder if my "throwaway" articles, the ones that take up just about one page of copy, really matter to anyone. After all, they can be read in a five-minute break from work and, when there is only one page to work with, as an author, there's not a whole lot of room for elaboration or examples.

Still, sometimes things go right—even in 500 words or less. This brief article details the life of Kerry Thompson, a subject in one of my books, *Kidstories* (Free Spirit, 1992), which was a set of biographies of 20 young people who had done something noteworthy. Kerry was my one international entry, hailing from Australia.

I never met Kerry, but we spoke by audio recording quite often. She would entertain me, and the then-fourth graders I was teaching, with the poetry she wrote about her home in the Outback. Accomplished even at the age of 9, Kerry and her parents had to suffer through people who disbelieved someone of her age could compose poems of such beauty and depth. This article, and the biography in *Kidstories*, documents both her frustration and her eventual triumph.

Still . . . the prejudice continues for kids like Kerry—kids who know more than they are supposed to, or think at levels that uninformed others label as

115

weird. And it is the parents of kids like Kerry who must be there to bolster them when their self-opinions falter.

I never met, or even spoke with, Kerry's parents. But, I empathize with their confusion over why gifted kids like Kerry can't just be accepted for who they are, instead of being seen as different from other kids in the neighborhood . . . or the Outback.

When Kerry Thompson was 3 years old, she began to compose poetry. Since her mind focused more quickly than her fingers, Kerry's mom transcribed her words into print. At age 5, Kerry entered her first poetry contest. Sadly, her work was returned to her unjudged; however, a note accompanied her rejected submission: "Please submit children's original work *only*. Obviously, a 5-year-old could not have written this piece."

How frustrating for Kerry and countless other highly gifted children whose work breaks the bounds of typical development. The ultimate insult to one's self-concept, no matter how young or old, is to have talent denied by "placekeepers" whose assumptions are wrong. With Kerry, this was the case; her verbal fluency was suspect because most other children her age did not share her talents or insights.

Parents of children like Kerry are as frustrated as the children themselves when it comes to being taken seriously. Surely, Kerry's talents are special; but, they are not so unique as to make them unbelievable. How can parents and their children cope when adults get stuck in a mindset that disallows excellence before it is "supposed to" be attained?

* *Encourage your children's efforts for their own personal satisfaction.*

Children as young as Kerry often need to release their talents and energies more for self-satisfaction than for recognition by others. Encourage these attempts and acknowledge how important it is to release one's creative energies in such positive ways.

* *Locate other children whose talents and interests match those of your child.*

Even if these children are chronologically older than your child, such a difference will be of little importance once their "like minds" connect on a common goal. Seek out these talented children through your local or statewide gifted education advocacy group.

* *Find adult role models who take your child seriously.*

One of Kerry's fondest memories was meeting a favorite children's author, Pam Ayres, at a day-long writers' conference. Encourage your talented children to write to individuals they admire and allow them to participate in community or cultural events that highlight the work of people whose interests they share. Even if he or she is the only child present, your encouragement to associate with these authors/artists/"doers" will be appreciated.

* *Provide an ear of understanding.*

It can be frustrating to have a talent that is not appreciated by one's agemates. By serving as a noncritical "sound board" for your child's wishes, dreams, and frustrations, you may be providing more support than you know. Be willing to listen, be willing to laugh, be willing to cry; no matter what, take your children's comments seriously, for that is, no doubt, how they made them.

Back to Kerry. Yes, her work was finally taken seriously, and, at the tender age of 8, she already has had her work published by the Fellowship of Australian Writers and she has presented her poetry in the Australian Parliament. As Kerry relates, "I am happy, excited, and proud."

As all of us should be, for Kerry represents just one child among thousands whose work precedes its "expected" emergence. Finally, she is being seen as the creative young poet she truly is.

Understanding Our Gifted
March/April 1993

Reversal of Fortune

How Parents Unintentionally Undermine a Gifted Child's Self-Worth

Introduction

Talk about guilt! Every time I distribute this article to parent groups with whom I speak, I hear moans of recognition from the audience. We *all* strive to be the best parents we can be, and when an article like this reminds us that we have made mistakes along the way, we want to retreat to a private corner to lick our parental wounds.

But, the only reason I was able to *write* this article is because I have uttered the same dumb statements that are listed *in* this article! If nothing else, this recognition that we are all human (and, therefore, frail) puts us all behind the same collective eight-ball. Still, despite our dumb statements, our kids forgive us our trespasses and love us as the caring moms and dads we are ever-striving to be.

So . . . as you read this piece and feel the pangs of guilt emerge, take a deep breath and realize I am not speaking directly to you.

Oh! And just one story that correlates with the statement "You did a great job in school, but . . ." A couple in Texas approached me to tell me what happened the first time their son, Danny, received a B on his report card, in fourth-grade music (Horrors! What will Julliard think?) Although Mom and Dad were very cool about the B and were actually happy that the first chink in perfection was finally achieved, they felt compelled to be empathetic. So, while their almost-perfect son was crying a sea of tears, Mom and Dad pulled out their own elementary school report cards, which they had stowed away for just this occasion. They shared this less-than-perfect performance rating with Danny who, upon reading them, began crying even harder than before! After a few minutes of uncontrolled wailing, Danny confessed to his misery. He looked at his parents and uttered: "With you two as parents, I'm doomed to be stupid!"

Sometimes, there is no winning.

---

 reader from Erie, PA, writes: "Sometimes I feel that I say and do the exact opposite of what I should be doing with my gifted child. I don't want to undermine my child's sense of self-worth, but it seems to happen. What kind of advice can you give to help me say and do the "right" things for my gifted child?

Imagine if being a parent were an easy job. You would speak, your child would listen, and every night would end like a rendition of John-Boy's good night on *The Waltons.* Do I have to tell you this is not going to happen?

Enter the gifted child: You know, the kid who asks why snow doesn't melt white if chocolate melts brown and butter melts yellow . . . the one who asks at age 3, "Mommy, do people feel the same way right before they're born as they do right after they die?" . . . the one who sees the grays of life while remaining unabashedly oblivious to the blacks and whites of scheduled bedtimes and required homework.

Gifted children and their parents can come to loggerheads when the topic is discipline, school, household tasks and responsibilities, or the relative benefits of attending to Play Station® for hours on end. But, there are ways to circumvent the verbal tanglings that often erupt when the parent of a gifted child tries to coax a reluctant son or daughter into believing or acting in a certain way.

As a primer from one who has been there—I have taught gifted children for 20 years and raised one at home—here are some things to remember not to do and not to say when you talk with your gifted child.

- *"You're not working up to your potential."*

Is there a more stifling, inhibiting, or demeaning comment as this? It is often said with the best of intentions—to get the gifted child to perform better in school. But, there's a snag: No one ever explains to the gifted child what "working up to your potential" actually means. No one ever says, "Okay . . . you've reached your potential, so you can relax now." Success is rarely defined for gifted children, leaving them without directions for success. Like a ship in dark waters seeking a safe harbor, the gifted child floats adrift among a sea of unexplained expectations.

But, consider this: Which of us, as adults, is working up to our potential? Which of us is capitalizing on our innate gifts or learned talents to such degrees that everyone around us says, "Wow!"? My guess is that very few adults would admit to working up their potential, blaming the constraints of too little time and too many responsibilities as the rationale behind their less-than-perfect performance. Well, guess what? Many of our gifted children feel these same restraints.

My advice? Lay off the "potential" theme and start asking more refined questions like "What did you learn in school today?" instead of "What did you earn in school today?" By realizing that *potential* is a term that exists individually in the eyes of the beholder, we may come to appreciate our children more in the present tense than in the future tense.

- *"You did a great job in school, but . . ."*

It is natural for people to want to reward excellence in others about whom they care. Unfortunately, it is also human nature to couple this praise with an urge to do better. Thus, a glowing comment like "You're doing a great job in school" is often reduced to a faint ember by adding ". . . but, if you worked a little harder, you could probably earn high honors."

Ouch! That burns! That single word—*but*—is one of our language's greatest natural depressants, as it diminishes the importance and worth of the genuine praise that came before it. Indeed, when a compliment is following a *but* statement, it really becomes a "kick in the butt," erasing any semblance of pride that a child might have accepted as credit for a job well done.

The solution, though, is easy: Just be quiet! When you give your child a compliment ("I like your outfit," "Your project shows a lot of effort"), leave it at that. Period. Don't complicate matters by inserting an urge to improve as a follow-up statement. Should you strongly feel that you need to prod your child to do better despite some success, that's fine—just do it at another time (the next day or the next week) and do not tie it in with the prior praise that was so well deserved.

- *"This'll be easy for a smart kid like you."*

Here's the scenario: Your child has decided to take an advanced class at school and you're very pleased, especially because the subject is calculus—your specialty. Finally, you will be able to help with homework in a meaningful way.

So, the class begins and, shortly thereafter, so do some problems. What used to be learned without even opening a textbook is now a struggle for your child. The content is more difficult, the challenges more frequent, the self-doubts more prominent than ever.

"Time for me to intervene," you think. And you do. Dredging up your knowledge of things mathematical, you begin to help your child with homework. When your captive student hits a snag, you arm yourself with advice and suggestions. But, it doesn't help. Your child is still struggling to grasp a concept that you mastered long ago.

So, you give some advice that you are sure will work. Hugging your child's shoulder, you say, "This'll be easy for a smart kid like you." Then, you watch as your child walks away in disgust, anger, or frustration, and you wonder what you did that was so wrong.

Unintentionally, you made a smart kid feel dumb by suggesting that a concept that was personally difficult to grasp was actually a piece of cake. Your child's inner thought: "Hey, if this stuff is so easy and I can't get it, I must be pretty dumb. Maybe I should drop this class." It may have been inadvertent, but the words still sting, especially if your child was honestly trying to grasp an elusive concept that was crystal clear to you.

Instead, try saying something like "I can see that you're having some trouble in understanding this concept. That's okay. Together, we'll work on it until you feel comfortable with it." This message gives validity to your child's efforts and merit to your child's beliefs that learning something new can be difficult. Also, it validates the idea that, just because you are gifted, that does not mean that everything comes as naturally as swimming does to a fish.

- *"I don't care about your grades as long as you do your best."*

Every parent I know, and virtually every student, too, utters this phrase at some time. It is meant to provide comfort to a child who does not gain an automatic grasp of a concept or idea. The effect of this statement, though, might be quite the opposite because, if a child thinks he or she always has to do the best work possible—whether in academics, creative endeavors, sports, whatever—then this leaves little room for mistakes.

Think of it this way: Do you always "do your best" in all areas of everyday life—like work, cleaning, or exercising daily? Or, is it sometimes okay to have a house that is 70% tidy or a four-day-a-week workout schedule? By sending a message that high grades do not always count, but that high efforts always do, you are leaving too little room for the very real pleasure of just being average. Trust me, as a mechanic I am mediocre and, as an adult, I have the privilege and the prerogative of saying those two magic words— "Hire out!"—when faced with a task that I definitely do not want to exert my best efforts in completing. Your child needs the same degree of freedom that you and I have when it comes to not being a top performer in everything he or she touches.

Be cautious of your admonitions to always do your best. Instead, ask your child to be selective in his or her attempts at excellence because there just is not enough time in anyone's life to excel at everything. Remember, less than perfection is more than acceptable.

A Final Word

As parents, there are many things we do and say that we wish we could take back later. We, like our kids, are imperfect beings, and it would be silly to believe that even our best-intentioned efforts are always interpreted in ways we meant them. This primer on some of the "don'ts" of parenting is not meant to make your feel guilty or dumb— only human. If you find yourself falling victim to using one of the above statements, just backpedal a little bit and be honest with your child: "Sammy, I'm sorry if what I said made you feel bad. Let's go back and try again."

An apology, if meant sincerely, can erase the impact of prior statements or actions, especially if your child understands what should be obvious: that, without the benefit of a sure-fire recipe book on childrearing, there will be an "oops!" or two along the road. In an odd sort of way, that's comforting.

Parenting for High Potential
June 1999

Profoundly Gifted Guilt

n 1999, one of the most significant events in gifted child education in the past 50 years occurred: The Davidson Institute for Talent Development (DITD) was founded. Unlike any other support organization for gifted kids and their parents, DITD looks out for the needs of profoundly gifted children, those 4–11-year-old children who have IQs above 160.

I have had the privilege of working with and getting to know more than 60 families associated with DITD, as well as Jan and Bob Davidson, the founders of this organization. For reasons that are both understandable and humane, Bob and Jan do not reveal the names of these families to the public, nor to they want those of us who know them to disclose who they are. I respect and admire this stance.

However, I learned so much from this group of Young Scholars (as they are called) that I needed to write an article about the specific concerns faced by exceptionally gifted children and their parents. That's where this article emanated: from the heart of people searching desperately for someone, anyone to understand their profoundly gifted child and the social, emotional, and intellectual issues that surround this level of ability.

The editor of the *Gifted Education Communicator*, good buddy and educator extraordinaire Margaret Gosfield, let me know that she wanted to publish this article. But, she also wanted to note that some of the issues raised in it, to a degree, are faced by parents of children who are not as profoundly gifted as those in DITD. As usual, Margaret was right.

I am proud of this article, as I believe it shows my own growth as a professional dealing with the issues involved in both educating and living with a gifted child.

Matt, I hope I "done you right" on both counts.

I've been involved with the care and feeding of gifted children for almost 25 years—longer than I've been a dad, longer than I've been a husband, and almost as long as I've been literate! So, of course, I thought I'd seen and heard it all in this field of study that has become my life's passion. I wouldn't call myself jaded, but I was, perhaps, a bit too smug about the completeness of my knowledge of gifted children.

But, during the past year, I have had the privilege of getting to know a large number (more than 60) of profoundly gifted children and adolescents. These powerfully bright and intense young people presented me with realities that I had not experienced previously: a 7-year-old girl taking college courses; a 14-year-old boy whose need to help others caused him to raise thousands of dollars for cancer research; two 10 year olds whose knowledge of physics far surpassed any college student I know; and an 11-year-old whose high school graduation prank (with several other seniors) involved releasing three pigs into his suburban high school, each of which was adorned with a number: 1, 2, and 4.

"I think they're still searching for Pig #3!" Ken giggled.

Perhaps the most touching story came from the mother of a 5-year-old who spoke to me at one of my seminars in Texas. She wasn't sure whether Jeffrey was "truly gifted" in the test-taking, IQ sense, but she was definite about one thing: His emotional sensitivity to everyone and everything around him. To illustrate, Mom spoke of Jeffrey's reaction to getting a pet kitten. About three days after receiving this living plaything, Jeffrey was holding the kitten as it slept, rocking it back and forth, tears streaming down his face. When Jeffrey's concerned mother asked what was wrong, her young son calmed himself enough to tell her this: "This is the most beautiful creature that has ever existed." Jeffrey's mother's question to me? "Will he ever *not* be this sensitive?" The answer was obvious.

This Texas mom, and other parents of profoundly gifted children I have had the good fortune to meet, share the concerns of all parents: "Will my child be happy and successful?" and "How can I help my child to become a good person?" But, there are also some unique concerns to being the parent of a child who may, indeed, be the family's smartest member. I have noticed what I have come to call PGG, "Profoundly Gifted Guilt," which is the feeling that, in some important ways, parents of extremely gifted children feel unable to raise adequately the child they have been given. These genuine feelings of inadequacy are, simultaneously, well-meaning and ill-placed, for when we downplay our competencies as parents, we do a disservice to both our children and ourselves as we underestimate the effects of our own importance on the lives of our children.

What are some of the statements that I've heard from parents of profoundly gifted children? Here are some samples.

• *"I'm not smart enough to help my child."*

From a very young age, profoundly gifted children have both knowledge and insights that can realistically be described as "uncanny." With very little direct instruction, and often limited exposure to the wider world around them, profoundly gifted children just seem to know a fact, a theory, a concept, a truth. To many of their parents, this is scary, for they are unable to point to the genesis of this wisdom in their children. How, then, can these parents "take credit" for what their children know or how they learned it? When this situation repeats itself often enough—as it will with profoundly gifted children—some of their parents begin to feel a loss of ownership in their parenting. This is only one small step away from feeling inadequate as a parent.

At some point, almost all parents realize that their children know more than they do about particular topics. Generally, though, this occurs when the children become teenagers, when it is "safe" for parents to admit that they don't remember enough algebra to help with their 10th grader's math assignment But, when this situation presents itself time and again when the child is 6 or 8 years old, a different parental attitude prevails, generating the onset of inadequacy that is woven into the statement, "I am not smart enough to help my child."

The thing is, parents are not necessarily seen by even the most brilliant of children as the font of all knowledge, the annotated bibliographer of all that is true and wise. Instead, kids—even profoundly gifted ones—see Mom and Dad as the people who give them baths, prepare their meals, pick them up at soccer, and embarrass them in front of company. Sure, it is a bonus to be seen as an adult who *knows* a little something about this and that, but the Academic Decathlon is seldom run in the family room or the kitchen. Wise parents know that it is okay to say "I don't know" in answer to even a young child's question. Whether parents then choose to learn the answer together with their child is up to them, but the reality is that effective parenting has less to do with "book smarts" and more to do with hugs. And these are things that *every* parent can dole out to their children with wild abandon!

• *"I'm sure if I do the wrong thing, I'll just ruin this child!"*

Maybe the suggestion has been made that a profoundly gifted child be accelerated several grades in school. Or, maybe the hint has been given that the child's high intellect complicates social issues enough that counseling should begin. Or, perhaps Grandma has warned that "If you don't get him out of that computer class and into a sandbox that boy will have troubles for the rest of his life."

Whom do you believe? How do you decide? To whom do you turn?

Parents of profoundly gifted children often feel isolated in seeking solutions to these and other life dilemmas. Even parents of "moderately" gifted children may not be able to give much advice, as the problems they are seeing or the situations they are encountering bear little resemblance to the enormity of the issues as perceived by parents of the profoundly gifted. Each dilemma seems dire and life-changing—how *else* could you describe the decision to allow a 10-year-old to begin taking college courses?—and parents of profoundly gifted children often feel as if the *wrong* decision will result in the most awful of circumstances.

What is often forgotten is that, in almost every case, a decision is reversible. So, if the grade skipping doesn't work out as well as it was assumed it might, or if the counselor chosen is someone who doesn't respect the child appropriately enough to help her, gears can be switched or a new direction can be taken. Just like the child who frets so much about the "huge assignment" due that he never begins to do it, parents of profoundly gifted children must realize that the worst decision is *no* decision. They need to consider the possible side effects—good and bad—of various options and go with the one that makes the most sense to them *at the moment*. No one can predict what lies ahead in two weeks, two months, or two years, but keeping an open mind to switching in mid-stream is one way to alleviate the guilt that any but the optimal choice will bring ruin on a brilliant young life. As my son would say, "Ain't gonna happen."

- *"I want to talk about my gifted child, but I seldom do."*

Every parent earns "bragging rights" the minute their child is born. When she first walked, when he first spoke a sentence, or which college accepted the twins are all legitimate milestones that parents are expected to share with their friends and relatives. Usually, there is a *quid pro quo* attitude about this among adults: "You talk about your child for a while, then I'll tell you about mine." And this social discourse generally runs smoothly, as the stories are believable and the range of embellishments are within bounds that parents can understand and appreciate.

Until you are the parent of a profoundly gifted child. Then, when you begin to say that your child began reading at 18 months, or that she asks questions about the origins of human life at the age of 3, or that he is going to start taking a high school geometry class instead of third-grade math, parents of profoundly gifted kids begin to get funny looks. Some think they are lying, making up stories just to make *other* children look bad. Others think that these are evil parents who push, push, push their child for their own selfish satisfaction. Still more (and this is often relatives) ignore the comments altogether, refusing to see the profoundly gifted child as being anything other than a typical child who is just "a little bit smart."

The effect of these reactions often leads parents of the profoundly gifted to say very little about their child's progress to anyone, for fear that they will be stereotyped as "that type" of parent. Perhaps there will be a neighbor or close friend who both believes and relishes the stories that are shared, but these understanding souls are rare. So, the parents choose to go "underground," talking only with each other, yet feeling frustrated that the birthright of every parent—telling stories about your kid—is being denied because the child they have is more unique than common.

A good solution is to actively seek out parents of other profoundly gifted children (the World Wide Web has made this easier). When a parent of a profoundly gifted child finally hears someone say those beautiful words—"Yeah, I know what you mean. That happened to us last year with our daughter"—a curtain is lifted and the play begins. Another answer is to write down the child's landmark events, witticisms, and insights. These can be shared, either moments or years later, with the spouse who wasn't there to hear or see them or with the child who asks, at the age of 30, "Dad, was I *always* like this?" And, finally, the strongest of parents might just choose to forge ahead and brag anyway, developing all the while a resilient shell that protects against the looks and the words that can hurt if they are taken too inwardly.

- *"I'd rather have a child who is 'normal' than one who is gifted."*

Some parents of profoundly gifted children are so alarmed by the animosity they feel from others toward their child's intelligence that they come to believe that giftedness is more of a burden than a blessing. Indeed, some even see extreme giftedness as a handicap that is as personally disabling as is a profound mental or physical challenge. How sad when the gift becomes a liability, as it denigrates the joy and wonder of early and deep insight.

What parents of profoundly gifted children need to realize is that, if their child is precocious far in advance of his or her years, this *is* normal behavior—normal for the child, as the individual that he or she is. This is not to say that the child's performance or depth of understanding is *typical*, but there is a vast difference between being "normal" and "typical," just as there is a major distinction between their opposites, "abnormal" and "atypical." No one wants to be the former—abnormal—but does anyone really care if they are atypical? It's a linguistic nuance that carries over into one's feelings of adequacy.

To be sure, there are major challenges to raising any child, but the added element of profound giftedness gives a whole new meaning to the word *complex*. Still, if parents can refrain from using the "n word"—*normal*—in front of their children, their playmates, their relatives, and their teachers, perhaps a whole new era of understanding can begin. It's worth a try.

Conclusion

"Drissle, drassle, drussle, drome
Time for this one to come home"

These classic words from an antiquated Saturday morning cartoon—*The Rocky and Bullwinkle Show*—remind me of just how old I really am! In case you were not, like me, around when the Earth was still cooling, the words come from a gifted scientist—the Professor—who sends his gifted lab assistant Sherman to different historical events via his "Way-Back Machine," a time machine that helped teach little kids like me about both ancient Greece and the Founding Fathers. Sherman's adventures almost always made an impact on history, but his curiosity often got him into trouble, causing the Professor to bring back his young charge with the "Drissle, Drassle, Drussle Drome" spell cited above.

It's weird to remember that spell after all these years, but I write it here because it seems to fit this article's conclusion. Parents of profoundly gifted kids, like Sherman, sometimes want to go back and rearrange history. They want to make the world a place where *all* gifted children are understood and accepted. They want to retrace mistaken steps, changing solutions that did not work and forging new directions that lead to better places. They want to learn as much as they can about who gifted kids are so that, when they get one, they will know what to do with him or her. And they want to go to Dr. Spock's office and ask him how you raise kids that don't fit the typical patterns he discusses in his books.

But, no parent of a profoundly gifted child wants to give back *the child*. Yes, profoundly gifted children may be challenging kids to raise, but most of the challenges come from clouding our own adult minds with fears that are unfounded or guilt that is not deserved. Like Sherman, it's time to "come on home" and recapture the magic that exists in the minds and hearts of our profoundly gifted children—and their parents.

Gifted Education Communicator
Spring 2001

Part Seven

Designing the Respectful Classroom

All three of my college degrees are in special education: a B.S. in mental retardation, an M.Ed. in emotional disturbances, and a Ph.D. in gifted child education. The most surprising thing about these three degrees is the incredible ways that they overlap and interweave.

For example, the first time I heard about Bloom's Taxonomy was in an undergraduate course titled "Methods and Materials for Teaching the Mentally Retarded." The first time I realized that one of the biggest reasons for school misbehavior is boredom caused by a curriculum that is too easy was in my "Behavior Management" class for my master's degree. When I reached the doctoral level, I read about gifted children with learning disabilities, hearing impairments, and, yes, emotional disturbances. I had come full circle, experiencing the full range of special education and finding more similarities than differences among the various labels and syndromes. This was surprising; it was also comforting.

Why comforting? Because it proved to me something that I had suspected from even those earliest college days: Before kids can be labeled anything, they must first be labeled as kids. Both the brightest child in the class and the one who struggles most to learn want a best friend they can trust. The kid who slams desks against walls out of frustration and the kid who keeps his hand down in class purposely so he doesn't appear "too smart" both want hugs and snacks and someone to talk to when they arrive home after school. Apply whatever labels you want, but kids will only live up (or down) to those labels after they have identified themselves as something simpler: children.

The following articles, for the most part, are "down home stories" of what has happened when I tried to disregard labels and simply enjoy kids as the individuals they were presenting to me. In our "travels," I believe the kids learned some skills that would help them in life, as well as on standardized tests. In any regard, I can only hope they had as much fun as I did, because curriculum and instruction, done right, can lead to all sorts of memorable mischief.

From Dead Wasps to Wonderment

I like this article for several reasons. Reason #1 is that it was the first article I ever had published in a national magazine with a circulation of over 100,000. Second, it is a true story of a classroom experience that happened to me during my first year of teaching gifted students. Third, it was the first time I ever got paid for something I had written—$150—which was like manna from heaven to a doctoral student juggling classes and two part-time jobs!

There is another reason I like it, though. It tells the story of what happens when we let children's interests guide the curriculum. In order to make this happen, we, as teachers, have to trust both our instincts and those of our students, assuming (until proven wrong) that they are as interested in learning new stuff as we are anxious to hook them onto the knowledge train.

"From Dead Wasps To Wonderment" also shows how the appropriate use of open-ended questions, higher level thinking, and advanced and varied resources can turn even the simplest learning task into a grand expedition.

Some of my favorite moments as a teacher started by accident when a student discovered something interesting and wanted to explore it further. Once enticed, the students gave me one of three options: lead, follow, or get out of the way. This article shows how doing a little bit of all three worked to our mutual advantage.

Weaving through my classroom, dodging children as able as a slalom skier avoids fixed gates, Randy charged to my desk, depositing his latest find: a dead wasp. Eyeing me through the ragged strands of his straight blonde hair, he asked, "Can I examine him with a microscope? I want to see why he died."

Children began circling my desk, peering into the Styrofoam cup crypt that held the wasp. Questions flowed: "Can we dissect him?" "Is it a he or she wasp?" "I wonder if it was stung to death." Randy grabbed for his wasp, again asking to examine it.

What a chance this dead wasp offered! Educational theorists speak of the importance of using a child's interests as a base for developing curricula. The Greeks referred to *heuristics* as learning through independent investigation. Sylvia Ashton-Warner, author of *Teacher*, asked, "Where is a better place for a teacher to begin teaching than from her pupils' own interests?"

But, neither the Greeks nor Sylvia Ashton-Warner work in *my* school. We have no microscopes (those are reserved for high school students doing "serious" investigations); we have no dissecting tools (only plastic spoons and forks for hot lunch); and Randy is not even one of my students (his teacher has probably marked him absent). We do have wasps, though, thanks to a nest that defies fumigation. And we do have several students in addition to Randy who seem to think they would enjoy examining a wasp. Maybe that is all that's needed to begin.

Randy left his wasp with me for safekeeping, and he returned during recess with more specimens and a few classmates. Each child cautiously poked and prodded his insect; no one was sure how dead his wasp really was. There was little talk during this probing stage, only the close examination of an object common to all children, yet unfamiliar in many ways.

Soon, two boys were at the encyclopedia matching the body parts of their own specimen with that pictured in the book. Another child had located a dead housefly and was comparing the two insects for similarities. Randy continued gazing at his find, moving in for closer and closer looks at the wasp's stinger.

Recess ended, and the children were pried away from their investigations to return to their afternoon studies.

"We'll be back tomorrow, Mr. D," said Randy. "Try to get us a few microscopes by then."

Clearly, I had homework to do.

Teaching is a profession for pack rats. No teacher worthy of his students has ever thrown out junk mail unopened; no teacher has willingly resold his college texts. Corcoran's law, somewhat paraphrased, prevails: "All things that you save will never be needed until such time as they are disposed of, when they become essential."

Keeping that maxim in mind, I returned home to search for possible tools that could be used in Randy's bug study. I quickly located a dissecting kit that had not been opened since Anatomy 213. It contained probes and scalpels sharp enough to dissect wasps, yet sufficiently dull to preclude slicing fingers. I also found a review of *Elementary Science Study* (ESS) that described a unit called "Small Things." Small

Things, the review noted, contained "miniscopes that used reflected light and glass tubing to highlight specimens." ESS, I knew, was the science curriculum used in our town's junior high school.

"You found some microscopes!" Randy exclaimed when he saw me the next day. "We'll be down at recess, okay?"

At 10:02 a.m., five 9 year olds—45 collective years of enthusiasm—were gathered around a common interest, with one 25-year-old teacher trying to juggle their potpourri of questions: "Do wasps go to the bathroom?" "Does a wasp sting me because he's mad at me?" "Is a wasp the same thing as a hornet?" "What do wasps look like when they're born?" And there was still Randy's continued concern: "Why did my wasp die?"

Obviously, what we needed were resources, so back to our available encyclopedia. Surely, wedged between *warthog* and *Waterloo*, wasps would command a paragraph or two, a picture, a photograph. And it did. But, the encyclopedia did not answer why Randy's wasp had died, and it neglected to mention the wasp's toilet habits. More than just the encyclopedia's impersonal facts, we needed raw data—the kind a *scientist* uses to gather and collect information. And we found it in the oddest places:

"I have an uncle who collects butterflies," volunteered one boy. "Maybe he knows about wasps, too." (He did.)

"The filmstrip I saw said that all animals go to the bathroom," said another. "I guess that means that wasps must, too." (They do.)

"This lab guide says that you can't take a wasp and dissect it—you've got to prepare slides if you want to see its insides." (He did.)

"This book says that wasps and hornets are in the same family. They're kind of like cousins." (They are.)

Because of an inopportune sneeze that irretrievably scattered the dismembered bug's remains, Randy never did discover the cause of death of his wasp. He did, however, hypothesize several ex post facto explanations, including cold weather, starvation, murder, and old age. Each hypothesis (a word Randy learned just for the occasion) demanded research into a wasp's physiology: its tolerance for temperate extremes, the kind and amount of food needed to keep it alive, its social patterns, the life span of a typical wasp. Each alternative also implied a personal quest for knowledge, a motivation so strong that Randy gave up recess kickball games to "do some science."

During the seven weeks of in-depth research that followed Randy's initial discovery of the dead wasp, my role changed from orchestrator of exercises to resource person—an annotated bibliographer who could show students that there is more to research than the finished data in *Compton's* and *World Book*. During that time, too, students learned that books need not be threatening obstacles and that science, despite the school schedule, was happening all around them, not just on Tuesdays and Thursdays following penmanship. Randy, in particular, learned to appreciate that, as a student, he can sometimes be his own best teacher.

Learning
February 1982

50 Ways
to Leave
Them Learning

Introduction

I n a way, this article reads like a series of those Arbus posters: colorful air-brushed images of nature or children with slogans that remind us, in one way or another, that life is worth living. Okay . . . it's not *War and Peace*, but, sometimes, all we want is a reminder that life is what we make it (which must *surely* be on at least one Arbus poster!). That's what this article does. For example:

- catch kids being good;
- reward attempts, not just perfection;
- remember that anyone can have a bad day; and
- realize that everyone's schoolday begins upon awakening.

Nothing Earth-shattering or blatantly original here, is there? But, sometimes, that is just the point. There are many good things we do (or can do) each day of our lives that infect our students with enthusiasm and hope. Each time we give an unexpected smile, or add an extra comment on a paper that a student turned in, or acknowledge a new haircut or pair of shoes in a genuine, quiet way, we validate the student as someone who is worthwhile, valuable, and responsible. If you get enough of these messages, it's hard not to believe that at least some of them are true.

By the way, you'll notice that there are only 45 statements listed in this article, not 50.

So, you already know what your homework will be, don't you?

Paul Simon (of Simon and Garfunkel fame) started it all with a song that detailed the 50 ways to leave your lover. Since then, Taco Bell has sponsored a contest highlighting the 50 ways to leave your burger. There seems to be no end to the 50 ways (at least!) we have of "leaving" various aspects of our everyday lives.

But, leaving does not always involve departing; it sometimes involves imparting. For example, as teachers, we impart a love of learning or a zest for new knowledge to our students everyday. Each venture into a classroom is another chance for our students to come away with something they didn't have before—an appreciation for science, perhaps, or maybe a new way to understand fractions, or even a strategy for making the "new kid in class" feel more comfortable during kickball matches.

When you think about it, there have to be at least 50 ways to leave your students learning. Here are just a few.

The Physical Environment: Creating Ownership of Your Classroom

1. *Design interactive bulletin boards.*

After a few days, if it's not changed, your bulletin board becomes just another classroom fixture, generally unnoticed by students. But, what if it is changed each day? A mystery word puzzle, for example, or a "guess this place" feature, taken from a travel article in your Sunday paper, could be adapted for use on a bulletin board. Each morning's "unveiling" of the day's feature would prompt attention and spark interest in many students.

2. *Use student-designed bulletin boards.*

You are probably assigned the task of designing the hallway bulletin board for a particular month. Why not cluster your students in small groups and assign each group a classroom bulletin board? This is a good way to enhance cooperation and creativity.

3. *Post your own accomplishments.*

Teachers often display their pupils' achievements, but seldom their own. Why not show off your latest evaluation, a complimentary letter you received, or a photograph of the patio you built last summer? Go on—show your pride!

4. *Allow students to display their accomplishments.*
Our classroom is often filled with students' work we've selected to post. That's fine, but do you give your pupils the chance to choose what they'd like to display? You might be surprised by their selections.

5. *Go on a mini-field trip.*
No permission forms required! Just go outside for a half hour and teach in this familiar, yet foreign, setting.

6. *Trade classrooms with a colleague.*
Both you and your students may get new ideas for classroom activities or environments.

7. *Provide a media center.*
Supply books, filmstrip projectors, marking pens, whatever! Great for those who finish their work early.

8. *Rearrange occasionally.*
A change in atmosphere often results in a change of outlook.

9. *Provide private space.*
This is especially important if your students share desks or change classrooms throughout the day. Even the smallest private storage space is sufficient for those treasures too precious or too special to share.

Classroom Discipline: Positive Reinforcement Revisited

1. *Catch them being good.*
Are your students behaving especially well today? Have you told them? You might say, "Class, I'm really pleased that you all worked so hard on your math exercises. Thank you for making my job pleasant!" This small investment of time could result in multiple dividends in your classroom climate.

2. *Reward attempts, not just perfection.*
Even a 70% "success" for a student whose usual grade is 60% is worth mentioning. Take care to notice and reward these improvements.

3. *Do not punish through curricular areas.*
If a student misbehaves—hits another student, for example—do not have him or her write "I will respect other people's rights" 100 times. The student may then associate *all* writing with punishment. Instead, take away a recess, or have the student sit quietly, or have him or her apologize to the person who was hurt.

4. *End the day on a positive note.*

Every day has its share of frustrations, but as you and your students close the books on another day, take 30 seconds to reflect on the good learning you have shared. Go ahead—find that silver lining!

5. *Reward safety.*

Last year, dozens of school children were hurt, some were killed, when they were given the "privilege" of transporting heavy classroom equipment. Reward appropriately and don't allow *any* child to handle something bigger or heavier than he or she is.

6. *Begin a "Student of the Week" program.*

Select that student whose behavior or performance improved the most since the last go 'round.

7. *Set rules together.*

With your students, decide upon some general classroom rules and punishments for infractions. It's harder to argue with self-imposed restrictions.

8. *Post and discuss free-time options.*

When students know what they can do if their work is done early, they'll rarely have reason to misbehave or to claim "I'm bored."

9. *Remember that anyone can have a bad day.*

Prevent some tears and outbursts by allowing students to tell you and their classmates if they're edgy or unhappy. You, too, can share this information, as necessary.

Curriculum Concerns: The "Meat and Potatoes" of the School Day

1. *Pretest and follow through.*

Many of your high-achieving students will know their weekly spelling list or basic math computation facts before the lessons begin. Pretest to discover these strengths and modify (i.e., shorten) the assignments for those pupils who can prove competency after very little practice.

2. *Adapt the curriculum to the child, not vice versa.*

If three of your second graders can multiply two-digit numbers accurately, don't "force fit" them into a grade-level text that emphasizes addition algorithms. Allow exposure to new, more complex material, and let their talents shine!

3. *Post a weekly "classroom stumper" that invites research.*

For example, "How far can the QE II cruise on one gallon of gas?" (answer: six inches) will rivet your students to available almanacs, newspapers, and other materials. Research becomes fun!

4. *Devote even 10 minutes a day to creative thinking.*

Once a day, ask your students to let their imaginations run free. Ask how many different uses they can think of for red bricks, or have them consider absolutely every way to make school more enjoyable. No holds are barred here, and there are no right or wrong answers, either. Remember: It's easier to tame a wild idea than to spice up a dull one.

5. *Do some science.*

A colleague of mine states that elementary teachers either hate science or are afraid of it. If that's so, we probably "do science" only when we have to. Buy a set of *Brown Paper School Books* (Little, Brown, & Co.) and get ready for the most exciting science to come your way since NOVA.

6. *Survey your students.*

Ask about their interests and hobbies and design learning stations around the most commonly cited areas.

7. *Avoid arbitrary limits on learning.*

If fourth graders can charge out only certain library books while first graders are limited to picture books, you may be stifling both ability and imagination. Disarm these arbitrary rules.

8. *Assign homework by reason, not rote.*

Telling your students "Anyone who scores 90% or better on today's language arts assignment will have no homework in that subject tonight" invites careful attention to seatwork. The results may surprise you.

9. *Allow "down time" after recess or special activities.*

Shifting from gym class to social studies requires a change in both subject area and learning style. Ease the transition with a minute or two of quiet time or deep-breathing exercises.

Making the Grade: Evaluating Student Work

1. *Use any color but red.*

The red pen has become an instrument of torture to many children. They know the correlation "The more red marks, the lower my grade." One solution? Alternate colors for grading papers—give the color red back its good name!

2. *Encourage self-evaluation.*

If your pupils complete independent study units, extra-credit assignments, or any special projects, consider the use of student self-evaluation. Questions like "What do you like about your work?" or "If you were to do this project again, what would you change?" will encourage a valuable personal critique.

3. *Make your first home-school communication a positive one.*
Near the start of the term/school year, send home a brief, positive note regarding each student. Something as short as "Sandy has really tried hard in her reading assignments—you can be proud of her efforts!" will let parents know that you care individually about their child. (Also, it makes any later, less-positive notes easier to take.)

4. *Praise and critique separately.*
We are all guilty of "kicking students in the *but*" with comments such as "Your essay is good, *but* I'd like to see some more elaboration." When we couple praise with criticism, it is usually the latter that is retained. (Consider your last teacher evaluation.) Both types of comments are important and appropriate; yet, it often helps to raise the issues separately.

5. *Find the number correct, not incorrect.*
If a student has a score of 90% on a 20-word spelling test, she has either "2 wrong" or "18 right." Which do you emphasize? Fractional equivalents, for example 9/10 or 17/23 are more useful than −1 or −6.

6. *Allow students to self-correct, using teachers' guides.*
This cuts down on your grading time, allows the student to note his or her own successes and failures, and sends the message "I trust you not to cheat."

7. *Don't grade creative writing for grammar or spelling.*
Sometimes, creative thoughts get messy. Don't let "mechanics" get in the way.

8. *Don't overcorrect.*
If an assignment is totally incorrect, write "See me" or "Let's go over this together." Then, follow through with the pupil.

9. *Don't read a student's grades or papers to the class without his or her permission.*
Success and failure are very personal—let the students determine individually if they want to share their work with others.

Being Good to Yourself

1. *Leave school at school.*
To be sure, this is easier said than done. There are always papers to grade or report cards to complete at home. But, the daily frustrations that accompany any career that involves interaction with others should remain behind school doors. Instead, enjoy your family, your friends, your freedom.

2. *Realize that everyone's school day begins upon awakening.*

A missed breakfast or bus can set the mood for a bad day, but a gentle smile or "hello" upon entering school can set things back on track. This is good advice for both teachers and students.

3. *Acknowledge that you don't have total control over your students' lives.*

Each teacher knows the pain of having a student whose time out of school is ill spent. Poverty and neglect, among other conditions, may breed problems over which you have little (if any) control. What you do have is six hours or so each day to teach and to reach each child. Take advantage of this time; for some students, your classroom will become a haven.

4. *Reward yourself.*

Show a movie that is both fun and educational. Showcase your talents by doing a mini-unit in your specialty area—photography, cooking, whatever. Go for a massage one day after school. Treat yourself!

5. *Advocate meaningful in-service.*

Ask your principal to survey the staff for suggested topics and speakers that will address real needs, not contrived ones. And please, if the meetings must take place after school, ask that some light refreshments be served!

6. *Rejuvenate your professional self.*

Attend a regional or state education conference, even if for only one day. And remember that good learning can occur at both formal sessions and informal gatherings—like happy hour!

7. *Allow your students to see the 3-D you.*

Be a person who laughs, cries, and isn't afraid to be a human in class. As children, our favorite teachers were often those who showed emotions and who talked *with* us, not *at* us.

8. *Don't be afraid to say "I don't know" or "I need help!"*

A teacher's job often requires skills in social work, public relations, and communications, to name just three. Use the support services provided by your school, however limited or vast these services may be. You are not alone!

9. *Consider your strengths.*

Do you want to get a Ph.D.? Become an administrator? Change from fourth grade to first? Don't sell yourself short—the first step in doing something is telling yourself you can do it. The second step is "I will."

Conclusion

Only 45 ways, you say? Ah, very perceptive of you, as there are five fewer suggestions than promised by this article's title.

That's where you come in. These hints for leaving them learning are only the beginning. Like a North Atlantic iceberg, only a small fraction of the whole appears above the surface. What remains is a mass of ideas for you to develop and explore. Start by naming five.

Abraham Maslow once wrote that every human being who is kind, compassionate, democratic, and accepting is a psychotherapeutic force, even if a small one. How true, and how very optimistic! We do have an impact on students by the little things we do for them and for ourselves on a daily basis. Indeed, *that* is the magic of teaching.

Challenge Magazine
January/February 1987

Empowerment
More Than Just a Buzzword

Teaching Kids to Care
*Character Development
and the Middle School Student*

Introduction

n working with gifted students over these past two decades, one quality about them I've noticed that is almost universal is an awareness of the world around them. They understand the implications of energy policies that favor big business over the environment. They hurt for people thousands of miles away who are caught in the middle of wars that are all about politics and power. They ask how the United States, the world's richest nation, can have homeless people living in cardboard boxes on street corners and on heating vents across from the White House. Gifted kids see the world for the paradox that it is: beautiful and needy. Sometimes, this scares them.

One of the most effective ways I have used to help address the issues brought on by this keen, premature awareness of reality is to put gifted kids in charge of making change. Too often, when children see an issue that bothers them, they are greeted by a comment like "Don't worry about that until you're older." If the child happens to be gifted, that comment might be followed with one like "Since you're so smart, I'm sure you'll be able to solve this problem yourself—you kids *are* our future leaders, you know!"

Ouch! Talk about pressure!

My goal is not to worry so much about solving problems in the future that may or may not even exist when these kids are adults, but to focus on what kids see now, right in front of them, as bothersome. These two articles address the very real and positive changes kids can make if someone is honest enough to say, "If you are old and wise enough to see the problem, then you are ready to address some solutions. Would it be all right if I helped you?"

Together, as you'll read, mountains can be moved.

Empowerment: More Than Just a Buzzword

When it comes to inventing jargon, educators have few equals. Often, the terms they devise sound more complex than they actually are. For example, *whole language* is little more than using literature and a child's experiences to teach reading and writing. And *differentiated curriculum* merely provides students with school experiences that match their talents and interests.

Another such term is *empowerment*, a trendy buzzword that has becomes popular now that the "Me Generation" is growing up and looking outward. In town after town, classroom after classroom, people are reaching out to others whose lives are filled more with despair than with hope. This focus away from self and toward others has caused many in their 30-somethings to recall their 1960s roots and the social movements that were spawned then.

Is it "*déjà vu* all over again"? Perhaps. But, this time, today, a generation after Woodstock, a new and valuable twist has been added: *This* time, schoolchildren are being brought along as participants, not just spectators. For example:

- In Middlebourne, West Virginia, middle school students "adopted" a hospital in Latin America, raising money to send both Christmas toys and medical supplies to children in need of both.
- In Walnut Hills, California, a high school social studies class rewrote voting instructions to make them more understandable for citizens with limited English proficiency (the State of California adopted these instructions for all election ballots).
- In Northampton, Massachusetts, a group of young children protested their city's plan to convert a park into a parking lot. Today, the swings and slides are still standing.

On and on these stories go—a Children's Crusade of sorts, spawned by the immediacy of our communication links with the entire planet. An oil spill in Texas? We see live coverage on CNN. An earthquake in Iran? Satellites beam back immediately the desperate plight of our global neighbors. Adults see the pain; so do the children. Adults want to help; kids do, too. So, they do. In ways both large and small, the children become empowered to make their world a better, safer, greener place.

There is danger in empowerment, but only if it is misguided or purposeless. No one person will solve all the world's woes—not even the most highly gifted child—nor should he or she feel obligated to do so. And to empower children may cause them to question the "balance of power" in their *own* schools and homes ("Isn't it unfair that *I* have to make my bed every day when you and Dad don't always make yours?"). But, still, no monsters need be created by showing our children the positive impacts they can have on their neighborhood and their world. And, besides, consider the alternative: If we refuse our children any attempts to improve our world "until they're old enough," they may grow up in fear, or feeling powerless, or (most insidious of all) apathetic.

Trends come and go. Buzzwords change to accommodate our present concerns. But, world health, global awareness, and neighbor helping neighbor are time-worn constants that never go out of style. Share this reality with your children and watch their minds and hearts grow.

Understanding Our Gifted
September 1990

Teaching Kids to Care: Character Development and the Middle School Student

I t had all the trappings of a bad soap opera: Brian, a young father of two with a budding career in telecommunications, suffered a stroke at age 29. Bravely, and with the help of his wife and family, he slowly recovered, only to suffer a second stroke after someone threw a rock through his car window, hitting Brian in the head, causing extensive neurological damage.

The news of this personal tragedy hit the airwaves of our local TV stations. This was no soap opera, this was an act of random violence in a world growing increasingly blasé toward personal acts of terror from which even the innocent cannot escape. As a middle school teacher of children old enough to be aware of terrorism and gifted enough to be sensitive to the ripples of pain that such an event stirs, I knew it was time to act; for, when children are old and wise enough to care, it is our job as adults to help children act upon that caring.

So, we began: Two classes of middle school students decided to let Brian know that 56 kids in a town 20 miles away were concerned about him and his family. The students each wrote letters, attaching them to "the world's largest greeting card," sending messages to hope and comfort.

We heard nothing back.

The next month, November, we delivered a "cornucopia of concern," more cards and letters for Brian and his children to read over Thanksgiving dinner.

Still, no response.

Then, for the winter holidays, the children wrote and produced a video of skits and songs and bad jokes, hoping that Brian might get a ho-ho-ho out of their collective antics.

And, on December 20, we heard back:

"Dear Boys and Girls," the letter began, "our family has been so very pleased and deeply touched by your wonderful notes of encouragement and get well wishes for my husband, Brian, following the incident of the rock throwing. You have been an inspiration to us and have helped to renew our faith in people by your care and concern. With this kind of positive support, we will survive this ordeal."

Thus began "Project Person to Person," our middle school's attempt to provide help or a "thank you" to those in our community who needed either.

Character Education and the Gifted Middle School Student

> "Down through history, in countries all over the world, education has had two great goals: to help young people to become smart and to help them become good."
> —Thomas Lickona, 1991, p. 6

For as long as structured society has existed, there have been calls to teach our young people the ethics of everyday living. In recent times, though, this idea has been met with concern or criticism by factions of parents and educators who fear that a particular set of values will be taught. Yet, when I consider the goals of character education— instilling a sense of community pride and personal integrity with a willingness to reach out to another human being—I wonder which political or religious sensitivities I am offending. I am not quite sure how to teach the life lessons of compassion, humility, perseverance, and hope apart from the everyday life experiences of others. If, indeed, service is the rent we pay for our time spent on Earth, then these life lessons must exist in both our homes and our schools.

This is especially true for middle school students, whose awareness of themselves grows with every opportunity they get to identify with others. And, when giftedness is added into the equation, the need for character education in the middle grades is even that much more stunning. Who among us has not met a 12-year-old who is "gifted in the heart," aware of the fragility of the human spirit? Who among us has not seen a gifted teenager angry at some arbitrary decision that reduces another individual's dignity or autonomy? Who among us has not comforted a gifted young person who saw vividly the dissonance between an adult's words and his or her actions? For the greatest reason of all—the preservation of hope in the human condition—character education is a basic skill. In today's complex world, learning to care is equally as important as learning to read. One of gifted child education's greatest and warmest thinkers, Annemarie Roeper, notes this necessary connection between the world of school and the world outside of the classroom:

Children need to live in a world that is relevant. They need to grow in an educational environment that prepares them to make sense of the real world and gives them the tools to change it. The difference is that gifted children know this and can articulate it, while others just accept it. (Roeper, 1995, p. 142)

So, how is character education done effectively in the schools? Where does one begin to act upon the caring that is inherently a part of childhood? Let me count the ways.

Character Education Begins From the Inside Out

It is difficult for children to care about the well-being of others if they do not feel safe, comfortable, and at ease with themselves. Indeed, in our world of increasingly fractured families and academic homage paid to statewide tests that compare children and schools, rather than envisioning each child as a unique entity, this sense of self is difficult for some children to find.

William Purkey and John Novak (1996) have recommended adopting school policies that invite children to learn, based on the following principles:

1. People are able, valuable, and responsible and should be treated accordingly.
2. Teaching should be a cooperative activity.
3. People possess relatively untapped potential in all areas of human development.

Purkey and Novak believe that school policies and programs can have a profound effect on children's self-concepts and school achievement. Everything from the way classroom rules are worded (see Figure 1), to the way students are greeted by the school bus driver in the morning, to the content of teachers' comments on students' projects and papers will have an impact on the way children see themselves as learners . . . and as people. Only when the power of the school climate is considered can one hope to institute a character education program. It might be a truism that "to give respect, one must first get respect," but, without this personal foundation of self-worth, there is little one can do to affect positively the lives of others.

Classroom Rules

1. Walking in the hall prevents accidents.
2. Be mature and serious during fire drills.
3. Enjoy chewing your gum at home.
4. When in groups, talk in six-inch voices.
5. Ask before you use.
6. People can be hurt by both words and actions, so choose both with care.

Please remember: Kindness is contagious.

Figure 1. Classroom Rules

Note. From *Growing good kids: 28 activities to enhance self-awareness, compassion, and leadership* (p. 6), by D. Delisle & J. Delisle, 1996, Minneapolis: Free Spirit Publishing Inc. Copyright © 1996 by Free Spirit, 1-800-735-7323, www.freespirit.com. Reprinted with permission.

Character Education Activities Share Some Common Elements

Classroom-based lessons to teach middle school children about their world share several qualities. First, *they involve both cognitive and affective learning opportunities*, calling on students to think, feel, and react simultaneously. Next, *they are experiential*, based on the belief that middle school children already know much about themselves and the world around them and that they are always curious to learn more. In addition, *they are product-focused*, allowing students to demonstrate in a concrete way the depth of their thinking and feeling. Finally, *they must be holistically evaluated*, removing from the students' minds the "curse" of a letter or number grade, which would be an artificial barometer of a project's quality.

An example of the above type of classroom activity can be seen in Figure 2. In response to the questions about inviting any three people to dinner who had ever lived, one sixth-grade student wrote:

> I would invite my real grandma because she died before I was born. Everyone says I look like her, but I don't even know who she is. I'd also invite my third-grade teacher, Ms. Heflin, because she retired during the year because of a heart problem. Next, I'd invite my little cousin, Eric. I'd like to get to know him as if he were my brother. (I do have another cousin, be he isn't allowed to do anything that'll get him hyper, like playing football.)

Figure 2. "Bug Myself"

Note. From *Growing good kids: 28 activities to enhance self-awareness, compassion, and leadership* (p. 27), by D. Delisle & J. Delisle, 1996, Minneapolis: Free Spirit Publishing Inc. Copyright © 1996 by Free Spirit, 1-800-735-7323, www.freespirit.com. Reprinted with permission.

When a classroom—or, better yet, a team—of students completes this activity and the responses are lined up side by side on construction paper and displayed for all to see (we arranged ours to look like a centipede; hence, the "Bug Myself" activity title), you have a visual display of children's dreams, hopes, uncertainties, and memories. From here, it is but one short step to seeing yourself as connected to others both inside and outside of the school environment.

Character Education is Best Taught Within a Community

In 1912, a recently arrived European immigrant wrote a letter home to his relatives. In it, he wrote, "When I came to America, I heard the streets were paved with gold. When I got here, I found out three things: First, the streets weren't paved with gold; second, they weren't paved at all; and third, I was expected to pave them."

As parents and other educators, it is one of our jobs to serve as the mortar while our children lay the bricks to the next generation. Taking character education into the community is one way to do just that.

This article began with the story of a man who was injured by an unknown assailant and the responses of middle school students to his injustice. Other "Project Person to Person" activities completed within a five-year period include:

- Students transported more than 2,000 teddy bears with personal messages of hope to families who had lost their homes and possessions in a hurricane (the mayor of Charleston, South Carolina, wrote the kids a *great* thank-you letter).
- Student sent thank-you letters shaped like playground equipment to a local toy manufacturer that had distributed $17,000 worth of free toys to local family shelters for the winter holidays (two months later, the company's CEO sent us some prototype toys, to see which ones we thought little tykes would like best).
- Students created 35 hand-decorated banners made out of muslin and distributed them (through the U.S. Army) to men and women stationed in Bosnia (soldiers wrote back their thanks, complete with photos of our banners hanging in their tents or barracks).
- For community residents who were just beginning a "stop smoking" program, students fashioned filtered cigarettes out of brown and white construction paper and wrote messages of support to these folks trying to kick the habit. The "cigarettes" were distributed the first night of class (weeks later, an older gentleman came to our class clutching our now-worn homemade cigarette, thanking us for being his "anchor" when he needed one).
- Working in cooperation with the Peace Corps, the students sold or raffled off food and gifts donated by local groceries and department stores to raise money to furnish a secondary school library in Nepal (months later, we received back a 10-page diary of the Peace Corps volunteers' four-day trek through the Himalayas to purchase and transport the books, as well as photos of the "library," which was little more than a storage shed filled with books, two tables, and many happy students!).
- Students invited into school the director of the local Animal Protective League, who spoke of the care and responsibility of pet ownership. She brought in Snuggles, a terrier mix puppy, and the students collectively wrote a letter for the local newspaper's "Adopt-a-Pet" column asking for someone to take Snuggles into their home (the letter was published and someone adopted Snuggles that same day).
- Students refurnished an entire home for a household of seven who had lost all of their uninsured possessions in a fire. Championed and coordinated by three sixth graders, the students solicited help from all members of the community—

friends, neighbors, relatives, businesses. Everything from clothing, to lamps, to a refrigerator was collected and distributed to the family, whose mother gave this message: "It sort of restores your faith in people. It's hard to believe there are such nice people in the world. Here are people who you'll never know and will never know you, yet they are willing to help."

. . . and that's the point of leadership, isn't it? Not responding to a call for help or a need for a thank you because of what you might get in return, but, rather, for what you might help *others* gain by your recognition that we all share the same space in this ocean of existence called life.

Character education programs may or may not help to improve scores on standardized tests, but what character education *will* do is bring together a community of learners who are seeking answers whose solutions begin in the soul and emanate outward. For those whose middle school students are "gifted in the heart," there is no better way to tap into the wisdom and kindness of childhood than through school-based

1. Start projects that will impact others outside the school community only after the students and teachers inside the school community have had a chance to get to know each other.
2. Involve parents as volunteers and idea generators for projects. Not only might they have great ideas, they may also have influential "connections" in the community with whom students can communicate.
3. Don't overdose the students on community service by doing one activity after another. Instead, have different classrooms or grade levels undertake different projects or pursue one or two (no more) large-scale projects each year that are schoolwide in focus.
4. If your school has a student council or other student leadership group, consider running at least some of these projects through them, as you already have students there who are committed to leadership and challenge.
5. Don't expect that every students will be excited about character education projects, and do not force participation upon all students. Often, the reluctant students get pulled along by the excitement of other students anyway, so try to let this occur naturally.
6. Do projects that are small in scale, but may still be large in impact. Sending get-well wishes to one individual is teaching students the message that the world gets better one day, one person at a time.
7. Don't focus solely on fundraising activities. This may limit participation to students who can "afford" to be charitable.
8. Keep a journal, diary, or scrapbook of the activities undertaken in successive years. Students—and others—will be amazed at the personal history that such chronicles represent.

Figure 3. Important Reminders
in Designing Character
Education Projects

activities that are best measured by using the yardsticks of empathy, compassion, and hope.

Back to Brian, our first "Project Person to Person" recipient of good wishes and sincere support. Brian's progress was slow (it still is), and he was not able to visit our classroom that year as he had wanted to do. However, his wife and children did visit, and they became our unofficial "room family," comrades in hope and bearers of Brian's messages to two classrooms of children who took the time to help a one-time stranger who had grown to become our friend.

From my perspective as the teacher, the greatest lesson learned that year is one that can never be measured by a test: the capacity to care.

Communicator: California Association for the Gifted
Spring 1999

Making
Social Studies
Social

his brief story chronicles another adventure I had with fourth graders. Instead of teaching social studies from our textbook, we put the texts away the first day of school and decided to learn about our country in a different manner. This article explains how.

It didn't take us long to figure out that the title "social studies" must, somehow, involve people—otherwise, why would the word *social* be in the name? So, in addition to learning about the history and geography of the U.S., we established a classwide series of events called "Project Person to Person," where our class went out into the community looking for people who deserved one of two things: help or a thank you. This article explains some of the projects we undertook that magical year.

One project that is not mentioned in the article that should have been was this one. In studying the impact of smoking on health, I learned that our school district was sponsoring a "stop smoking" program for school employees and relatives. So, as a means to show our support of this tough road ahead, my students used construction paper to create cigarettes—25 filtered cigarettes, each about two feet long, which we packed together tightly in a cardboard box that was decorated to look like a cigarette pack. On the inside of each paper cigarette was printed a hand-written message of support, something like "We know that it won't be easy to stop smoking, but we know that it will be one of your best choices ever. Good luck! We're thinking of you!"

About three months later, an older gentleman appeared at the back door of our trailer/classroom with the principal. None of the kids called out "Grandpa!," so I had no clue who this man was. Then I saw his hand. Clutched in it was a wrinkled, dirty, two-foot long cigarette.

"Ahem," he began nervously. "I just wanted you kids to know that I haven't had a real cigarette in over two months. In fact," he said coyly, "this is the only one that's been in my hand." He held up the cigarette, one of my student's creations. "Since I knew you were counting on me, I couldn't disappoint you."

Everyone clapped. I still do.

Now *that's* social studies!

After 12 years as a college professor of education, I returned to teaching fourth grade, hoping to find I could still cut it as a classroom teacher. In planning for the transition, I recalled the lessons and methods used by my best teachers when I was a student.

Oddly, I scarcely remember my textbooks. Instead, I remembered Mrs. Bradley, who interrupted second grade reading everyday so we could sing. And Brother Richard, whose tales of his summer working in Appalachia added depth to our religion class. Or Mr. Maloney, who played the Beatles' song "Hey Jude" and informed us, as a group of volatile 16-year-old boys, that the song wasn't about sex and drugs, as we had thought, but about "angst . . . a quality, gentlemen, from which you shall all someday suffer." (I wrote that down so I would recognize angst when it appeared in my life. Trust me, it helped.)

I realize that I, like these teachers, wanted to be someone who mattered to the children in my care, and textbooks would have little place in fulfilling that desire.

I jumped into teaching without a text the second day of school in a social studies class. Our curriculum was based on states and regions, so I asked my class, "Boys and girls, tell me something about the United States—anything."

"It's big," said Martha.

"There are *lots* of mountains in Colorado," ventured James.

"California has more people than any place else—and more money, too!" chimed in Erin.

"Okay, now tell me something you'd *like to learn* about the United States."

Michael answered first: "I'd like to know if Minnesota really has 10,000 lakes, like it says on their license plates."

Lydia was more practical: "I'd like to know how to drive from here to Disney World because my mom says it's too expensive to fly."

Carla wondered, "Why do homeless people always seem to live in big cities?"

Inside the heads of these 10 year olds was more information and inquisitiveness than in even the best-written textbook.

Beginning that day and continuing on through the warm days of June, our social studies theme became "The U.S. is US." We targeted people in our region or nation who could use our help or deserved a thank you, and we contacted them by letter or phone.

During the year, we communicated with victims of a hurricane; the governor of Ohio (he had cried at a press conference—we told him that was okay); the owner of a toy company who had donated $17,000 in toys to homeless children; a 9-year-old Haitian refugee who had found a new home in Miami; and the family of a local man who was paralyzed when an unidentified person threw a brick through his car window. We sent 200 of our own stuffed animals to a family shelter in Cleveland in February because, according to Billy, "People stop thinking about helping once Christmas is over."

We learned our states. Each student selected a favorite state and developed a brochure for visitors, complete with maps, sites of interest, and suggestions for appropriate clothing.

Throughout each lesson, we learned that social studies is only "social" when we get involved with other people. States and regions mean very little unless we learn about the individuals who inhabit them, and nothing feels better than thanking or comforting a stranger who shares our American home.

The textbooks? Yes, they came in handy as supplements when we needed an atlas or a fact sheet on a state's population or terrain, or if we needed to know the difference between a mesa and a plateau. But, our states and regions, our nation's people, our biggest problems, and our best solutions were out there, on the TV news and in the local papers.

We didn't finish our textbooks last year, and in June the bindings on them still snapped and crackled when we opened them flat. But, I hope that, when my students try to remember their teachers and what they learned, they will remember that the U.S. is us.

Educational Leadership
May 1998

The Lock-In

I f you have been a teacher for more than two weeks, you have been talked
into doing something by your students that causes you to say later, "What
was I thinking?" If you have had enough of these experiences, you are a fine
teacher, indeed!

One of my most memorable "What was I thinking?" moments came when my
seventh- and eighth-grade gifted students and I were discussing plans for the following school year's all-day seminars and field trips. We'd visited the FBI and the
Federal Reserve Bank in Cleveland, tromped through mud and swamp on a biology tour of a nearby arboretum, and feasted at a neighborhood outdoor ethnic
market to get the full flavor of cultural diversity. What new could the next year
bring?

"A lock-in!" was the unanimous response.

So, here we have more than 70 adolescents wanting to spend an evening
locked in to their school, with me as their lead chaperone. What was I . . . nuts?

Well, call me Skippy, because that's exactly what we have done, for two years
in a row, on an always-cold Friday evening in February. And, after the scheduled entertainment and speakers have left, the last snacks eaten, the boys and
girls separated into different wings of the school, and the poker games quashed

154

by 2 a.m., I look back on these nights as some of the best times I have ever spent with students.

Enjoy this recollection, and then break it to your principal ever-so-gingerly that this might be a good idea in your school, too. If you've got a principal as good as mine, he might even agree to stay overnight as a chaperone.

S ix months ago, it sounded like a good idea: 70 gifted seventh and eighth graders spending an overnight at our school, with me as the lead chaperone. Here's how it all began.

I direct gifted student services at the middle school level for a town not too far from my home. It's a one-day-a-week job that adds texture and life to my full-time university appointment as a professor of education. When I meet with my students, it is for a full day, and our time together is spent on field trips to hospitals, homeless shelters, museums, graveyards, and other community treasures.

As last school year's program came to an end, I asked my (then) seventh graders, "What haven't we done in *Project Plus* that we should do next year?" Their answers, of course, were expectedly exotic: high-cost excursions to faraway places to learn about science (Space Camp) and politics (the United Nations) and geography (the Grand Canyon). When I presented them the reality of our shoestring budget, their ideas shifted only slightly, until one idea struck a chord of agreement among all who heard it: a lock-in at our school.

"It wouldn't cost anything, except electricity and water," said Joel.

"And what would we *do* all night?" I asked.

Joel smiled his familiar, subtle grin: "That's up to you . . . you're the teacher!"

I must admit, the idea intrigued me. After all, even though I did get to know my students pretty well during our field trips, I was still a very-part-time element in their lives: the educational equivalent of a "Disney Dad," who brought them to cool places and paid the entrance fees. The extended time that a lock-in would afford us sounded both fun and challenging, and I thought it might give me a way to learn a little more about these gifted young people who had been a part of my life for almost two years.

My principal—the world's best!—agreed with our plan and even offered to stay overnight with us. So, it was official: *The Night of 1,000 Mysteries*, during which students would explore with professionals and college students the intricacies of mathematical, scientific, artistic, and visual problem solving, was scheduled for February 4th. Six months ago, it sounded like a good idea.

Like most notions that look simple at first glance, this one became more complex by the day: chaperones, food, required medicines to distribute, and a foolproof plan to isolate the boys from the girls once bedtime arrived, each needed to be considered. Still, when February 4th rolled around, all was in order, and our *Night* began. Students arrived with sleeping bags, headsets, soccer balls and a few cherished "blankeys" and stuffed animals that were hidden gingerly into pillowcases. My college students ushered the kids to their overnight accommodations and chatted casually about school and life. A "professional game player" arrived, a multitalented musician who caressed the idea of having fun as essential to a life well lived, and he introduced my students to a game so complex even computer programs could not master its intricacies. A leadership team of athletic trainers tied the kids into human knots and spider webs, showing them that the biggest ingredient in successful leadership is the ability to listen to others. The night's events, interspersed with continuous snacks and laughter, ended with 15 different games that tested the mind and the imagination. It was midnight now, and time to end until morning.

As the students shuffled off to bed, several of us teachers cleaned up and prepared for the onslaught of 7 a.m. Then, after the requisite warnings to "quiet down and go to sleep" were distributed among the sleeping rooms (with limited success), the teachers, too, snuggled into their sleeping bags on the too-hard floors. Unable to sleep much, I sat up and just looked around. It was 2:10 a.m., and all was quiet. Jake had hurled his last pillow at Bryan about 40 minutes ago, Roy's snoring was quickly extinguished by a well-placed poke in the side by Mario, and the only sounds now audible were the soft, rhythmic breathing patterns of 15 adolescent boys whose minds and mouths were finally at rest.

I began to take stock of what I'd seen earlier that night. The activities all seemed to be successful and participation in them was full. Giggles were common and a few high-fives and handshakes were traded between my middle schoolers and my undergraduates. But, other things were noticeable, too. For example, it intrigued me that the same students who generally kept to themselves during our days together also maintained their privacy during this night together. Even in a group of intellectual peers, outliers existed. Also, it was obvious that most of these students, who had been together in classes for up to six years now, knew each other as well as they did their siblings. This closeness had many advantages, as divisions between grade levels and genders didn't exist, and the ritualistic game playing, so common with adolescents bent on impressing one another, were nowhere to be seen. I also got to talk with students in a lighthearted, personal manner that only happens when the roles of "teacher" and "student" are put aside in deference to our common bonds of just being people. And, I got to see who appeared to need a little more time in getting comfortable with the social roles we all play in life. Being smart doesn't automatically translate into being successful if you feel you are a minority of one.

Morning came early, as my last recollection of the clock face read 3:34 a.m. Exhausted but animated, students appeared in the cafeteria for breakfast and a fast-paced game of trivia, complete with tacky prizes. Parents collected their kids at 8:30 and I assume that many students did exactly what I did when I arrived home: took a shower and went immediately back to bed—a real bed!

Before *The Night of 1,000 Mysteries* arrived, I would comment to colleagues that the biggest mystery of all was why I said "yes" to this "adventure" in the first place! Now that it is over, I realize that the benefits of such an experience go way beyond what the kids may have learned about math or science or leadership. The true benefit was seeing my students shine in the reflections of their own possibilities; to notice that underneath the collective demeanor of adolescent conformity lay individual hearts and minds that will change and challenge the world in years ahead; and to realize the connectedness shared between gifted young people and their part-time teacher, who now appreciates even more than before the very human part of growing up gifted.

Six months ago, *The Night of 1,000 Mysteries* sounded like a good idea. Six months later, it still does.

Gifted Child Today
May/June 2000

Part Eight

Gifted Children
in the Media

I t is so easy to exploit bright, young minds. Shifty entrepre-
neurs, many in the media, look for ways to put gifted children on display in ways that result in deepening the
stereotype that gifted kids are one-dimensional beings with a
mind, but few feelings.

I have so many cases in point, and three of them are written
about in this section. But, let me reveal to you some of the methods with which I have been approached to give out the names of
gifted children to various television or newspaper reporters.

"Hello, Dr. Delisle?"

"Yes."

"It's Joe Chips calling from XYZ-TV in New York. I'm sure
you've heard of our weekly news show, *Datetime?*"

"How may I help?"

"Well, we're doing a story on gifted children and we thought
you might be able to give us some names and phone numbers of
a few of these exceptional children."

" . . . Because?"

"We're planning a special segment to profile these kids. Nothing sensational, nothing negative. We'd just like to interview a few kids. Say, a 10-year-old who is in college, or a 9-year-old who is working on curing cancer."

"You realize that these are *not* examples of typical gifted kids."

Long pause. "You have to understand, my producer is going to want to know what new angle we will be taking in this story . . ."

"So, why not do a story on some more *typical* gifted kids? I'm sure your viewers know more of them than they do the exceptions, the geniuses. In fact, your story could go a long way on demystifying the whole idea of giftedness."

"I see what you're saying, and perhaps that would be a good follow-up story. Now, about those names . . ."

"Goodbye, Mr. Chips."

Sadly, many parents fall for this line of reasoning—that the exposure of their children in the news spotlight will somehow serve them well. Too often, it does not, as the following articles demonstrate.

Ghosts From Different Nightmares

The Unabomber, Jessica Dubroff, and the Fate of Gifted Children

Introduction

My hope is that the name "Jessica Dubroff" is still one you recognize. If not, if we forget who she was, we will probably relive through another gifted child the pandemonium of her short life. Jessica was 7 years old when she died in 1996. She was going to be the youngest pilot ever to cross the country, but her plane crashed in Wyoming while she was at the controls. In Jessica's death, the strongest proponent of her aviation quest was her mother, who believed that, since her daughter died in pursuit of her dream, it was not in vain.

When I heard that, I went into the bathroom and vomited. I could not imagine a parent with a style and set of values so different than my own that my own child's death would be pooh-poohed as the price one might have to pay for glory.

In this same article, I discuss another gifted individual whose life, from all reports, was never allowed to include a childhood. His name is Ted Kaczynski, now known as the Unabomber. I hope now, as I hoped then, that readers do not think it cruel or misguided of me to name him and Jessica in the same breath. In some ways, they had nothing in common at all. But, in other ways, they were both reflections of society's intolerance for letting gifted young children be *children*; boys and girls who are valued as much for their presence as their promise

161

and who are allowed to play with friends and teddy bears, neither of which Ted or Jessica seemed to do too often.

Let us never forget these two martyrs. Surrounded as they were by self-serving adults who adored and prized them for the wrong reasons, our world now has two more losses; two more reasons to cry.

For the past 18 years, I have been involved in gifted child education, that on again/off again field of study that our culture either loves or loathes. Much of my time has been spent trying to explain that I am not a bad guy, an elitist intent on hurrying bright children through their youth so that, collectively, they can better our society through their genius.

During my career, I have struggled to find the best ways to appreciate agile minds that are encased in the bodies of children who can read chapter books before they can even tie their shoes. "How much is too much?" and "How soon is too soon?" are questions that I ask myself each time I see a child whose intellect far outstrips those of his or her agemates.

Then, it happened. Not once, but twice, and in quick succession. Ted Kaczynski, the alleged Unabomber, vied for front-page coverage with Jessica Dubroff, the 7-year-old "pilot" whose life ended in a tragic crash. "Who killed Jessica?" blared the cover of *Time* magazine.

Call me crazy, but to me there is a connection between Jessica and Ted, a connection so strong that we ignore it at our personal and societal peril. It's a connection that entails what happens when gifted children are forced to grow up too fast or too alone.

How similar—and how sad—were their lives. Kaczynski lived in a family that demanded academic excellence and got it. While other 7 year olds played, Ted read *Scientific American* with his mom on their Illinois front porch. Skipping two grades and entering college at 16, Kaczynski was a *wunderkind*, but a lonely one. He was labeled the "Harvard Hermit." Jessica, according to interviews with her mother, never attended public or private school and never read picture books or owned toys. In fact, Jessica's mom said that, when she arrived at the primitive but sincere memorial to her daughter at the Cheyenne, Wyoming, crash site, she planned to remove all the teddy bears that had been placed there so lovingly by kind strangers. How sad that, even in death, Jessica was not allowed to be the child that she was.

I've tried to see these two cases from a perspective that voids my responsibility as an educator. After all, I never met Jessica or Ted, so what could I have possibly done to contribute to their tragedies? Call it guilt by association. Whenever I hear another story about the Unabomber or Jessica, I somehow get the feeling that I should have been more vocal in telling parents of gifted children that it is okay for their kids to enjoy childlike adventures, even if their minds are riper than most for academic pursuits. Or maybe I could have told the thousands of kids to whom I've spoken at awards assemblies that life is not a race to see who can get to its end the fastest; that sports and Nintendo and art and music each have challenges all their own. Perhaps I should have said more loudly that, even if you can read chapter books, picture books still hold much allure; or that, as the Water Rat in *The Wind in the Willows* reminds us, there is absolutely nothing so good as "simply messing about . . . simply messing."

From today on, I won't be so circumspect with my words. I'll remind both parents and educators that gifted children, first and foremost, are children; that, even though a gifted child might be able to spell the word *exhausted,* he or she still might not know when he or she is. I'll remind them that, even though a gifted child can jump through academic hoops with the greatest of ease, it's more important to be known for who you are, rather than for what you can do. Perhaps this is why we are a species called *human beings*, not *human doings*.

But, even if I do suggest that able kids are "children first and gifted second," I'll still be bothered when I see 5 year olds who read independently being forced to "learn" their colors and numbers in kindergarten. I'll still wonder why a seventh grader who gets A's on all his science tests earns a report card grade of D because he won't completely home-work that he regards (accurately) as meaningless. I'll still question the logic behind forcing a National Merit Semifinalist to pass a state-ordained proficiency test before she is allowed to earn a high school diploma. However, I'll still search for answers to those questions I asked earlier: "How much is too much?" "How soon is too soon?"

In retrospect, it is always easy to notice when the line has been crossed between "nudging" and "pushing." Looking back, it seems criminal that 7-year-old Jessica would be at the controls of a plane for no reason other than the attainment of a cross-country flight record, and it is absurd that 10-year-old Teddy would be encouraged to work alone in the basement at the expense of playing a little one-on-one at the nearby basketball court. Jessica and Ted, in ways only now visible, were victims of child abuse, induced not only by their overzealous parents, but also by a society that demands its ablest children to perform, perform, perform. We often hear that gifted children owe a debt to society in exchange for the gifts they've been given. Does anyone take the time to ask what it is that society owes to them?

In the end, with all traces of anger and bitterness aside, I feel tremendous compassion for the teachers of Ted Kaczynski, as well as for the parents of him and Jessica Dubroff. I'm sure each struggled, at least occasionally, with the question of balancing intellect with childhood. Sadly for these two families, that balance was never found.

Unless our society starts noticing that gifted children need the same nurturing, structure, friendships, and guidance that all other children need, I'm afraid any lessons we may have learned from the tragedies of Jessica and Ted will be short-lived. In our continual quest for more, better, and faster, I'm afraid that we're losing the most important race of all: the human one.

Gifted Child Today
July/August 1996

Neither Freak
nor Geek

The Gifted Among Us

Okay . . . the truth can now be told: I wrote this article about a now-defunct TV show, *Freaks and Geeks*, before I had even seen the series. But, as I read its description in *TV Guide*, I was surprised to read that gifted kids would be portrayed as real teenagers who were equally as concerned about STDs as they were with SATs. And, for the most part, they were. So, anytime giftedness can be portrayed as a three-dimensional phenomenon, I feel encouraged.

The real point of this article, though, had little to do with a TV show. Instead, I wrote it as a slam (I admit it) of Howard Gardner's work on Multiple Intelligences, that trendy and politically correct notion that allows everyone to be gifted at something. In devising his "theory" (I often use quotation marks when I brand an idea as illegitimate), Gardner has done more to discount and dismiss true giftedness than any other individual who came before him. Unfortunately for us, his work became popular overnight, before many people had a chance to digest its worth. Now, the "MI Bandwagon" (note, again, the quotations) is chugging along like a runaway train, fueled by illogic and wishful thinking.

I have taken an untold amount of heat for my strong views in support of gifted children and my equally strong beliefs against Multiple Intelligences. Even

Howard Gardner's wife, Ellen Winner, wrote a letter to the editor of *Education Week* calling the publication (and me, by association) irresponsible for having the gall to write and publish such drivel! On the other hand, I have people come up to me after I read this article in a public forum and thank me for having the courage to put into words what they have long wanted to say themselves. Many of these people, parents and educators both, have tears in their eyes as they are saying thank you. Ellen Winner never had tears, just anger.

I will continue on my Don Quixote crusade against the MI myth and hope that others join me in my quest to return legitimacy to the construct of intelligence that Gardner has so wrongly shoved aside.

The new television season has barely begun, and already viewers are confronted with an age-old stereotype that just won't die: the gifted kid as nerd. *Freaks and Geeks*, the NBC creation that rewards bullies with their own sitcom, pits the smart kids (the "geeks") against the jocks, with the stoners (the "freaks") characteristically occupying their own Never-Neverland. Pitting the athletes against the "mathletes," the show assumes viewers know that the road to social acceptance will always be tough for kids who value brains over brawn.

As a teacher and counselor of gifted students for more than 20 years, I have only two things to say to this show's producers: "welcome" and "thank you."

Huh? As an advocate for gifted kids, shouldn't I be hurling brickbats instead of bouquets at this show's designers? Why would I appreciate a program that trivializes and demeans the very students who are already among the most picked on in our nation's schools? I'll tell you why: because the presence of *Freaks and Geeks* on Saturday night's television lineup re-establishes the existence of gifted kids as a visible entity in America's classrooms. For the past decade, thanks to the myopic work of Howard Gardner, who wants us to believe that "all children are gifted at something," I was beginning to feel that gifted kids no longer existed in the make-believe world of Multiple Intelligences. *Freaks and Geeks* might just be the vehicle to refocus our attitudes toward an essential truth: In a world of equals, some are more intellectually equal than others.

Case in point: Jason. At the age of 7, while lunching at McDonald's with his dad, Jason asked why the Duplo blocks that had always been on the restaurant's tables during previous visits were missing. Dad's "I don't know" response to this basic question led Jason to head home and write the following essay, which he titled "Disintegration":

Have you ever noticed that all things seem to disintegrate piece by piece? McDonald's restaurants are disintegrating. They are taking the Duplos out. They have taken all the slides out of our McDonald's because someone got burned on one. Sometimes I feel like I'm disintegrating when I have to do worksheets and worksheets at school and when I have to answer silly questions. When I have to sit there and do what I already learned instead of something new and interesting, I feel like I'm in a battle and being torn apart bit by bit—the battle of work. Sometimes I feel like I'm disintegrating and leaving parts of myself in the past. I'll never be small enough for Daddy to carry me up the stairs again, and I am too big to be on Mommy's lap while she rocks. Disintegration!

The Multiple Intelligences adherents might qualify Jason's essay as an example of linguistic intelligence, one of the many separate intelligences that seem to grow in number with each new edition of a Gardner book. Advocates of curriculum differentiation for every student might attest that all children are capable of Jason's level of prose, if given the proper curriculum and instruction. Full-inclusion proponents would say that Jason's presence in a heterogeneous classroom would give other students a model to emulate in their own writing assignments. To these assertions I respond thusly: You are missing the point. Instead, I would argue that what distinguishes Jason's work from that of other second graders has little to do with the work itself and much more to do with the person who wrote it; someone whose intensity, insights, and ability to conceptualize at abstract and complex levels distinguish him as a breed apart from other 7-year-olds. Not a freak, not a geek, Jason is merely an example of a now-neglected truth: Giftedness is not dependent on something you do; rather, giftedness is determined by someone you are.

This approach to viewing giftedness as a psychological trait rather, than one manifested in outstanding projects or high test scores, is not new, merely forgotten. In the early 1900s, when Lewis Terman began his longitudinal study of 1,500 children with IQs above 140, giftedness was noted as being a confluence of intellect, emotions, and insights. As Terman wrote in 1905:

Heroic effort is made to boost every child just as near to the top of the intellectual ladder as possible, and to do so in the shortest possible time. Meanwhile, the child's own instinct and emotions . . . are allowed to wither away. No adjustment of clock wheels, however complicated and delicate, can avail if the mainspring is wrongly attached or altogether missing.

Lewis Terman knew then what our current emphasis on Multiple Intelligences has caused many to forget: The gifted child thinks, acts, and feels differently than other children. Giftedness is a trait no more universal in people than being tall or blue-eyed, and no more present in everyone than having an ear for music, an eye for art, or a heart for empathy. Most importantly, you can't "train" children to be gifted; you can only cherish and protect the insights and visions they possess naturally. In essence, gifted children simply are.

Yet, in today's schools, with the hue and cry for "high standards for all" and "talent development for everyone," it is ironic that the students missing out the most on these reforms' benefits are gifted students like Jason. Because of the misguided notion that giving more to a group of students who already appear to have so much—gifted kids— is elitist or wasteful, everyone gets clumped together in the name of equality. The results? Gifted kids get bored, special programs that serve them are resented, and *Freaks and Geeks* becomes part of a culture that is increasingly intolerant of unseen yet obvious human differences. In Jason's word and world, "Disintegration."

There are solutions to serving gifted students well, and we need look no further than our own history to find them. Starting with our attitudes and beliefs, let us first acknowledge that children like Jason exist in our schools. Like Jason, they may question the value of their own existence, ponder the existence of God, or talk about their ideas and dreams at a depth that is both uncanny and uncommon among young children. Next, let us return to Terman's notion that giftedness is not just an intellectual trait that can be captured by more and harder curricula, but rather, that being gifted is fraught with social and emotional elements that will require "advanced training of the heart" for the child to function fully and well. Then, let us put our egalitarian biases behind us and admit that the most economical, efficient, and beneficial placement of gifted children in our schools is with intellectual peers who will both enrich and challenge them.

We do not force star athletes to compete against intramural squads every day of each year, nor do we cluster the most refined musicians in an orchestra with those just beginning their music lessons. How, then, can we assume that grouping gifted students with less-able agemates for the duration of their education will benefit them in any legitimate ways?

Without a doubt, giftedness is a worthwhile trait for both the individual and our society, but we should be honest enough with ourselves to admit that not everyone has it. This artificial show of egalitarianism denies everything we know about the sanctity of human differences.

Finally, let us respect gifted children enough that we will acknowledge their abilities and insights as a natural part of who they are—not better or worse than anyone else, neither freak nor geek, but merely a member of our diverse human family, where "one size fits all" just doesn't fit anyone.

Education Week
October 27, 1999

The Smartest Kid
in America

Introduction

O f all the articles I have written in the past 20 years, I would say that this one is my favorite. Again, it focuses on the media's inane quest to oversimplify a complex idea like giftedness, reducing it to a two-hour TV show that is as exploitative a venture as any I have ever seen.

Here's the scene: You have more than 40 children, ages 10–12, vying for the title of "Smartest Kid In America" on Fox TV. Each child gets a chance to introduce himself (male contestants far outnumber girls; Whites, by an even greater margin, outnumber other ethnic groups). They say things like "My name is Steve, I live in Michigan and my IQ is 143."

Following this, each child is asked a trivia question in math or geography— you know, the kind of dumb stuff you learn in school and forget immediately after the test is finished. If you answer correctly, you move on; wrong answers are dealt with harshly, as the kids are banished backstage and you never see or hear from them again. This goes on until the final two contestants—remember, they're 10 years old—vie for the title of "Smartest Kid." The child who is defeated sees himself as the first loser, never again to be known for anything else except coming close to winning.

I wrote to Dick Clark, the show's producer, enclosing a copy of my article and explaining in further detail how I thought his show was both cruel and wrong. He wrote back a one-line letter that read "Your comments are noted." Dissatisfied with this response (you don't mess with me, Dick Clark!), I found the e-mail address for the president of Dick Clark Productions and spread it out over the gifted network that I have established nationwide. Let's just say they got a lot more messages about this show then they ever wanted to get.

If Dick Clark is shameful enough to have a third "Smartest Kid" contest, I will once again pick up my pen and begin anew this quixotic crusade against cruelty to children.

Stay tuned . . .

The *Smartest Kid in America* was an intellectual trial that bordered on abuse. Recently, the Fox Television Network, in a bold and misbegotten attempt to garner high ratings during the "sweeps month" of May, decided to locate the smartest kid in America. Call it a pint-sized version of *Who Wants To Be a Millionaire?*, for the questions dealt with the kinds of trivia important only on game shows or their educational equivalent, those silly state competency tests that inflict pain on students and teachers nationwide.

So, the smartest kid nominees paraded onto the stage; a beauty pageant of the mind, with the contestants wearing just a tad less makeup than JonBenet Ramsey often wore to events like these. Each spoke about academic accomplishments that would make viewers go "Wow!" and, like their Miss America equivalents, some of the kids spoke of their future goals and ambitions as scientists or technicians or doctors.

The competition began, the questions were asked, and child after child fell victim to one of the most common maladies of being human: They made errors. When it got down to the last two contestants, the tension was as high as the stakes. Face it, in the world of competitive TV, there lies a big gulf between being named "The Smartest Kid in America" and being named . . . well, nothing.

It was then I noticed the tic. One of the two finalists, obviously showing signs of nervousness (who wouldn't?), had a noticeable twitch in his eye, a nonverbal indicator that he was not comfortable. He didn't win.

Applause, applause for the victor. Break to commercial. Add up the ratings.

Just one question: Were you proud, Dick Clark, that you had just presided over an intellectual trial that bordered on abuse? Shame on you. Shame on Fox.

I'm not sure what upset me more, the fact that a contest based on silly questions could actually qualify as the sole indicator of finding America's most gifted child or the willingness of millions of viewers to believe that, indeed, this was possible.

But, then I began to think. If I had been asked to locate the smartest child in our nation, what criteria would I have chosen? So, I put myself to work, coming up with the following.

First, I'd have to determine what is meant by "smart." Does it mean answering multiple-choice questions about math and reading and science? Does it imply a deeper knowledge of the concepts that underlie the facts, like knowing that the reason people choose to fight wars has as much to do with economics as it does ideology? Or, does "smart" mean having the common sense to know that, although I may win at the blackjack table often enough to entice me to stay, the odds are with the house no matter how lucky I appear to be? "Smart" is not as easy to define as it appears, despite what Fox TV might want us to think.

Since defining the word *smart* didn't seem to be getting me anywhere, I decided I would merely revert to the experiences I have had with children over the past 22 years as an educator and look there for guidance in *describing* "smartness." In doing so, I relived some fond memories and found some interesting data:

- *The kids who left the biggest impact on me were seldom the ones who got every answer right on their tests or turned in all their homework on time.*

To be sure, my most memorable students were generally conscientious and motivated, but occasionally, they just blew off or forgot an assignment because something else ignited a passion that they just had to explore. If I argued with them about "setting priorities" or "acting responsibly," they'd look back at me with glazed eyes, asking without words whether I understood the true meaning of being turned on to learning.

But, when I was wise enough to ask what they were doing that prevented them from completing their assignment, I was often rewarded with an animated review of an area of knowledge or fun that taught them more than any of my assignments ever could have done.

- *The students who looked beyond the school and the classroom for their learning arena were both better informed and more interesting than the "bookwise" kids.*

I'll never forget how Brian, a sixth grader, took on a social studies project that involved furnishing an entire household for a family of seven after they lost all their possessions in a house fire. Brian corralled his classmates and made them care as deeply about these strangers as he did—and he did so without ever opening a social studies book or a "how to do it" guide on community service. What he opened, instead, was his heart, and the beneficiaries were seven people who now sit in chairs, sleep in beds, and cook on a stove that were all due to Brian's initiative in combining his loving heart with his fine mind.

- *The boys and girls who were the best thinkers always had more questions than they did answers.*

For proof of this, I looked at 4-year-old Lisbeth, who asked her mommy if people felt the same way right before they were born as they did just after they died. I also thought of Justin, one of my current eighth graders, who asked out loud which property of matter—gas, liquid, or solid—did a fire's flame fall under. And I looked at 5-year-old Matt, my son, who asked for clarification on the following: If butter melts yellow, and chocolate melts brown, why doesn't snow melt white?

It is these kids, the question *askers*, who always appeared much brighter than did their counterparts, the question *answerers*. With both people and ideas, their innate curiosity caused them to take nothing and no one at face value.

- *The children who were my most memorable scholars understood that their learning would neither end nor expire.*

Every fact these students learned got stored alongside others like it, eventually causing them to make generalizations about ideas and people. Each learning opportunity was seen as just that: a chance to pick up something new, so that, even if these kids knew how to *spell* the word *bored*, they didn't know how to *feel* it. They could always find something intriguing behind even the most mundane activity or lesson.

Using these criteria, I'm afraid I'd never be able to spin off a two-hour Fox TV special on picking America's smartest kid. That is because, in addition to the above qualities, I'd also need something that the medium of television is loath to give: extended time to know these children from the inside out; to determine how "smart" they really are using the multiplicity of definitions of intelligence that we now have at our disposal; to ask the finalists not only "*What* do you know?" but "*How* do you know it?"; and to publicize not only these kids' test scores, but also the contributions they have made to a society very much in need of tenderhearted kindness and honest compassion.

The Smartest Kid in America? I have no idea who it might be, and I wouldn't know how to begin to make that choice without adequate exposure to the "candidates" over a long, long time. But what I *do* know is that this choice cannot be made in two hours, waffled between commercials for athletic shoes and promotions for *That '70s Show*.

Perhaps a bigger question is why search at all for the Smartest Kid in America? What does it prove? I can't imagine whom this contest helps, but I already know two children it hurts: the boy who was selected as the "smartest" and who will now be living down that reputation for decades to come and the runner-up, the boy with the tic in his eye, for whom second place was seen by millions of viewers as a sign of inadequate brainpower on a TV show that should never have been aired.

Education Week
June 21, 2000

Part Nine

The Emotional Parts of Growing Up Gifted

Since a majority of the articles in this compilation deal, in some way, with the emotional components of giftedness, this section may seem superfluous. Still, I wanted to include these articles apart from the others, as they provide something of a "primer" for the specific adjustment concerns of gifted people

If I were to dedicate these next few pages to anyone, it would be to Dr. James Mehorter, the most influential person in my career that I have never met.

Huh?

Dr. Mehorter was a graduate student at the University of Virginia under the guidance of my esteemed friend and colleague, Dr. Virgil Ward. Like many doctoral candidates, Jim had trouble coming up with a researchable topic for his dissertation. After several attempts that went nowhere, Dr. Ward suggested that Jim look into the work of Leta Hollingworth, a woman who was a contemporary of Lewis Terman and whose work focused on serving highly gifted children. A specialty of hers was the emotional aspects of growing up gifted. Reading her work, Jim became convinced that this was a researchable topic, and he began to adapt Hollingworth's work in a most fascinating way. Taking six of Hollingworth's main points about growing up gifted—for example, kids don't understand what giftedness is; they have trouble making friends their own age because of their advanced intellectual development; career selection is difficult because of too many choices—Jim developed a self-guided curriculum for gifted secondary students. In it, students read excerpts from classic literature and philosophy, answered questions about these excerpts that were pertinent to their own lives, and sent their responses back to Jim for comment. This was bibliotherapy with a twist: The person helping you sort out yourself was a trained psychologist.

Jim's work fascinated me for several reasons. First, it was very complex yet simultaneously quite personal. Second, his work introduced me to the life and achievements of Leta Hollingworth, the most prominent (yet underrated) figure in our field. Third, his work has guided my own for almost a generation, and for that I thank him.

I never met Jim Mehorter. He took his own life before I even became involved in gifted child education. His work was never published; his dissertation was all I had to work from. Yet, this man is a cornerstone—an almost forgotten cornerstone—in our understanding of who gifted children are, as I am fond of saying, "from the inside out."

Emotional Hitchhiking

Understanding and Appreciating Gifted Children From the Inside Out

Introduction

I f you're looking for a "Gifted 101" version of the specific emotional needs of gifted children, this article should suffice. I questioned whether I should put it in this collection at all. Its references are old and the writing style is too choppy, thanks to my frequent inclusion of bulleted items and pithy quotes. Still, if you are an educator, the main components of the inner lives of gifted children can be found in this piece.

There is just enough history to tantalize readers who may want to know more about why insanity was closely linked to genius in the 1800s and enough specific activities that can be done with gifted children to cause those practical ones among you to get out your highlighters. Lastly, there are references to books as diverse as Stephen Manes' *How to be a Perfect Person in Just Three Days* to Sir Francis Galton's *Hereditary Genius*. Quite a variety!

It's probably about time to write another article like this, outlining anew the issues often faced by gifted students and updating the references to include Web sites and other helpful resources. Interestingly, though, the central emotional issues involved in growing up gifted have not changed since this article appeared. Indeed, they have not changed since Leta Hollingworth wrote about them in the 1930s. I take comfort in stating this fact: It means that each generation of gifted individuals shares commonalties with those who have come before them.

T en-year-old Matt could barely contain his enthusiasm. For a classroom assignment, Matt's teacher had said that students "could do a project on anything." At last! A chance for Matt to share his knowledge and love of nuclear physics.

Matt's presentation was squeezed between Beth's (on Dalmations) and Jeb's (on indoor soccer). Their presentations lasted about 20 minutes each—lots of questions and visuals piqued the interest of classmates. Matt's talk took about six minutes. Interspersed with classroom giggles and comments like "Speak English, Matt!," the presentation fell apart one word, one term at a time. Matt didn't even bother to show his collection of toothpick-and-marshmallow molecule models.

By recess, Matt had covered his embarrassment with a cloak of stoicism: "Lots of scientists have trouble getting their points across. People just won't think too hard about anything." Then, off he strode to discuss the latest Nintendo tricks unlocked by his buddies.

Matt represents gifted children in two important ways: He owns some unique talents and interests far above those of his agemates, and he fits into age-appropriate discussions about video game hijinks. He is a child, a young adult, and a scientist simultaneously.

As Matt continues to mature, he will need the guidance of caring adults who understand him. These life guides, these emotional hitchhikers, can provide Matt with both concrete advice and soft shoulders of support in dealing with a world he may not fully understand.

Nothing New Under the Sun

Despite our nation's on-again, off-again interest in providing appropriate educational challenges to intellectually gifted children, the fact remains that highly able children have always existed, and, until cloning becomes commonplace, they always will.

Since the earliest days of the studies of genius (Galton, 1869; Lombroso, 1891), a nonintellective "differentness" about gifted persons has often been noted. Some researchers and diarists have focused on the negative, the "weirdness" of gifted people. Perhaps these views exist most vividly in media caricatures of gifted individuals—Urkel on the TV show *Family Matters* or the Professor on *Gilligan's Island*, both of whom need crash courses in social skills. Other writers have chosen a higher road and have explored differentness in a more positive manner. In reading the work of Hollingworth (1926), one is struck by her acceptance of the social and emotional distinctiveness that often accompanies talent. Roeper (1990) sees the tenderness and empathy expressed by even young gifted children as an asset in a world where selfishness sometimes overshadows compassion. In their minds, an appropriate media model of giftedness might by Doogie Howser, M.D., a man-child possessed of a big brain and a tender heart.

Even though both research and common sense point to the importance of social and emotional development of gifted persons, it is rare to find school-based provisions that address these areas. Instead, gifted program specialists focus on higher level thinking, independent study, and seventh-grade calculus. The brain and its development take precedence over all other endeavors, and affective nurturance—concerns for one's relationship with the world and those in it—is relegated to a Friday afternoon timeblock when the "real work" is completed. If, as a society, we truly cared about our children's ability to love, as well as to reason, it would be reflected in our curriculum guides and in our classroom practices. Omission speaks louder than words.

What are we to do, individually and collectively, if we truly believe that social and emotional development is at least as important as intellectual stimulation? The first step is to raise this very issue with our colleagues—educators, parents, students—to ascertain their beliefs and prejudices about this topic. We must emphasize that the affective dimension pervades all our work. For example, if I loathe group projects, my attitude will probably affect my academic performance on such tasks.

Next, we must define carefully the intent and scope of our efforts, so as to dispel the myth that programs or activities with an affective dimension are attempts to indoctrinate students to accept a certain set of values of beliefs. Indoctrination would be intellectual child abuse. It would usurp the family's right to raise children in accordance with their own values and morals. Our task instead is to allow students to ask questions and raise issues about themselves, others, and their world—questions that help to clarify matters of individual importance or concern. Sometimes—in fact, often—students will not require answers to their queries; many times, just voicing their concerns or beliefs is enough to resolve a quiet, internal crisis about school, friends, or family.

These two steps are the most difficult parts of addressing social and emotional development. Once they are accomplished, then specific programmatic concerns can be addressed.

Implementing an Emotional Curriculum: Topics, Strategies, and Resources

The most basic concern in implementing emotional education for gifted students is a sense of perspective: "What does this label of 'gifted' really mean, and does it change who I am?"

This most fundamental of topics is often sidestepped by parents and other educators who assume that such discussion will lead gifted children to believe that they are better than those not quite as talented.

Au contraire.

We should review the child's answers to such questions as these:

- Are *you* gifted? If so, in what ways? If not, name someone who is.
- What misperceptions do people have about giftedness?
- Are gifted people better than other people?
- Are you gifted all your life, or can it go away and come back?
- What are the best and worst parts about being gifted?
- What do you think of the term itself—*gifted*? Is there another word you prefer? Why or why not?

These questions can be asked of students in several ways. A teacher may begin with a paper and pencil, asking students to write their opinions, anonymously if preferred. The students' comments can be shared with partners or in small groups for a comparison of responses. This option works well with students who do not know each other too well. Or, a group of students comfortable with each other can hold a "circle group" open discussion. In either arrangement, the teacher reserves personal judgment and acts more as a bridger of student ideas or as an encourager of reluctant participants (vocal participation, though, should always be the student's prerogative).

Resources helpful in prompting these discussion are offered by Delisle (1984) in *Gifted Children Speak Out*, a compilation of hundreds of responses to questions similar to those suggested, or by Galbraith (1983) and Delisle and Galbraith (1987), whose *Gifted Kids Survival Guides* are written specifically for gifted children and teenagers.

Once discussions (note the plural) of giftedness have taken place, the teacher has several choices of the next topic to address:

- setting expectations;
- getting along with friends;
- benefiting the most from school; or
- dealing with feelings and beliefs.

Each of these topics, which are addressed below, commingles with the others; the arbitrary distinctions provided here are for purposes of illustration only.

Setting Expectations

A pensive Charlie Brown, trying to cope with yet another failure, expresses a view held by many gifted children: "There is no heavier burden than that of a great potential."

Failure and success are in the eyes of the beholder. Each of us knows someone for whom a grade of B+ is bad because it could have been an A. Each of us also knows someone for whom a D- is acceptable because, "Hey . . . it's still passing!" Such individual interpretations of performance would be problem-free were it not for an additional variable: Significant others let children know they disagree with their interpretations. When a children believes that, "Since I'm gifted, I should get straight A's," and a parent comments, "It's okay if you get a B, I know you tried your best," the lines of communication are fractured. With the best of intentions, parents and teachers try to reassure the budding perfectionist that "less than perfection is more than acceptable." But, the comments and pleas often fall on deaf ears because the real issue, "my personal view of success," is the undiscussed core of the problem.

Several resources are helpful in reviewing this vital issue. *Understanding Success and Failure* (Roets, 1985) uses a series of classroom activities that help students confront the underlying issue of setting realistic expectations. *Mistakes Are Great* (Zadra & Moawad, 1986) uses contemporary actors and athletes in addressing the importance (and, yes, fun) of messing up. *Mistakes That Worked* (Jones, 1991) identifies common products—

Crazy Glue, Silly Putty, Post-It Notes—that were invented by accident, and *How To Be a Perfect Person in Just Three Days* (Manes, 1983) is both a children's book and a movie extolling the benefits of being less than perfect.

Understanding personal expectations and accepting failure as a by-product of being human are important. If left unaddressed, these concerns can lead to the most serious problem of adulthood. Discussing such issues during childhood may relieve some of the rampant stress that results when children see their personal efforts and their personal worth as identical.

Getting Along With Friends

T. Ernest Newland did our field a great favor when, in 1976, he wrote a book called *The Gifted in Socio-Educational Perspective.* Among other gems, Newland coined the term *peerness* to explain that one's agemates are not necessarily one's peers. Thus, an able 9-year-old may have more in common with a 12-year-old in terms of interests and intellect than with a 9-year-old classmate. Our society generally frowns upon mixed-age comraderie—look at how our schools are structured—for fear that such alliances will stunt a child's social growth. Children need to get along with their peers, we say, without thinking that peers can, in fact, differ in chronological age.

Gifted children confront this dilemma regularly: the 6-year-old who hears calls of "Huh?" from agemates when he wants to play games by the rules, not just for fun; the 10-year-old who endures taunts of "bookworm" because she's in love with words; the teenage boy who is a "fag" because he listens to classical music. Each is engaged in behaviors that adults consider appropriate, but that agemates construe as weird. To help gifted students better understand the difference between peers and agemates, several strategies are suggested:

- Ask gifted students from a higher grade level (two or three years above works well) to review with younger students some techniques they have used in creating friendship bonds. These "near peers" can share valuable life lessons with younger students.
- Ask students to list ways they are the same as and different from their classmates. Ask them to do the same with a group of students who are three years older.
- Encourage students to interact socially and intellectually with students who are both younger and older than they. Combine classes with another teacher, perhaps, and do some hands-on activities that allow individual talents to emerge.
- Ask parents to consider whether chronological age is the most important criterion used in the selection of their own personal friends. If not age, then what factors are more important? By reminding parents of the relevance of common interests and intellect in their own selection of friends, perhaps you can show them how this principle applies to their children.

Of course, gifted students can and do have friends who are the same chronological age. This discussion of peerness is meant merely to indicate that age is not the only factor worth considering when choosing friends; it is meant to take some of the "weirdness" away from preferring, at times, the company of older or younger people.

Benefiting the Most From School

More than at any other recent time, our gifted children now appear at risk from the structure and operation of our schools. Recent movements away from ability grouping and toward total heterogeneity in classrooms; the overuse and misuse of cooperative learning strategies; and the economic recession, which has once again raised the issue of whether gifted education is merely a frill to be cut, have combined to create benign neglect, at best, or animosity, at worst, toward the intellectual needs of gifted students. The maxim that "everyone is gifted in some way" is hard to argue against without sounding elitist, and the continued provision of resource rooms for gifted students is hard to argue for now that educators agree that creative, critical, and independent thinking should be a part of every child's curriculum.

Frankly, I believe our field needed to be shaken up in this way. For too long, gifted child educators have holed up in worlds of their own, sharing little of their knowledge with regular class educators and, even worse, ignoring the talents possessed by our colleagues in the classroom. Now, more than ever, gifted child educators need the support of the very professionals they have often neglected. And, since it is not forthcoming in any identifiable mass movement, we need to convince our colleagues one at a time that they need us as much as we need them.

Given our past track record, the "sell" will not be easy. Here are some suggestions:

- Acknowledge the very good ways that most regular classroom educators devote at least some time and energy to open-ended assignments and individual student goals.
- Willingly share expertise and, as importantly, resources that you have found helpful in reaching the talents of gifted students. When asked, work with colleagues in coteaching a lesson or unit. When not asked, volunteer to do so.
- Be "armed" with current information on the benefits and drawbacks of ability grouping (Kulik & Kulik, 1991), cooperative learning (Rogers, 1992), and middle school reform provisions for gifted students (Robinson, 1990). Opinion, backed up by evidence, can carry clout with some important audiences.
- Get out of the resource room and return to the mainstream. When we work alongside teachers, rather than away from them, they are more likely to see us as partners in the learning process.
- Have a vision for the future of gifted child education. Perhaps now is the time to get serious about programs and services for underachievers, gifted students with learning disabilities, preschool-age gifted children, gifted children from diverse cultures, and highly gifted children. Despite big talk, we have had little action in these aspects of gifted child education.

You may notice that, in this section of the article, I am on a soapbox, spouting opinions, rather than offering curricular strategies. My tone is intentional and underscores the importance I place on refocusing our efforts toward redefining our field of study.

If you need specific strategies for working with gifted students in a school setting, consider the work of Colangelo and Davis (1991) or Winebrenner (1992). There you will find specific activities to enhance the education of gifted students. Still, unless we address the overall concerns presented in this section, the good work of these authors and others may be largely irrelevant.

Dealing With Feelings and Beliefs

The last area of focus is the most elusive to define and to address directly with students. It comprises intangibles and immeasurables:

- How will I know if I am a success?
- What do I do if I disagree with one of my parents' strongly held beliefs?
- How do I decide what I should be when I grow up when I am good at so many things and interested in them all?
- Why is the world so unfair?
- Why are smart people—even leaders—sometimes so cruel?

Bordering on the philosophic and existential, such questions can torment able people from very young ages. Equally as frustrating, students can sometimes cite remedies for these personal or global problems, but their solutions may be "pooh-poohed" by others as immature, shortsighted, or quixotic. The resulting angst experienced by thoughtful young people may result in cynicism or, worse, self-imposed exile from the human family. It is easier to be an isolate than an agent of change.

Of course, there are no quick solutions or activities to address these internal dilemmas. There are, however, important models that help us respect the student's right to ask deep questions. Betts and Knapp (1981), in their Autonomous Learner Model, provide strategies to address issues as complex as those raised here. And, Roeper's *Educating Children for Life* (1990) shows specific ways that her school for gifted children has addressed these issues for 50 years.

In his treatise, *Education* (1883), Ralph Waldo Emerson reminded readers that

the secret of Education lies in respecting the pupil. It is not for you to choose what he shall know, what he shall do. It is chosen and foreordained, and he only holds the key to his own secret.

No tricks, no magic elixirs, no one right answer. Share these realities, too, with your students, and you will be on your way to meeting their deepest emotional needs.

Conclusion

One vital factor that has gone unstated is the importance of the teacher in helping to secure a gifted child's self-worth and promise. Frequently, teachers of gifted children are just large-size versions of the pupils in their care. The questions, frustrations, and joys of students and their teacher overlap greatly; we identify with our students because they are us, only slightly younger.

Take advantage of these similarities by "sharing the ride" of their development. Such emotional hitchhiking benefits both driver and passenger, who, as partners on this trip through life and learning, often change places before reaching the final destination, satisfied that the road just traveled, complete with detours and speed bumps, was one worth driving together.

Educating Able Learners
Spring 1993

Gifted Children

The Heart of the Matter

Introduction

J ust as artists go through their own transformations—Picasso had his "Blue Period"—so do writers. This article was written during my "Duality Period." And, while I am not comparing my work to that of the great artists, it is one of the eras of my writing styles that has withstood the test of time.

Just read "Essential element #1" in this article: *Giftedness is someone you are, not something you do.* And then there is "Essential Element #2": *Gifted students want to belong more than they want to be smart.* Notice the catchy play on words that each duality illustrates; these one-liners grab people's attention, and they are easy to remember.

Just as importantly, though, these "Essential Elements" really are that—essential. Talk with gifted kids and you will learn that they reinforce each of the three main points of this article. For example, few kids want their entire sense of self wrapped up in the accomplishments they complete or the achievements they master. There is more to them than production, and they want to be recognized for just being themselves. Likewise, I don't know a kid—gifted or otherwise—who goes out of his or her way to be a social leper. We *all* want at least one friend to converse with, to share secrets and stories, wishes and fears. As stated by Hollingworth years ago,

"Isolation is the refuge of genius, not its goal." The dualities presented are nothing more than effective sound bites in an era that is used to hearing them.

Watch out, though, for that third "Essential Element": *Parents and educators must appreciate their own giftedness if they expect gifted children to do the same.* Not as catchy a tune as the previous two, but an important piece of the gifted pie: to recognize giftedness as a lifelong phenomenon, not a school-based one.

As a long-ago teacher of gifted children, I made many mistakes. Armed with all manner of curriculum guides and problem-solving models, I saw gifted children as human machines capable of lots of production. Projects flowed out of my resource room, as interested student devoured subjects ranging from astronomy to botany, algebra to Amelia Earhart. I was doing a good job, I thought, because my students were busy, engaged, and learning.

But, then Katy wanted to drop out of my gifted program. She couldn't come up with a project idea, and she didn't think she "deserved the privilege" (her words) of working in my class. Mike also chose not to return to a second year with me. He blamed his friends and the teasing he got from being a "cg" (cognitively gifted) kid. His classmates said his "cg" *really* stood for "chicken guts." Another program casualty was Benny, who said he used to feel smart before he entered my class, but now everyone else seemed smarter than he. The pressure to keep up was just too much for him; he didn't want to feel that he was the "bottom of the top" anymore.

It was then I realized that curriculum guides and fancy projects were not the essential elements of educating gifted children. The true essence lies someplace else, someplace deeper. It was only when I learned that the way to gifted children's minds is through their hearts that I became able to legitimately call myself their teacher. And that has made all the difference.

Gifted Children 101: Understanding Their Basics

When the field we now call *gifted education* began to get much attention in the early 1900s, it was because psychologists—not educators—began to get interested in young people whose intellectual and emotional functioning far surpassed those of their age-mates. Today, it seems that the only time a psychologist sees a gifted child is either to do a one-time intelligence test to "prove" giftedness or to pave the path for a formal diagnosis of ADHD by a physician.

Today, educators are both the main identifiers of gifted children and the primary professionals responsible for their intellectual well-being. And, while I applaud the efforts made by teachers, most have a limited background in psychology, leaving them to use either common sense or past experiences as the bases on which to consider the social and emotional needs of gifted children. Sometimes, this is enough; often, it isn't.

What follows, then, are three elements of the psychological needs of gifted children. Gathered over the years by my observations as a teacher, counselor, and parent, these basic needs must be considered if we are to address fully the special needs that exist within the mind, hearts, and lives of our gifted children.

- Essential Element #1: Giftedness is *someone you are*, not *something you do.*

Since the mid-1970s, the concept of giftedness has been shaped by researchers who equate it with an activity you do (Renzulli, 1978) or a talent you possess (Gardner, 1983). In fact, a debate has arisen recently (Feldhusen, 1995) on whether the term *gifted* should be discarded completely, substituting it with the word *talented.* Gifted behaviors have increasingly become the measure of choice to determine one's intellectual prowess.

Such talent-based conceptions of giftedness seldom address the psychological or social needs of gifted children. In fact, it is not uncommon to find a gifted student dropped from an honors course or resource room program because he or she is not producing adequate work. Such policies as this produce many psychological land mines for the children involved, as they may begin to believe their self-worth is measured against an external barometer of success or competency. When this occurs, a lowered regard for one's own uniqueness may result and a standard for perfectionistic work in all endeavors established:

> I personally never felt like anything I did was good enough
> —Angela, age 17

> [Gifted kids] expect themselves to be perfect in all areas of study, therefore, when something goes wrong, they undermine any prior success.
> —Sonja, age 13 (Galbraith & Delisle, 1996)

Parents and educators must help gifted children realize that the ability to understand complex ideas and emotions qualifies one as "gifted," whether or not they produce consistently at school-based tasks. The psychological construct of "giftedness" was never meant to be interpreted in relation to academic success. Isn't it time we returned to the idea of giftedness as a *personal trait*, not a *standard of behavior*?

- Essential Element #2: Gifted students want to *belong* more than they want to *be smart.*

As loathe as some gifted students may be to accept this reality, they are part of a species for whom socialization is both natural and important. We grow and learn to a large degree because of our associations with others; "no man is an island" is as true an expression for gifted students as it is for everyone else.

However, gifted students are often placed in a self-imposed either/or position that is very awkward: "Should I be gifted or just a regular kid?" The assumption, of course, is that you can't be both simultaneously:

We are expected to be pretty and popular, and it is so hard to be intelligent and let it show in school.
—Girl, age 14

How does a person avoid being ridiculed for having an advanced vocabulary or whatever? I mean, saying "I can't help it, I'm gifted" isn't exactly a good comeback, is it?
—Peter, age 12 (Galbraith & Delisle, 1996)

To help gifted students "fit in" while maintaining their very important sense of individuality, they must understand a few key points:

1. *Agemate* and *peer* are very different terms. A peer is someone who accepts, understands, and enjoys you. An agemate merely shares you birth year.
2. Many gifted students' peers are younger or older than they are themselves—and that's okay.
3. The toughest time for gifted students in social relationships is also the toughest time for most *all* kids: the early adolescent years, from ages 11–16. After that (and especially in college), peer pressure to conform lessens considerably.

Given these realities, gifted children and teenagers can plan their actions—and reactions—accordingly. Figure 1 gives specific ways to approach an impending social relationship, with class and confidence providing guidance in an area that is too often left to the painful method of trial and error.

Can you be gifted and socially well adjusted, too? Most gifted kids are, but it's the exceptions (and the popular media) that have led us to believe otherwise.

• Essential Element #3: Parents and educators must appreciate their *own* giftedness if they expect gifted children to do the same.

When I am presenting to adult audiences on the topic of the social and emotional needs of gifted children, I get them comfortable before tossing in a zinger: "How many of *you* are gifted?" The most common responses are nonverbal: shuffling of feet, downcast eyes, and an uncomfortably wiggling in their seats, fearing, no doubt, that I will call on them to personally "own up" to their unique gifts.

Educators and parents of gifted children often present themselves as poor role models with regard to the acceptance of personal giftedness. With comments like "You don't have to *be* gifted to *teach* the gifted" or "I don't know where she got her giftedness; I think it skipped my generation," we are sending a *very* mixed message: Even though I want you to be proud of your giftedness, I'm embarrassed to acknowledge my own.

There is abundant research showing a strong genetic predisposition for giftedness, and, even if they are not well-schooled, parents of gifted children present themselves generally as an intelligent, curious, intense lot. Yet, too seldom are these adults willing to admit openly that giftedness has an impact on their lives, too, not just on those of the children in their care.

1. Reach out. Don't always wait for someone else to make the first move. A simple "hi" and a smile go a long way. It may sound corny, but you'll be amazed at the response you'll receive when you extend a friendly greeting.

2. Get involved. Join clubs that interest you; take special classes inside and outside of school. Seek out neighborhood and community organizations and other opportunities to give service to others.

3. Let people know that you're interested in them. Don't just talk about yourself; ask questions about them and their interests. Make this a habit and you'll have mastered the art of conversation. It's amazing how many people haven't yet grasped this basic social skill.

4. Be a good listener. This means looking at people while they're talking to you and genuinely paying attention to what they're saying. (A long litany of "uh-huhs" is a dead giveaway that your mind is somewhere else.)

5. Risk telling people about yourself. When it feels right, let your interests and talents be known. For example, if you love science fiction and you'd like to know others who feel the same way, spread the word. If you're an expert on the history of science fiction, you might want to share your knowledge. But . . .

6. Don't be a show-off. Not everyone you meet will share your interests and abilities. (On the other hand, you shouldn't have to hide them—which you won't, once you find people who like and appreciate you.)

7. Be honest. Tell the truth about yourself and your convictions. When asked for your opinion, be sincere. Friends appreciate forthrightness in each other. But . . .

8. When necessary, temper your honesty with diplomacy. The truth doesn't have to hurt. It's better to say, "Gee, your new haircut is interesting" than to exclaim, "You actually paid money for *that*?" There are times when frankness is inappropriate and unnecessary.

9. Don't just use your friends as sounding boards for your problems and complaints. Include them in the good times, too.

10. Do your share of the work. That's right, work. Any relationship takes effort. Don't always depend on your friends to make the plans and carry the weight.

11. Be accepting. Not all of your friends have to think and act like you do. (Wouldn't it be boring if they did?)

12. Learn to recognize the so-called friends you can do without. Some gifted kids get so lonely that they put up with anyone, including friends who aren't really friends at all. Follow tips 1–11, and this shouldn't happen to you.

Figure 1. 12 Tips for Making and Keeping Friends

Note. From *The gifted kids survival guide: A teen handbook* (p. 209), by J. Galbraith & J. Delisle, 1996, Minneapolis: Free Spirit. Copyright © 1996 by Free Spirit, 1-800-735-7323, www.freespirit.com. Reprinted with permission.

Blame this lack of openness on personal modesty or the cultural belief that you don't "blow your own horn." But, whatever its source, it is sending a signal that the only *acceptable* gifted person is the *humble* one; the gifted individual whose pride in his or her own uniqueness must be closeted or hidden. Such self-effacing is but one short step away from denying that you are gifted at all.

It is vital that adults talk with gifted children about their own giftedness. They can mention the benefits of being able to understand concepts quickly or the joy and pain of feeling emotions with an intensity not always appreciated by others. They can talk about their own struggles with personal identity and acceptance and the self and social expectations that often go along with growing up gifted. Also, they can help gifted kids recognize the distinction between being *better at* some things than others their age and being *better than* other people because of these gifts. "Better at" is nothing more than an acknowledgement of reality. "Better than" is a false statement of superiority that has no place in any individual's belief system.

The simple, honest, direct route is usually the best approach for explaining an issue that has many layers. Discussing giftedness with your children at home or your students at school begins with your own willingness to be open about your own gifts, whatever they may be.

The Essence of You(th)

Lily Tomlin wrote, "When I was growing up, I always wanted to be somebody, but I see now I should've been more specific."

Gifted children have the needs of safety, love, belonging, and self-acceptance shared by all other people. These universal desires, when coupled with a unique gift to see the world from an enhanced perspective, take on importance earlier in life than one might expect.

As caring adults, whatever our personal or professional roles, we must give our children some essential elements through which they can live their lives with honesty, integrity, and joy. As their life guides, we have more abilities to do so than we sometimes realize.

So . . . begin talking to your gifted children about these three essential elements. You'll end up in some very interesting places.

Understanding Our Gifted
Spring 1997

Zen
and the Art
of Gifted Child
Education

Introduction

I am still *appalled* at the number of people who have not heard of the amazing book *Zen and the Art of Motorcycle Maintenance*. It is a *Catcher in the Rye* for the more mature among us; a *Prince of Tides* for those not so prone to schmaltz. What Robert Pirsig does in this, his first and best novel, is nothing less than strip our collective souls clean to the bone, exposing our flaws and our inconsistencies. He orchestrates this all carefully, interspersing life philosophy with repairs that need to be made to his motorcycle during a cross-country trip with his 10-year-old son and a hero/villain named Phaedrus. All the while, Pirsig is on a quest for one elusive element of life: quality.

Using his theme for my own brief article, I strip away discrete elements of quality from gifted child education. Student identification has to go—too messy and arbitrary. So does the need for training teachers how to work with gifted kids—hey, if they're smart kids, let them learn on their own, right?

Okay . . . you get the idea. The more we take away from a field that has unique elements to it—as gifted child education does—the more quality we erase. I contend here (and elsewhere) that that's exactly what Howard Gardner and his compatriots have done since they entered the gifted child education field. Now, using Gardner's logic, we can just say that everyone is intelligent in some way, which means no one is really any better off than anyone else. We're all the same, just with different gifts.

Horsefeathers!

Anyway, enjoy this little article, which actually drew quite a bit of positive attention from readers when it was first published.

When I first read it in the early 1970s, Robert Pirsig's *Zen and the Art of Motorcycle Maintenance* left an impact on the way I lived my life and analyzed my thoughts. Ostensibly about two very different subjects—motorcycles and meaning—it is really about the search for quality in one's everyday existence.

Nearly 25 years later, I still find comfort and wisdom within its pages.

Its main character is a college professor who finds himself teaching undergraduates in Bozeman, Montana. He has difficulty with students who question his grading practices because his main directive to attaining an A is to do work that contains quality, a term that cannot be defined, yet is discernible when one is presented with it. To prove the existence of this fuzzy trait, he reads two samples of student writing—one that is bland and typical, and another, filled with significance, meaning and . . . well . . . quality. Even his students detect the differences between the two papers, as 28 out of 30 students select one of the two essays as superior. Pirsig then goes further to prove his point, by removing quality from different aspects of life. First, he removes the fine arts:

> If you can't distinguish between good and bad in the arts, they disappear. There's no point in hanging a painting on the wall when the bare wall looks just as good . . . Poetry would disappear, since it seldom makes sense and has no practical value. And interestingly, comedy would vanish, too. No one would understand the jokes, since the difference between humor and no humor is pure Quality. (p. 193)

Taking a cue from Pirsig's logic, I thought it might be an interesting exercise to remove quality from various aspects of the field of gifted child education, to see what remains after these excisions. Let's begin:

The first aspect we could remove from gifted child education is the one that often gives us the most problems anyway: student identification. If we figure that all children are gifted in some way (the Howard Gardner approach), then there is no need to separate some by calling attention to their differences, for there would be no differences. "All children are smart," we tell ourselves. "They all have similar learning needs." So, farewell to those messy identification problems and our need to justify why some children are selected as gifted while others are not.

The second thing to go would probably be special training programs and college courses that teach people about the special needs of gifted individuals. General courses in child development would be sufficient for all, so why bother talking about children who do not fit the established norms? And courses in teaching strategies that are beneficial for gifted students, too, would be superfluous—since everyone can learn through memorization and rote, why bother talking about other time-consuming methods? And state and national conventions on educating gifted children? There would be no need for them, either, because how could you justify the expense of such specialized training opportunities for a group of children that no longer existed? Even *Gifted Child Today* would disappear, but it could keep its acronym of *GCT* by getting a new title: *Generic Child Today*.

The next obvious step is to eliminate gifted programs entirely. Since we've already determined that gifted children need the same things as everyone else and that everyone has a gift or talent at something, why bother with providing special provisions for a select few? We could easily maintain academic quality by focusing our efforts schoolwide (because everyone benefits from enrichment, don't they?), rather than providing those silly gifted programs, honors courses, Advanced Placement options, and so forth. Or, perhaps we could offer these provisions (to make our schools look like they promote quality), but just eliminate any criteria needed to gain access to them: All who apply get in, which brings us back to the first excision of student identification. A perfect circle of concordance; everyone wins when each is treated the same as the others.

How ironic to me that my first reading of Pirsig's book was just slightly in advance of my initial entrance into the field of gifted child education and that now, more than 20 years later, I see more clearly than ever how right he was about quality and how wrong we have been in gifted child education about letting that aspect of life and schooling—quality—almost disappear from our classrooms and our thinking. If I look for reasons behind this monumental shift in thoughts and practices in gifted child education—and I do—the reasons lie in three trends that have overtaken our field of study as quickly and efficiently as do locusts devour plants:

1. the field of gifted child education's shift in the 1970s from one that was enmeshed in the psychology of intelligence to one that is now entrenched in politics and schoolwide improvement;
2. the misinterpretation and misuse of the work of Howard Gardner on Multiple Intelligences and his selfish decision to fail to correct those who embraced his ideas as *the* way to serve gifted children; and
3. the recent proliferation of self-titled "talent developers," who are succeeding more than they have the right to do in convincing educators and legislators that *gifted* is a bad word and that, by focusing on visible talents alone, the needs of intellectually gifted children will be fully met.

If we are to return quality to the field of gifted child education, we need to reexamine the reason we exist at all as a field. This will require some deep thinking and some rigorous attention to detail. For example, we will have to admit that our efforts to embrace all children as gifted has done a disservice to highly able children who differ markedly in intellect and emotions from their agemates. Also, we will have to admit that our well-intentioned efforts—including many of my own—to reform schools by introducing gifted child education strategies for all students has watered down the offerings for many of our most gifted children. We will have to admit that by trying to improve services for all, we have lost sight of the fact that our field is dedicated to the few.

Pirsig ponders a thought:

Correct spelling, correct punctuation, correct grammar. Hundreds of itsy-bitsy rules for itsy-bitsy people. No one could remember all that stuff and concentrate on what he was trying to write about. It was all table manners, not derived from any sense of kindness or decency or humanity, but originally from an egotistic desire to look like gentlemen and ladies. (p. 162)

It may all be well and good that our field has focused for more than two decades on embracing giftedness as more of a universal trait than a distinctive one. But, even if we have gained adherents and increased our visibility, even if we have acted more like gentlemen and ladies by refusing to admit that some children are more gifted than others, we have done so at a high price: quality, the "betterness" that, though hard to define, definitely exists in the minds and hearts of children we once knew as gifted.

Gifted Child Today
November/December 1998

Striking Out

Suicide and the Gifted Adolescent

Introduction

erhaps it is a morbid fascination, but I have always been intrigued by people who would willingly take their own lives. Never having felt depressed or lonely enough to contemplate the act of suicide seriously, I have generally looked at the suicidal gesture from a professional, distant vantage.

Until recently.

In my former role as a counselor, I worked with families who had fears that suicide was considered a viable option by a gifted adolescent about whom they cared. The teen and I would talk, sometimes just once or twice, but often over a period of months. In the three years I did this work, I was unaware of any suicides that occurred with any young person I had counseled. An unblemished record of "saves."

Until recently.

I know what the research says—and does not say—about the confluence of giftedness and suicidal behaviors. The statistical evidence just doesn't bear out the popular belief that gifted kids, due to their heightened sensitivities, are more prone to suicide. I always pointed out this research to my audiences, letting them know that suicide is an issue impacting all adolescents, not especially rampant among the highly able. I said this, and I believed it.

Until recently.

This article points out both the prevalence of suicide and the unique combination of intellectual gifts and vulnerabilities that raise concerns in those who care about gifted adolescents in crisis. Although almost 20 years old, the same statistics and underlying reasons for suicidal gestures among able youth remain true today. Little has changed, at least not for the better.

Perhaps it is a moot point to argue the statistics of suicide, especially when you have a teenager at risk for such behavior sitting across from your desk or the kitchen table. Do what you can to listen—that helps so much—and ask if suicide is an option that he or she is considering. I have found that, almost always, the teenager will tell you the truth.

Until recently.

I love you, Matt.

The death of a child, above all else, prompts a stunned regard for our own mortality. We look around and are forced to see that life itself is transient. When that child's death is by suicide, our sorrow turns to shock, our pity to rage (Calhoun, Selby, & Faulstich, 1980); we recoil at the thought that someone so young could hurt so deeply.

And then we flip the page or switch the channel, for death—especially suicide—is not pretty to look at, and, besides, "It can't happen to me."

Statistics That Shock

But, it *can* happen, to ever-increasing numbers of bright adolescents. Yale University's School of Medicine estimated 8–12% of college students' deaths to be suicide (Parrish, 1957), a figure that it surely greater today (Garfinkel & Golombek, 1977). Over a five-year period, the University of Michigan cited an 85% increase in student suicides and attempts (Grollman, 1971). The "wrist-cutting syndrome" is most prevalent among females who, among other facts, are under 20 and have a higher-than-average IQ (Grueling & DeBlassie, 1980).

Led only be accidental death, suicide claims 5,000 young victims per year, a loss of 13 children per day (McKenry, Tishler, & Christman, 1980). But, suicide—like underachievement, success, or divorce—seldom occurs without prior notice. Instead, suicide manifests itself in cumulative clues that are, at times, obvious. However, as with Monday morning quarterbacks, hindsight often prevails.

Jean Casey: He was our oldest. . . . In hindsight, we see some things. . . . Then we thought, "This must be what adolescence is like." Unfortunately, with a gifted child, [as] either a teacher or a parent, you say, "Wow, they [sic] are gifted" . . .

and you don't realize that they intellectually may be very intelligent, but socially and emotionally they may be seven years old.
Bill Casey: Yeah, but emotionally, you know, . . . that aspect we didn't figure into it. He is [sic] a big smart kid. He's an adult. He wasn't. (Multimedia Program Productions, 1981, p. 4)

Precipitating factors of adolescent suicide differ from those of the suicidal adult as the child more often expresses *behaviorally* feelings of strife and personal dissatisfaction (Poznanski & Zrull, 1970). Internal difficulties with peer relations, imperfections, and social incompetence become manifest in boredom, a drop in school performance, and a push to be alone.

For the teacher and parent, an awareness of these and other factors may help in clarifying for the child the right to be imperfect. Yet, 13 times each day, this reconciliation fails; lives shatter like candyglass.

Living in a Social Vacuum

> How empty I feel, how empty. To be totally alone, with others but
> alone. But what is left except for that quiet desolation.
> —Diary entry, 17-year-old girl (Morgan, 1981)

The emotional and social developments of gifted teens often lag behind their academic aptitudes. Thus, the child who is intellectually capable of high performance in school subjects may be immature by comparison when dealing with social interactions. And, although this lag between emotional and intellectual development is recognized, it is often ignored. As teachers and parents, we assume that the intelligent boy or girl learns the unwritten rules of life and love as rapidly (and independently) as he or she masters chemical equations. But, such assumptions confine the gifted child to an emotional limbo where "acting your age" is childish, yet "behaving as an adult" is preempted by imposed bedtimes. More than just growing pains, the hurt and isolation caused by this intellectual-emotional rift cause the child to believe he or she is a "minority of one" (Torrance, 1961), a distinct unit with no true peers, an expendable child in the family complex. For the gifted child with social problems, everyone is an outsider.

Several authors point to this lack of true peer identification as a precipitating factor in adolescent suicide (Grueling & DeBlassie, 1980; Peck, 1968). Goertzel and Goertzel (1962) examined Salvador Dali and others whose childhood suicide attempts seemed prompted by a lack of friendships. John Gowan (1972), though, put it more bluntly: "If you're one kid in a hundred, you have to find one hundred other kids to find one like yourself—and half the time she's a girl, and you're sunk" (p. 6).

But, as stated, signals do flare up to warn of impending extremes. Through study of case histories and suicide notes, some common characteristics emerge:

1. self-deprecation ("I'm the bad one," "I'm doomed to fail," "I'm better off dead"; Finch & Poznanski, 1971);
2. a sudden shift—upward or downward—in school performance (Morgan, 1981), coupled with
3. increased study and almost total absorption in schoolwork (Grollman, 1971); and
4. frequent mood shifts, manifested more in anger than in depression.

All are signs of a progressive failure to adapt to social expectations; all are based on the teen's impression that life's good times are not good enough. Hope expires, and death becomes a viable alternative.

The Fear of Being Human

> Too early in life, I felt that I didn't want to be human anymore. I didn't want to die, yet continuing on in the state I was in wasn't hit-tin' on nothin'. The hard core fact that life has limitations hit me like a baseball in the eye, and I cried. (American Association for Gifted Children, 1978, p. 18)

Coupled with emotional isolation is the gifted teen's fear of intellectual ineffi-ciency—the fear of being imperfect. As Grollman (1971) stated: "A terrifying concern of the student is his inability to compete successfully in school. Failure brings not only disappointment and disapproval from parents, but also a shattering of personal confi-dence" (p. 46). What is *not* done naturally outweighs what *is* accomplished; what is *desired* ends in unmet expectations.

The internal pressure toward perfection is the most influential, yet overlooked, aspect of being gifted (Whitmore, 1980). The striving to succeed becomes the struggle to continue as the challenge of untried options decays into unattainable possibilities.

This fear of failure is active in both high school- and college-age students (Jacobs, 1971; Seiden, 1966; Teicher & Jacobs, 1966), but, ironically, contrasts vividly with the excellent academic achievements of suicidal students. Peck (1968) contended that the real pressure to succeed comes from the student's attempt to attain parental—*not* inter-nal—standards of perfection. Again, from the parents of a "successful" suicide:

> Jean Casey: We were trying to raise him as we had been raised, to be the perfect, perfect student. . . . We said, "If you want to be in medical school, you have to earn A's."
> Bill Casey: We leaned on him too much. We expected too much of him. If I had it to do over again . . . I would spend more time hugging him than nagging him about his grades or whatever. (Multimedia Program Productions, 1981, p. 7)

The prevention, in this case, is the same as the cure: a genuine awareness of the gifted teen as being composed of more than intellect; an examination into *whose* goals the child is trying to reach; a willingness to speak of one's own imperfections and personal foibles; an atmosphere that allows—indeed, encourages—mistakes, followed by an honest discussion of both the hurt and growth that accompany them. The reconciliation between being bright and flawed must be addressed as the serious issue it surely is.

Developmental Immaturities: Going to Extremes

> The crescent moon was fading into a cloudless dawn sky when [they] drove into an abandoned graveyard. . . . Before walking away from their car [the boys] had torn a scrap from a paper bag and written notes. They asked for forgiveness for what they were about to do.
> State police have called the deaths a murder-suicide by two willing teenagers. (Robinson & Samek, 1981, p. C-1)

Children develop in a sequence of spurts—voices and bodies mature along established paths; logical and ethical reasoning proceeds as if on a preplanned itinerary. Yet, when gaps exist in the maturation of both mind and body, the adolescent is the first to notice. At a stage of intellectual development that *should* allow for individual differences, the bright teen often accepts these personal nuances for everyone by him- or herself. Having fewer inner strengths and internal solutions for confronting these imperfections (Anthony, 1970), the gifted youth may turn to extremes: drugs, dropping out of school, the abandonment of family and peer camaraderie, suicide.

The marked rise in adolescent suicide at 14 years coincides with a major developmental stage. The onset of the teen years brings a shift of both responsibility and influence from parents to peers. Concomitantly, anxiety, too, increases as the bright adolescent fails to reconcile which behaviors are acceptable for his or her present and past spheres of influence. Resultant behaviors and attitudes are frequently interpreted as rebellion against anything constructive—teens are often blamed for overreacting. In fact, it is *normal* for early adolescents to experience feelings and reactions to events much more intensely than adults (Blos, 1962), and denial of these increased emotions surely leads to yet more inner strife and confusion.

For example, a junior high student whose grades of A's have slipped to B's is faulted for lack of effort by teachers and chided for "knowing it all" by peers. The student then retaliates against parents by insisting that they "quit pushing" while protecting peer credibility by explaining good performance as "luck" or "careful cheating." The dilemma then becomes internal, as the youth knows he or she is being honest to no one. As explained by one student:

> Though I realized learning was a thrill, I suppressed the yearning or transformed it, in some cases even degraded it in order to be accepted by peers. Consequently, frivolities won over. (American Association for Gifted Children, 1978, p. 15)

The developmental immaturities of *all* teens seem insurmountable and unending and, for each child who fails (e.g., the suicide, the dropout), millions succeed. Statistically, the loss seems insignificant. In real terms—for the teen, the family, the society—the cost is dear.

Conclusion: The Obvious Solution

> Just as there are those who at the least indisposition develop a fever, so do those whom we call suicides, and who are always very emotional and sensitive, develop at the least shock the notion of suicide. Had we a science with the courage and authority to concern itself with mankind . . . these matters of fact would be familiar to everyone. (Hesse, 1974, p. 55)

The Beatles and Madison Avenue would have us believe that all you need is love and Band-Aids to mend life's bruises. But, as sure as a small scrape, untreated, invites infection, so does the neglect of emotional hurt cause grief to fester. The wound felt by the fear of being alone and imperfect is tender and deep for the bright teen; the saddened or angry adolescent feels powerless in a world where even self-worth is out of reach. Suicide, then, is elevated to a "step in the right direction."

There are preventive steps, camouflaged by their simplicity, yet potent when applied:

1. *Respect* for the child and his or her hurts; for the self-doubts that accompany growing up; for the imperfections in thoughts and actions. The respect from us, as parents or teachers, to involve our children in our own defeats; to acknowledge that tears are okay and that more will inevitably follow.
2. *Awareness* that, indeed, bright children *are* different; that conformity for the sake of companionship does not necessarily imply a lowering of personal ethics; that isolation from peers is, too, acceptable. The awareness that being gifted is easier at some times than at others.
3. *Tolerance* of mood shifts and the desire to experiment with sexual and societal taboos; of academic ups and downs caused by in-school boredom or the need to be a "regular kid." A tolerance for the idealism of adolescence and the subsequent depression caused by recurring reality.
4. *Participation* as both spectator and coach, referee and guide. As a parent or teacher, to participate in the events that are benchmarks to our child's future. The ability to ignore actively or overlook; and the concomitant perceptiveness to intervene when needed.

It all sounds so sketchy and "sugary," as if the answer is to be found in everyday occurrences of simple affection. But, affection works subtle miracles. A pat on the back implies approval; a laugh in the right direction says that life is fraught with potential good times. Even cursing, if it counts and you mean it, reveals an honesty and openness that should be shared between adults and their children.

The potential suicide is a child already troubled with an overabundance of self-made and external fears. The intensity of these problems is universally underestimated by parents and professional educators (Teicher, cited in Schoolar, 1973), and suicide—or its attempt—shocks all who hear of its occurrence. But, the clues are there—always—if the time is taken to notice them and the courage garnered to address them face-front. As parents and teachers, we must acknowledge *our* parts in the onset of teenage suicide. To defer to professional outsiders for expert guidance ("Band-Aids") is a misplaced effort without also interrupting our own lives enough to care ("love").

As a start, that *is* all you need.

1988 Update

Since 1982, when "Striking Out: Suicide and the Gifted Adolescent" appeared in *Gifted Child Today*, approximately 35,000 teens and young adults have killed themselves. Collectively, this figure equals the population in such cities as Ithaca, New York, or Beverly Hills; individually, our world is now less a place than it might have been had each of these young people chosen to live.

How many among these 35,000 adolescents were intellectually gifted or creatively talented? How many of the additional 250,000 "unsuccessful" adolescent suicide attempts during this same period were young persons whose scholastic achievements or original accomplishments surpassed the expectations we generally hold for high-school-age students? The answers, now as then, are still elusive. For despite some recent research showing a positive correlation between high intellect and severity of suicide attempt (Sargent, 1984) and a summary of research by Husain and Vandiver (1984) showing that "children who attempt suicide are usually bright—average or above average intelligence with several of superior intelligence" (p. 215), there are still little data amassed concerning the specific frequency of suicide among gifted adolescents. Still, the reality of suicide exists for some talented youth, including Ted, a gifted high school student who, shortly before his suicide, had received a presidential nomination to West Point:

My IQ is 142
My mind is diseased
   That I know
I am going to kill myself
What a relief it was
I am so much better now
You cannot do wrong when you are dead
Time is infinite
   You are at the beginning (Leder, 1987)

The frequency of suicidal gestures among gifted adolescents remains an unanswered question. And, due to both the difficulty in data-gathering procedures and our naïve cultural attitude that any discussion of suicide is going to prompt its occurrence

(Laufer & Laufer, 1984), it seems unlikely that accurate statistics will be forthcoming. However, to be concerned more about the specific number of suicidal acts by gifted teens than about preventive strategies to discourage such attempts is to lose sight of the primary issue: Death by suicide results in a tragic loss, whether the victim is gifted or not.

However, as cited in "Striking Out," we are aware of particular personality and attitudinal characteristics that may be debilitating for the most emotionally vulnerable of our gifted youth. Perfectionism; significant discrepancies between intellectual acuity and social, emotional, and physical developments; and an attitude of hopelessness regarding future events (whether personal or global affairs) appear to contribute negatively to the fruition of talents among our most able youth. In extreme (but by no means rare) cases, suicide becomes an acceptable route; the gifted adolescent chooses life-threatening actions, a permanent solution to what is usually a temporary problem.

Issues of mental health are never easy to discuss between adults and adolescents. However, before we can expect a decline in suicide occurrences among our young people, we must accept the sad reality that some of our most able youth, despite their heightened abilities to analyze hypothetical situations using creative problem solving, still suffer from "tunnel vision" in terms of alternatives to personal emotional trauma.

Further, we must educate our emotionally healthy teens on the typical warning signs they might receive from a friend in need of immediate care. More than three-fourths of all suicidal teens express their unhappiness verbally (e.g., "If I died, I bet nobody'd notice" or "If I killed myself, that'd solve all my problems at once"), and the majority of these comments are directed to peers, not adults. Thus, it is imperative that adolescents understand that, in the case of a potential suicide, it is okay to "overreact" by seeking guidance from an adult who will listen. *No* threat to human life should be taken lightly; persons who claim they are going to kill themselves often do. Adults and students need to understand and accept this grim reality.

A New Beginning

Some claim that suicide is a cowardly act, a vain attempt to gain attention from a world growing increasingly blasé toward death, destruction, and the importance of human individuality. Others see adolescent suicide as "someone else's problem," a situation that surely affects everyone's kid but their own, everyone's student except those they teach.

If you have read this far into this article, you probably see the importance of, and need for, attending to the problem of adolescent suicide among *all* youth, including those who are gifted and talented. Now, I ask that you go one step further. Find out what your school and your community provide for preventing this problem and discover, too, what resources exist—hotlines, support groups, and so forth—for children, teens, and families in crisis. Then, share this information with people who need to know it.

It is rare that I get the privilege, in print, to editorialize on a "cause" as vital as this one, and I thank the editors of *Gifted Child Today* for providing this forum to me. Yet, my words will be purposeless if all they do is "leave an impression." Instead, my goal—my hope—is that follow-up will occur and that, due to *your own* involvement in bringing attention to this issue, at least one talented young life will be saved in your community.

Gifted Child Today
January/February 1988
(originally published September/October 1982)

Psyched Out

Searching for the Soul of Gifted Child Education

Boy, did I get in trouble when *this* article appeared in print!

It was my last year sitting on the Board of Directors of the National Association for Gifted Children (NAGC). I'd been a board member for three terms—nine years—and decided not to run again, based partly on what happened at the meeting that was the genesis of this article.

As usual, our 20+ board members were arguing some small point regarding the upcoming publication of some board-sanctioned position statements. It seemed the media often called the NAGC office looking for our association's written statement on ability grouping, acceleration, cooperative learning, or some other general issue involving gifted kids. It seems there was no statement on the emotional issues involved with growing up gifted and what we, as an association, suggested that educators do to address these issues.

That's when a discussion began that can only be described as surreal. Here we were, a board of recognized leaders in the field of gifted child education, and we were arguing whether there was evidence to state that the gifted actually *had* any unique emotional issues in their lives.

I thought: "Has no one read Terman? Hollingworth? Roeper? Has no one here taught gifted kids or been the parent of one?" The longer the discussion continued, the more perturbed, and then disgusted, I became.

That next month, fortunately or otherwise, I had an article due to the editor of *Gifted Child Today*. What follows is the article that came out.

I got letters and phone calls (thank goodness, this was before the existence of e-mail in my office!) from NAGC mucky-mucks chiding me for publicly embarrassing the board. Mind you, no one denied that the discussion took place; the objection was to my airing the discussion, and my thoughts about it, in a public forum.

As true today as when this article was written, the heart and soul of gifted child education has been removed from discussions of what to do to help gifted kids emotionally. Oughtn't we to know better by now?

At our most recent meeting of the National Association for Gifted Children's Board of Directors, several of us got into an extended discussion of "best practices" that are used with able learners. When the issue of affective concerns arose, some board members questioned whether there really were any social and emotional needs that were unique to gifted children. They wanted to see research—hard data—that proved the existence of such issues.

I sat there, puzzled, and wondered if the question, perhaps, could have been raised in jest. It was not. Later, upon reflection, I came to realize a sad truth: The field of gifted child education (GCE) has become so enmeshed in curricula, instruction, and educational reform that it has lost its soul.

The GCE field was founded by psychologists, individuals like Lewis Terman, Leta Hollingworth, and George and Annemarie Roeper, who came to support special provisions for gifted learners precisely because the emotional make-up of these children differed markedly from that of their agemates. Without proper attention to their "emotional education" (Hollingworth's term), gifted children would only progress so far. The mind, as keen as its insights might be, needed to have the company of the heart in order for it to be put to its fullest use.

So, how did we get to the point where even some of our field's leaders (if, indeed, that is what the NAGC Board of Directors represents) question the validity of unique emotional needs of gifted students? The culprit, I believe, is in our own search for professional respect among fellow educators. Always on the fringe, rather than in the mainstream of education, GCE experts have sought ways to bridge their goals with that of general education. In the 1970s, we seemed to find that niche, as we proposed an array of curricular models and instructional practices that served us very well: Creative Problem Solving, radical acceleration, the Enrichment Triad, and Odyssey of the Mind were all conceived with gifted children in mind. The trouble is, in our quest for academic recognition from our colleagues, we neglected the very essence of our field: psychology.

The 1990s have fared no better, I'm afraid. Although we can take a degree of deserved pride in knowing that many of our instructional strategies and concepts are now embraced as an important aspect of overall educational reform, we are still off-course when it comes to recognizing the social and emotional needs of gifted children. Indeed, some "experts" have even "progressed" to the point of substituting the term "gifted child" for "a child with gifted behaviors"! In just two generations, the monumental work of Terman and Hollingworth has regressed to the point where the gifted *child* is no longer a part of our philosophical equation! Behaviors matter—nothing more, nothing less.

How sad for us all, but especially for kids like Matthew, who, at 10 years of age, attempted suicide because "everyone told him his ideas were weird and his questions stupid." Or Vamir, whose parents decided to teach him at home because he complained that educators "don't respect a kid who may know more than they do about some things." Or Toya, whose overexcitable personality caused her to be seen as a behavior problem by the very teachers who say they're not quite sure how to challenge her.

Perhaps each of these children could use some curricular modification, yet academics are not the main reason for their school problems. Instead, it is a lack of respect for, and understanding of, the ways they differ psychologically from others their age. In loosening our grip on this, the very foundation of the field of GCE, we have lost countless children to the mediocre middle.

A relatively new "buzz term" for GCE is that our field is experiencing "a quiet crisis," a subterranean attempt by advocates of inclusion, middle school reform, and cooperative learning to eviscerate our field as we know it. To me, focusing on this "quiet crisis" is a shortsighted and self-serving attempt to resurrect a field that was caught off-guard when reformers embraced GCE curricular strategies as good for all students. Instead, my concern goes deeper and, rather than a quiet crisis, it is a "whimpering plea": Please, let us return to the very reason our field came to exist in the first place—the *psychology* of gifted children, which addresses social and emotional issues of giftedness that have, for too long, taken a backseat to academic concerns.

The bridge between education and psychology of gifted children may not yet be burned, but it is definitely charred. Reconstruction must begin immediately to prevent any further damage to our field and the children it serves.

Gifted Child Today
July/August 1995

Portrait of a Nonartist

Introduction

This short article focuses on an area of education I have written about very seldom—probably because I don't feel I am good at the subject: the arts. It begins with an admission that my Catholic school education caused me to believe that a good artist was one who could copy pictures that looked like the ones in our books and the only good singer was one with perfect pitch. Since I had neither the hand for drawing nor the voice for crooning, I became a practicing nonartist.

In reflecting on this sad situation from my childhood, I recognize now that art and music teachers today seem much more sensitive toward students like the one I used to be. They make accommodations, partner us up with someone whose work is *not* embarrassing to display, and tell us to sing a little softer in the chorus. I thank them, in absentia, for their tolerance.

More than anything, I want my own son and my own students to see themselves as authentic *consumers* of art, if they feel they cannot be successful *producers* of it. This is something I never learned was okay.

The world needs both those who create great art and those who appreciate its beauty, don't you think?

Beginning in first grade, my weekly art lesson went something like this: Nancy, our school's most talented artist, was given a picture by the teacher. Nancy drew as close a reproduction as possible on the blackboard, using the colored chalk taken out expressly for this special occasion. We, in turn, were to use our crayons and reproduce *her* reproduction as best we could. Grades were given on how accurate our artistic portrayal matched that of Nancy's.

I hated art class.

In music, Marcia played the piano (very well, I might add) while John's angelic voice led us in a chorus of whatever song for which the teacher had sheet music and available lyrics. This continued until eighth grade, when John's voice deepened and we sang along, instead, to records. I don't recall how we got graded.

I hated music class.

Today, when I walk into a museum, I still have trouble detecting a Monet from a Renoir; at a symphony, I can't tell a fugue from a movement (isn't one part of the other?) without consulting my concert program.

Now, I love art and music, but, like a child who enjoys magic while having no knowledge of legerdemain, I listen or look in ignorance. I know what I like, but I have no knowledge to compare it against that which I don't.

Elliott Eisner, one our world's most poetic writers, artists, and educators, is concerned that our nation prizes SAT scores above aesthetic awareness, and Lorin Hollander, a pianist who played Carnegie Hall before his 10th birthday, bemoans the fact that every society but our own has made it a priority to teach children about cultures—their own and those in past centuries—as a way to introduce young people to the connections we all share.

To me, functional illiteracy means more than being unable to read; it means, too, that some of us (myself included) are incapable of appreciating the true beauty of sculpture, classical music, or ballet because early on we learned that what Nancy did was "art," and what I did was "not art." Marcia could play the piano and John could sing, but I could do neither. As a child, I hated "the arts," and, as most of us will, I distanced myself from those activities that caused me to look silly or unaccomplished. I ridiculed boys like John by calling them "sissies," and I rolled my eyes at Nancy, thinking "teacher's pet, teacher's pet" every time she picked up a log of chalk.

My background in the arts, my illiteracy, is shared by too many of my generation. Collectively, we learned long ago to avoid that which we did not understand or appreciate. Now, as adults, we have learned compensatory strategies: We hold our applause at concerts until we hear others clap, lest we appear uncultured by acknowledging excellence at the wrong time; we roll our eyes at the "guys in tights," knowing secretly that a ballet dancer's athletic skills and strength far surpass our own.

I recall vividly art class in second grade, despite years of telling myself that the teacher was naïve and her lessons contrived. How I wish, though, that my memories of art class were fond ones, instead of recollections grounded in fear and shame.

Elliott Eisner is right, and so is Lorin Hollander. We must convince our nation, our children, and ourselves that "the basics" in life go far beyond basal texts and ditto sheets. For once those reading and writing skills are mastered, we need something onto which they can be attached, like a musical score, a lyric poem, or a painting by Monet (or is Renoir?).

Understanding Our Gifted
May 1991

Part Ten

Just Trying to Get Your Attention: Continuing Controversies in Gifted Child Education

If you can't upset somebody,
what's the point in writing?
—Mark Twain

When I first began writing articles and books about gifted kids and their lives, I never presumed to take on the role of vocal critic. I wanted my words to inform, not inflame. Still, when I read over the pieces I have written over the years, there is an element of suspicion of the status quo that is present in many of my articles.

Sometimes, I question what is going on (or not going on) on behalf of gifted children. Other times, I write to dismantle a politically correct opinion that giftedness is nothing to worry about or to act upon—you know, the ol' "these smart kids will make it on their own" kind of attitude. And, most recently, I've railed against the dilution of our field by self-titled "talent developers" and advocates of Multiple Intelligences.

Do I take on these roles out of retribution or petite jealousies? I certainly hope not. Instead, I would like to think that what I write is based upon my belief that gifted children deserve more than our society and our schools are giving them. No one's abilities or needs deserve to be ignored, but that is exactly what I see happening to gifted children *more than any other population of special needs children.* Hence, my chagrin and my criticism of what often gets labeled as "gifted education."

I know I can write a good sentence, and I realize, too, that a well-chosen verb can state better what a string of lithe adjectives can only hope to accomplish. So, my writing is direct. Also, during my career I have chosen not to conduct the type of research that results in extended articles in *Gifted Child Quarterly.* Many of my colleagues do this much better than I, so I applaud their efforts. Instead, I prefer to err on the side of practicality, which is probably why many of my writing ideas germinate in the public school classrooms I teach in weekly.

So, that's the story behind the stories. I believe I am still too young to be considered a curmudgeon, but if that's the label I need to wear to get gifted kids the attention and programs they deserve, fine by me.

The Top 10 Statements That Should Never Again Be Made by Advocates of Gifted Children

Introduction

Sometimes, we can be so dumb. As bright as we are intellectually, as a collective, many folks in gifted child education say some things that just don't make much sense. They utter these statements passionately, with all the conviction of a zealot, and they sound silly when asked to back up what they just said.

Here's an example: An experienced G/T teacher had been hired to take over a waning gifted program in a wealthy school district. On the first day of school, as she was being introduced to already-suspicious teachers, she said this: "Hello, my name is Kate, and I just have one thing to say: I'm here to make you look good."

This assumes, of course, that every one of the teachers in that room needed Kate's remediation. To this day, that G/T program is floundering.

On a grander scale, I have heard a very popular gifted child education consultant ask her audiences of classroom teachers, "Guess who is going to learn the least amount in your room this year? Answer: your gifted students." It is incredulous that someone would have the *gall* to presume this is the case for every teacher at a workshop session. Smart woman, dumb statement.

The following article reviews 10 more *faux pas* made by so-called experts in this field: ourselves. If you find yourself guilty of saying any of these . . . join the club.

But, now is the time to reform!

A memo crossed my desk last month. It contained the minutes of a meeting held by a group of regional coordinators of gifted and talented programs. Among the dozen agenda items highlighted in these meeting minutes was a section titled "In-Service." The only sentence under this category was one that read: "Good way to introduce topic: Ask teachers, 'Who do you think will learn the least in your classroom this year?'" No answer was given to this query, but I suspect the "correct" answer was supposed to be "your gifted and talented students."

A month before receiving this memo, I was attending a meeting of teachers, parents, coordinators, and university personnel whose main professional interests are in educating gifted and talented students. Our combined mission was to determine some guidelines for distributing $600,000 to school districts for the purpose of enhancing understanding about the special needs of able learners. When a suggestion was made that gifted specialists work with classroom teachers by demonstrating some techniques of incorporating higher level thinking into their lessons, the following comment was made by a coordinator: "I don't know about anyone else, but when I am asked to help classroom teachers improve their teaching skills, I feel a lot like the gifted student who is asked to help a less-able classmate. It's not my job to be their tutor!"

I sat silently, awaiting a disavowal from one of my colleagues about this misplaced analogy. It did not come. Instead, I hard a chorus of agreement from at least a half-dozen others who saw such in-classroom services as a "watering down" of the role of the gifted specialist. Finally, unable to be silent any longer, I spoke out with my belief that to sidestep this collaborative role is to deny today's reality of inclusionary practices. The few who responded positively to my comment shared with me the minority view.

I've been around gifted education long enough to recall when "pull-out programs" were considered innovative and giftedness was determined by little more than a high IQ. Also, I've been in contact with thousands of individuals in gifted education—in person or through print—and I realize that not all people feel as do those whose examples begin this article.

Still, I believe that there are enough gifted education specialists who desire a return to the "good ol' days" (when "gifted stuff" took place in an isolated classroom of high achievers) that it would be helpful to have some guidelines for fulfilling our mission within the context of educational reforms.

Therefore, in an effort to provide some guidelines toward our future direction and growth, I offer (in late-night television fashion) the Top 10 Statements That Should Never Again Be Made by Advocates of Gifted Children.

#10—Only gifted students can really do in-depth, independent projects.

I've known identified gifted students who couldn't care less about long-term investigations of "real problems" and nonidentified students who shine when given the chance to explore an interest in depth. Let's stop kidding ourselves that only identified gifted students have the wherewithal to complete complex assignments and instead realize the obvious: Doing well depends as much on attitude as it does on aptitude.

#9—Twenty percent of all high school dropouts are gifted.

This myth has been perpetuated for years and, for the life of me, I can't determine where this figure comes from. The only rational voice on this issue was presented by David Irvine in an *Educational Leadership* article, "What Research Doesn't Show About Gifted Dropouts" (1987). He determined numerically that, if this 20% figure were accurate, it would mean that every gifted student in our nation drops out of high school. I'm all for getting people to support gifted education, but citing false data is something I cannot support.

#8—Gifted students are more prone to depression and suicide than nongifted students.

Related to the myth about dropouts, this "scare tactic" has been cited for years even though there is no research evidence to back it up. Having studied both of these issues extensively, I can assert unequivocally that, although suicide and depression among gifted students are serious concerns, their prevalence is no more frequent than it is for nongifted adolescents. If we are to advocate for mental health education for teenagers and children, let's do so for all children.

#7—Today's gifted students are tomorrow's leaders who will solve the world's problems.

I'm not sure who should be most irate about this assertion—the gifted students who seem obligated to save their world or the "nongifted" students who apparently are bystanders to global change. Either way, the statement is both unfair and unfounded. We can no more predict that today's gifted children will remedy their world as we can assert that today's politicians and "change agents" were all involved in gifted programs when they were youngsters. When will we realize that history and social improvement are not as predictable as we sometimes make them out to be?

#6—Cooperative learning should not be used with gifted students—they're just made into "little teachers."

I will be the first to admit that many practices that occur under the guise of "cooperative learning" are detrimental to gifted students. However, the idea of cooperative learning, in which students work as teams to draw out each others' academic strengths and interests, should not be considered bad. In fact, when done well and appropriately, I can think of no better way than cooperative learning to integrate gifted education principles into the repertoire of skills useful for classroom teachers. Don't fault a good concept because it is being implemented poorly. Instead, change the method of operation so that it becomes advantageous for all its participants.

#5—Underachievement happens because children aren't challenged in school.

Granted, there is some connection between academic rigor and one's desire to achieve at a high level. Still, the topic of underachievement is so complex and it involves so much more than purely academic conditions (e.g., self-concept, family relations, school climate) that to blame underachievement on a lack of intellectual rigor is to oversimplify a very complex problem. Children who underachieve in school must be looked at individually, not as a conglomerate, intact group if positive changes are to occur in their lives.

#4—We need to identify children who are truly gifted.

First of all, "truly" or otherwise, many gifted children identify themselves through their behaviors, vocabularies, emotions, or actions. To state that we seek to identify only "truly" gifted children implies that somewhere out there exists a cluster of capable children who can be found as long as we use the right tests or performance scales. I prefer a simpler mode: Let's look at what children need in school and other places and give them the opportunities they need to enhance their individual talents. Then, identifying giftedness becomes less of an issue while providing appropriate services becomes paramount in importance.

#3—Classroom teachers cannot possibly meet the needs of gifted children in a regular classroom.

When this falsehood is stated, the speaker usually exhibits an aura of compassion: "Oh, pity the poor classroom teacher. He or she has *so* many children, *so* many requirements, *so* little time." Well, sorry. Rather than take away one of the few remnants of respect that classroom teachers still hold—that is, that they know how to plan instruction based on the needs of students—I'd rather assume they are trying the best they know how and that it is my role, as a gifted education specialist, to help them become even better than they already are.

#2—Gifted students are bored in regular classrooms.

Boring is one of those buzzwords that sends teachers into spasms. How often a child has told me that he or she was bored in school, and how often I followed this assertion with a classroom observation in which said "bored" student was smiling and participating to the max. Before we ascribe as strong an adjective as *boring* to a teacher or classroom, let us first determine what this amorphous word really means.

#1—Without a gifted program, this student will never reach full potential.

First of all, who among us has reached his or her "full potential"? And, if you have, how do you know that you did? *Potential* is perhaps the most misused word in our gifted lexicon, as it implies that someone other than ourselves know the limits of what we can accomplish. To add an even bigger measure of insult to this assertion, we sometimes state that the only way to reach one's potential is to be in a gifted program. Forget parents and excellent classroom teachers and personal aspirations—it's the gifted program that makes us reach for the stars. Sorry . . . that's probably not entirely true.

So, there you have it: A listing of 10 sentences and sentiments that should be stricken from our collective vocabulary. With what does this leave us? Perhaps nothing more than this reality: Gifted children cannot and should not be pigeonholed due to their talents or the school programs in which they are placed. Only when we begin to work together as teams—kids, parents, gifted education specialists, and classroom teachers—will we realize that our bottom-line goal is the same: We all want the best for the child in question. So, forget the platitudes about boredom and dropouts and potential. If such talk hasn't gotten us anywhere so far, it's unlikely it will move forward now.

Gifted Child Today
March/April 1994

The Gifted, You Know

The "G" Word . . . Sssh!

Every time I have read either of these Dr. Seuss-like poems to an audience, I get loud applause and more than an occasional tear. Here's how one of the poems, "The Gifted, You Know," came about.

I was speaking at the convention of the National Middle School Association in Denver. After a rather long day of trying to defend how gifted child education *can* mesh with the then-hot "middle school movement," I sat down in my hotel room with a glass of wine (okay . . . two glasses) and just started writing. I wanted to compose something snappy, something that advocates of gifted children could grab onto as their own and read at time-strapped school board meetings. "The Gifted, You Know" emerged after only two hours.

All the elements of a good Dr. Seuss poem are there: the rhyming cadence, the attempts at humor, the final poignancy of a message well-stated. It is about as jargon-free as one can get and still make a statement. But, even if someone is unfamiliar with Gardner and his work (there must be one or two educators who have been huddled under a rock for a couple of decades!), the main point is driven home: Gifted kids exist, even in an era of Multiple Intelligences drivel.

"The 'G' Word. . . Sssh!" is not quite as overarching, focusing more on our field's reluctance to use the term *gifted* anymore. I mean, really: Schools now have

216

"talent development" programs or "enrichment clusters." Gifted has become, again, that bad, bad word that sounds so elitist. You know what? Get used to it! It's a term that has withstood more than a century of use, and it deserves to keep its place in the lexicon of both educators and every citizen.

The Gifted, You Know

hat's wrong with enrichment for all?" you might ask.
"Young minds are astir, committed to task.
It's all well and good, and our schools have a mission
That every child's gifted—that's part of their vision.
Computers are buzzing, minds are awhirl

Proclaiming all kids, every boy and each girl
Are learning the things they will need to succeed.
What's wrong with enrichment for all, I do plead?"

I sit and I think and I think as I sit
Why this fitness for all is a really poor fit.
For our children in schools who used to be gifted
Now sit untouched, 'cause the focus has shifted
To schoolwide enrichment and plans that equate
One's mind to a project on which one can rate
A child's depth of knowledge from zero to eight.

Eight! That magic number that changes quite often
When Gardner and friends begin their a coughin'
up a new intelligence for this talent or that,
"Naturalistic!" "Spatial!" with the drop of a hat,
A new way to be smart, a new way to be lifted
Into this land of enchantment we used to call "gifted."
But no more, not now, never again, for you see
With these new kinds of smarts, "you ain't better
    than me"
(Or, should I say, "aren't," and should I say "I"—
My linguistic panache has just gone bye-bye.)

When everyone's smart, per Gardner's rules
Something big needs to happen in everyone's schools.
Talents need to develop, products emerge

So we can all handle the on-coming surge
Of projects and puppets and plays and productions
And other concoctions and various functions
That prove gifts are present in everyone's mind.
Just one thing's the matter, does anyone find . . .

That the gifted are missing from this rosy picture?
The gifted, you know, the kids whose main fixture
Is a presence of mind that's more complex than most.
It's not that they're show-offs; they don't mean to
    boast
But their minds race ahead while others just coast.
The gifted, you know, those kids whose emotions
Are more up-and-down wavy than the world's greatest
    oceans.

The gifted, you know, those kids with a passion
To question and probe in their deep need to fashion
A world in their minds and a world in their hearts
That doesn't distinguish itself into parts
Like "artsy" or "mathy" or "wordy" or any
Of those multiple intellects that can't hold a penny
To an overall sense that few are like you,
Alone in your feelings, alone in your view
Of a world built for many tho' you're one of the few.

I'm afraid for the gifted, the ones we once knew
As vibrant a bunch as this Earth ever grew.
They've gone underground, to escape
    from the masses
Who think that all students belong in
    all classes
Be you smarty-smart Suzy or not-so-apt
    Sammy,
Our gifted, in schools, are receiving a
    whammy
From those who have come to the foregone conclusion
That all can get served by this beast
    called "inclusion,"
or "enrichment for all" or "multiple
    talents,"
Whatever you call it, we've now lost
    our balance,
For when all are as many, and all are as one

The kids who lose out on all of the fun
Are the kids on the edges, the ones on
    the side
The gifted who ask, "When's the end of
    this ride?"

"What's wrong with enrichment for
    all?" you declare.
Ask a gifted child somewhere; the answer lies there.

Gifted Child Today
July/August 1999

The "G" Word . . . Sssh!

It used to be, when folks were bold
And words weren't minced, and truth was told,
That people spoke a common tongue
When talking of their able young.
They used a term we all once heard,
Simply put, the big "g" word.

But now . . . shhh! . . . you can't say "gifted,"
For if you do, you will have drifted
To a place of ill repute
Where malcontented folks refute
There's such a thing as a higher state
Of mind, of heart, of depth or rate
Of thinking, feeling, knowing, being,
Sensing, asking, crying, seeing.
These "g" word critics have lost their balance.
They think that "gifted" equates with "talents."
And, thus, have come to the errant view
That the "g" word (shhh!) is just taboo.

Away! Away! They say to gifts
Thinking this denial lifts
All children to a common place
Where people do not have to face
The truth, that some have deeper thoughts

Than others, not by plans or plots,
But just by being born and trained
To use their wits and thus have gained
A higher ground of greater knowing,
A deeper depth, a profound showing
Of empathy, knowledge, wisdom, wit
That "g" word (shhh!), it still doth fit
These children, who've become a part
Of a world that's known right from the start
That some are gifted, in both mind and heart.

Sadly, though, too few take heed,
They spout "All children can succeed!"
". . . Yes, that is true!" in haste I add
But when did it become so bad
To use the "g" word to define
Those able few whose intact minds
Race forward, faster, ever strong,
'Tis not a question of right or wrong,
Or better than, or me 'gainst you.
"But I know that the gifted, too,
Have special needs" we must now say
For if we don't, they'll go away
To a place where "gifted" equates with "bad."
It's way too wrong, and downright sad.
For when all are treated just the same
In this "multiple talents" or "inclusion" game
Then no one need be tagged or labeled,
That "g" word (shhh!), it can be tabled,
Pushed far into the deep, dark past,
That "g" word (shhh!) might breathe its last.
(Some may be happy,
I'm aghast!)

For the gifted (shhh!) have always been
They always shall, for it's no sin
To be smarter than some, more able than most.
My dream? To someday serve as host
Of a feast where famous athletes talk
Of that new sensation, the "knowledge jock,"
Who tackle big issues and wrestle down rules,
And swim for miles in big, deep pools
Of learning, hoping that others see
That knowledge jocks, yes, they deserve to be

Applauded and cheered, as their minds are set free.

And if it should happen that this day should come.
I'll lead a parade with a big, bold bass drum
With a rat-a-tat loudness that gives out a cheer
That the gifted are with us, they've always been here.
They won't go away, never will, never can,
So let us just hope that each woman and man
Will embrace the idea "It's OK to be smart."
And my idea of a good place to start?
Let's deliver the "g" word from persona non grata
And make it a good term, for it truly does matter
That the "Shhhing" end soon, so our children can know
That it's OK to be gifted; it's OK to grow.

Understanding Our Gifted
Spring 2001

Gifted Girls

Who's Limiting Whom?

Introduction

What surprised me the most about this article's publication was the *lack* of response I had to it. I had assumed that there would be a brigade of individuals accusing me of being one of those male chauvinists who wanted to keep gifted girls in the kitchen cooking hardy meals for their men. But, the criticism, if any, was muted and limited. I'm still not sure why that is.

Truth be told, I've never been real fond of the gifted girls' literature. Some of it makes good points about salary inequities of women, historical depictions of girls in children's literature books, and the need to expand career horizons for girls talented in math and science. But, I don't see this as a gifted *girl* issue, I see it as a gifted *person* issue. Anytime anyone is stereotyped—boys can't cry, girls can; boys are mathematicians, girls are linguists—we *all* lose a little bit of our individuality. I guess I would be more sympathetic to the researchers who work in the area of gifted girls if they even once spoke of the specific concerns, stereotypes and vulnerabilities of gifted *boys*.

Again, my preference is to forgo altogether the gross generalizations about gender and giftedness made by researchers in this field. Honestly, I see a lot of bias afoot, with the researchers finding exactly what they set out to locate: examples of inequities.

222

Give me a few weeks and I'll be able to do the same with a bunch of gifted guys I know. Or a bunch of nongifted girls. Or any group that is pigeonholed by one or two criteria like age, gender, or intellectual ability.

Maybe *now* the letters will pour in!

I am the father of a son, a legal-age young man whose career pursuits cause many of my adult friends to cringe. Matt wants to be a writer, an artist, a creator. Math and science, early talents both, did not hold Matt's interest once he discovered the more ethereal life options of film and painting and prose.

To my face, folks smile when I tell them of my son's career interests. When they turn away, their eyebrows raise. I've heard some mutter, "What'll he do for a real job?"

How could the fact that I am the father of a male, an only child at that, and the sole brother of a brother, possibly qualify me to write about gifted girls? And how dare I criticize (as I am about to do) both the work and the underlying premise of much of the research that focuses on the collective underachievement of gifted females in our culture?

I'll tell you why. After having read the opinions of noted researchers whose work on gifted girls has become their stock in trade, I have come to the conclusion that many of them are pigeonholing gifted girls into career paths that may bear little resemblance to individual girls' actual interests and passions. By lamenting the fact that too many of our brightest girls are eschewing math and science in favor of the more "typical" female areas such as the arts and languages, these researchers are sending a loud and clear message: to be authentic and self-fulfilled, gifted girls must measure up to the standards of success adopted by the White, male majority—high prestige, high power, low affect occupations. In a subtle display of reverse sexism, advocates for gifted girls have made the desire to become anything less than a surgeon or scientist taboo for intelligent females, much as a career in art seems to be "verboten" for my son. It brings to mind a quote from one of my favorite adolescents, who told me that "the only thing worse than being denied opportunities is being forced to take them."

I am sure that my views on gifted girls' research will be ridiculed by many, especially the researchers themselves. Some may read my comments as having portrayed their intentions inaccurately; they will correct my assertions by stating that it was never their intent to limit gifted girls' aspirations to those of science, math, business, and politics.

But, if this were so, where is it stated in the research—specifically and explicitly— that teaching and nursing and other traditionally female careers are appropriate if girls' hearts, minds, and passions lead them in these directions? As parents, most of us would prefer that a child of ours become a professionally fulfilled fourth-grade teacher than an unhappy, high-salaried chemist. This is even true, I would suspect, for those who study gifted girls for a living. But, then, why hasn't that point been made louder and clearer— if at all?

Some may argue that my remarks are little more than "sour grapes" from a dad whose own son shuns the world of science for art; as if this were some sort of mind game where I am seeking psychological revenge by taking my parental disappointment out on the females who do aspire to become what my son does not. Yet, this, too, would be false, for when I see the smile in my son's eyes as he discusses his latest screenplay idea, I admire the choice that he has made: to follow a path of greater, not lesser, societal resistance. Gifted girls, too, should have this sparkle in their smile, wherever their career paths may lead them.

Has it come to the point where gifted children in our culture—boys and girls alike—are having their dreams limited unintentionally by a group of "experts" who remind them that success is measured primarily by the selection of one's occupation? Are gifted young people being taught, subliminally but effectively, that their lives will be less fulfilling if they choose to become mechanics instead of mathematicians, or painters instead of professors? Have we lost the vision and the wisdom of John Gardner, who reminded us almost 40 years ago that the world needs both gifted plumbers and gifted philosophers, or neither our pipes nor our theories will hold water?

In trying to equate the genders in relation to the opportunities open to gifted adults, I'm afraid we may be sending the wrong message to both sexes: that self-worth is defined by the career you choose and that personal success is measured by prestige, not happiness.

Perhaps this was never the intent of the research done on behalf of gifted girls; still, it seems to have become the result. My guess is that much of the literature produced about gifted girls was written so that capable young women would know that course selection in high school often determines the availability of particular academic majors in college. Still, in reading the gifted girls' literature closely, between the lines where the messages are most clearly written, I believe you, too, will see a definite bias: "Take calculus . . . it will serve you better than another elective in English."

Pretty presumptuous, wouldn't you say, as this comment makes assumptions about a young person's dreams that might be more ours than theirs.

My hope is that, in the years ahead, we will speak less about the special problems of gifted girls and come to realize that both genders face difficult choices on the path to adulthood. We will lecture less and listen more, giving academic and career guidance based upon individual interest patterns, rather than preordained societal benchmarks of success that may or may not apply to a particular boy or girl. And finally, we will come to realize that one measure of success seldom mentioned by test scores or credentialed experts is the most vital statistic of all: the measure of personal fulfillment our children feel as they pursue their passions in whatever endeavors most make them smile.

A high-profile career that is rooted in someone else's reality sustains an individual for only so long. But, when the adolescent dust has settled and gifted young adults are left only with themselves as barometers of their personal worth, what a shame it will be if they look back on their career choices and ponder "what might have been."

Gifted Child Today
July/August 1998

ADD Gifted

How Many Labels Can One Child Take?

Introduction

T hank goodness, once again, for Annemarie Roeper. She and I began a dialogue back in the mid-'90s about how uncomfortable we both were with the prevalence of the ADD/ADHD label among gifted children, especially young gifted boys. Where a generation ago, kids with excess physical or mental energy were told to run outside or read a book, today's kids are asked if they remembered to take their Ritalin (90% of which, by the way, is prescribed in the United States).

Annemarie saw this phenomenon firsthand, much more so than I did. As co-founder of the Roeper School for the Gifted in Michigan, Annemarie had worked with gifted children for more than 50 years. She had seen her students become parents and then grandparents. After retirement to California, Annemarie continued to make annual pilgrimages ("visits" just don't do justice to her presence!) back to Roeper, and it was in the late '80s that she began to see the ADHD label beginning to rear its head. As time went on, the diagnosis of ADD/ADHD became even more common, both at Roeper and nationally, until now, where we have seen a 600% increase in its diagnosis in America in just 10 years.

This article emanates from our dual concern about what we are *giving up* when we *give in* to the label of ADHD for gifted young people. Neither

Annemarie nor I are downplaying the significance of this behaviorally identified syndrome (there is no medical "test" for ADHD), but we do question why it has become so prevalent in students who used to be called "active."

I received a letter from Will the other day. Now a seventh grader, he was 9 when I met him. He was one of my fourth-grade students during the year I returned to full-time classroom teaching.

From Will's self-report, he was doing okay. His loves of math and hockey remained strong, and his aversion to cursive writing was still evident in his printed script. "And I don't get into fights anymore and I don't bawl out loud when I lose a game," he reported. Ah, Will, how you've changed!

The Will I knew was on Ritalin and hardly made it through the afternoon without lashing out verbally or physically at someone. Ten minutes, tops, was the limit of his on-task, stay-in-your-seat attention span, and his avid curiosity and knowledge base about absolutely anything scientific was my first clue that this child was bright—very bright.

"But, his behaviors!" I thought. "I wish he (and I) knew how to contain his behaviors!"

That was in 1991, and it seems that Will did change over time. Calmer, more mature, and medication-free, who would ever now suspect that Will was almost mislabeled "ADD Gifted"?

Applying the ADD Label

Attention-deficit disorder—ADD—has quickly become a professional sounding term to apply to any gifted child whose behaviors, like Will's, are nonconforming and disruptive. This increasingly ubiquitous label—often self-applied by parents or teachers without benefit of a formal and thorough diagnosis—has taken on the aura of chic: "Oh, yes, she is very bright," a caring adult explains, "but the ADD problem just doesn't allow her to get the grades she is capable of."

How sad, how trite, how potentially harmful: We are beginning to raise a generation of students who may believe themselves to be victims of their own behaviors, incapable of high achievement due to a demon called ADD.

As a former special education teacher, I fear that the ADD/gifted label is unjust, unfair, and overdone. Too often, it is a convenient excuse that prevents an in-depth exploration of what the *real* "problems" may be—an unchallenging curriculum, perhaps, or social immaturity, or a lack of consistent discipline at home or at school. By relinquishing our responsibilities to a Ritalin quick fix, we are disguising the issues instead of dealing with them.

In discussing—and, at times, debating—this issue with colleagues, I have found that Annemarie Roeper asks the most poignant and pointed questions about the ADD/gifted syndrome. Specifically, she wonders why:

- ADD/gifted assumes that all difficulties belong to the child only, rather than to possible external reasons, such as inappropriate teaching methods, unrealistic expectations, or teaching styles that do not compliment a child's learning styles.
- ADD/gifted explains learning difficulties as being biologically based, excluding the possibility of unconscious emotional reasons within the child that can lead to inner resistance or a lack of motivation.
- ADD/gifted discounts the possibility of natural developmental lags often noted in gifted children (e.g., social or motoric immaturities in comparison to intellectual development). Often, the ADD/gifted label is "outgrown" over time. In this case, should these developmental lags be pegged as "disabilities"? And, if so, what is the long-term impact of this label on the child?
- ADD/gifted is currently diagnosed through evaluation and testing methods that are purely cognitive and often conducted under stressful testing conditions. What effect does this have on the child's development?
- ADD/gifted focuses on the child's weaknesses, rather than the many strengths that must have existed for the child to have been identified as gifted in the first place. "Half empty," not "half full," seems to be the prevailing ethos.

In addressing the "problem" of ADD/gifted, the first issue we have to confront is whether or not so generic a label should ever be applied at all. There will always be children, like my fourth grader Will, who need something different from school than what is generally offered. But, even when these children don't "fit in" with other identified gifted children, the problem is not necessarily theirs.

Before assigning a label of ADD/gifted to any more children, we must seek alternatives that lie *outside* of the child. As Annemarie Roeper has stated, "I would rather see children 'dislabeled' than 'disabled.'"

Back to Will. The reason we still keep in touch is that our fourth-grade year together ended on a much happier and more rewarding note than it began. Instead of trying to "contain" his behaviors, I began to "channel" them more appropriately. So, after I admitted—to myself *and* to Will—that some of my expectations were inappropriate, and after I allowed him to learn about reading and writing through science and math projects, rather than through the literature approach that he loathed, things did improve. Behavior and grades were both within reasonable limits.

So, Will still writes me—that's a triumph in itself! He shares with me his successes and his trials, and he gave me the greatest compliment of all when he wrote recently that he liked my class because I "treated him like a big person who was smart."

I'm thankful every day that the ADD/gifted label wasn't as prominent in 1991 as it is today. I shudder at the easy route I and his parents could have taken by applying that false label to Will.

Gifted Child Today
March/April 1995

For Gifted Students, Full Inclusion is a Partial Solution

I had the highest of hopes for the inclusion movement when it first emerged as a programming option for gifted students. It seemed to have it all: Gifted education specialists would work with gifted students both in and outside of the regular classroom. Classroom teachers would become close colleagues in designing curricula that were advanced and open-ended and relied on high-level thinking skills to complete. Gifted child education programs would be seamless, with a variety of options used to address the specific needs of individual kids; thus, acceleration would be allowed, early entrance to kindergarten encouraged, and high school options for gifted adolescents would be secured. Wow.

Er . . . wrong!

Instead of taking the best of what resource rooms and self-contained classes for the gifted had to offer, these options were scrubbed in deference to an *entirely* classroom-based model. Worse, the teacher of the gifted, who used to work with 50 or so kids a week in a pull-out program, now saw these kids spread out over a couple dozen different classrooms, because "we want to be fair and give every teacher one or two gifted students." The task of managing and teaching gifted students became unwieldy, and "enrichment for all" was the fall-back position taken by many schools and gifted child educators. How sad.

This article, published in *Educational Leadership* (never a publication that was real big on gifted programming) provides specific examples for taking the best of inclusion-based programming and combining it with what already works well. Call it a happy medium, or just call it common sense, but a "one-size-fits-all" inclusion-based gifted program is as warped an idea as requiring all third graders to wear size 6 shoes, no matter the width or length of their feet.

I magine that you are a good tennis player. In fact, you're so good that you have difficulty finding a partner who can consistently return your volleys. Now imagine this: Every time you play tennis, your opponent is a beginner whose skills are far below your own. Challenge is rare and, even if you do get to refine a few good moves, the net result is a game that doesn't let you break a sweat. Pretty soon, you wonder whether playing tennis is worthwhile at all.

School is not a tennis match, but, if it were, many intellectually gifted students would find themselves returning lob after lob with little challenge to hold their attention. Inclusionary practices for gifted students and schoolwide plans to upgrade curricula for all students (Renzulli & Reis, 1985; Winebrenner, 1992) may make the idea of gifted education more palatable to its many critics, but they have actually caused a decline in the rigor of academic options for a school's most able learners. Further, with many gifted students now being served in general education settings, rather than in pull-out programs or ability-grouped classes, they have fewer opportunities to challenge one another intellectually. Just as important, today's inclusionary classrooms allow virtually no time for gifted students and their teachers to discuss growing up gifted in a world that often values brawn over brains (Delisle, 1998).

Gifted child educators and classroom teachers have the job of planning school-based experiences that address the intellectual, emotional, and social lives of gifted students while offering teaching methods and strategies that benefit a broad array of students. We can achieve this balance—providing excellence in an atmosphere of equity—only if we include the possibility of academic options that are more segregated than integrated and more focused on the needs of some than on the needs of all. Indeed, it may entail a return to some of those program options—pull-out programs or ability-grouped classes—that we have eliminated or curtailed in the rush to appear nonelitist. This notion may not be as politically correct or as popular as today's emphasis toward full inclusion, but it is based in the reality of students' lives; like it or not, some children and adolescents *are* more able than others. Just listen to 15-year-old Vamir:

> I was classified as gifted in 2nd grade. This was really driven home when I skipped two grades, going from 5th grade to 7th over winter break. I am interested in science (especially physics), mathematics (algebra), philosophy (logic), and finance (futures trading). I like to read about these topics and some science

fiction and espionage, as well as the classics that I started reading in my human-
ities and social science classes. . . .

Here are some of my concerns as a "gifted student." I hate it when adults are
condescending to me simply because of my age. . . . I hate it when I have so many
thoughts that I lose one (which has happened at least a dozen times while writing this). I also hate it when I cannot think of anything and when I have a really
neat thought that I can't investigate more deeply because I just don't have the
educational background.

I worry too much. I worry about losing my talents. I worry about becoming
average. . . . I worry I will burn out or overspecialize. I worry about how successful I will be in my career and whether my colleagues will accept me (and
whether they do now). (Galbraith & Delisle, 1996, pp. 20–21)

Vamir is experiencing the self-doubt that is as natural a part of adolescent as acne,
but he has the ability to express his fears and hopes at a level far in advance of his agemates. In inclusionary high school classes where futures trading and logic are not everyday topics, students like Vamir can find themselves absorbed by boredom, wondering
when it will be *their* chance to shine.

Only a rare teacher would be able to personalize Vamir's learning needs in a heterogeneous classroom. Especially with today's heavy emphasis on high-stakes assessments
that stress lower level content that students can spew back on state-ordained tests, students with Vamir's insights and abilities often find themselves languishing intellectually.
Their personal reach surpasses the grasp of curricula built for competency instead of
accomplishment. The net result?

Failure to help the gifted child reach his potential is a societal tragedy, the extent
of which is difficult to measure but which is surely great. How can we measure
the sonata unwritten, the curative drug undiscovered, the absence of political
insight? They are the difference between what we are and what we could be as a
society. (Gallagher, 1975, p. 9)

The field of gifted child education can offer much to all students—creative and critical
thinking, problem-solving opportunities, self-selected project work, and so on—but this
does not diminish the accuracy of another truth: Gifted students can also benefit from time
spent alongside their intellectual peers in settings that allow them to express their individuality with others much like themselves in ability and intensity. We must reconcile today's
inclusionary practices and yesterday's emphasis on more homogeneous groupings of students if we are to meet the diverse needs of gifted students in a school setting.

A Key to the Solution

How *can* we meet the needs of gifted students in today's climate of inclusion? As
a researcher in this field for more than 20 years and as a part-time teacher of gifted

students in grade 4–8 for 7 years, I have found three solutions: *flexibility, acceleration*, and *variety*. As is true with any complex process, no "one-size-fits-all" approach is possible. Our suburban middle school of 1,025 students serves gifted students in multiple ways:

- Our school places identified gifted students in grades 4–6 in two-teacher teams where at least one teacher is licensed as a gifted education specialist. Within these teams, students participate in homogeneous groups for language arts, mathematics, or both, which allows both content acceleration and enrichment opportunities. Because the identified students can be gifted in math or language, specific strength areas are recognized and programmed accordingly; in other words, students can be gifted in one subject, but not in another.
- Identified gifted students in grades 7 and 8 attend a series of 16 daylong, off-campus seminars on such topics as architecture, psychology, college planning, chemistry, and the judicial system. During each seminar, the students meet with professionals from these fields. An additional component of these seminars addresses some of the emotional issues that gifted students often raise: "How do you decide a career choice when you are good in so many areas?" "What do teachers, parents, and classmates expect from you when you have been identified as gifted?" An added benefit of this daylong seminar structure is that students are not pulled from their regular classes on a weekly basis, but only two days each quarter. Make-up work—the bane of pull-out programs, from students' perspectives—is kept to a minimum.
- Our school invites identified gifted students, and others, to participate in community service projects involving local agencies or individuals who need, as the kids say, "help or a thank you." Often, these events tie in with the curriculum. For example, sixth graders participated in "The Academy Awards of Literature and Science," for which they read dozens of books and then nominated titles, authors, book characters, and scientists for awards. The "Oscars" were presented at a fundraising event for a local homeless shelter. Another project involved language arts classes in a letter-writing campaign to survivors of the Columbine High School shootings.
- A licensed gifted education teacher in a regular classroom teaches lessons on creative and critical thinking that tie in with core-subject learning objectives. Thus, the gifted teacher, along with classroom colleagues, can help design and implement lessons that require higher level thinking and can assist in informally assessing students' interests and abilities. Several students not previously identified as gifted have been selected for testing after their classroom teachers observed their interactions with this high-level content.
- Students whose IQ scores are in the superior range but whose classroom work is mediocre meet weekly with the gifted education specialist to determine reasons behind the low achievement and to design strategies for reversing this pattern. Although specific comments by students are kept confidential, the gifted education specialist communicates frequently with the students' parents and teachers about any changes in behavior or classroom performances.

- Students exceptionally able in core-subject areas, especially mathematics, participate in out-of-grade-level experiences in different schools within the district. Thus, a third-grade student whose mathematical abilities are exceptional attends a seventh-grade math class one period a day before returning to her elementary school.

These curricular experiences, in addition to enrichment opportunities offered to all students (field trips, guest speakers, and such academic competitions as Power of the Pen), provide the "cascade of services" envisioned in 1985 by Cox, Daniel, and Boston. In their study of more than 1,100 school districts throughout the United States, these researchers discovered that, of the 16 programs found to benefit gifted students, only four school districts offered at least 10 of options listed in Figure 1. Indeed, nearly 45% of these districts offered only one or two of these alternatives, with the most popular being a pull-out resource room in the elementary grades. Calling this a "part-time solution to a full-time problem" (p. 43), Cox, Daniel, and Boston contended that gifted students need school services that address their needs every hour of the school week, not just once or twice a week. "Gifted on Tuesdays" is not adequate.

Still, a resource room can be one viable option for school districts that are not willing to make the philosophical commitment to group gifted students in self-contained or ability-grouped classes. The resource room often serves as an intellectual and emotional haven for gifted students, allowing them to review issues that are not common to other classmates. For example, an activity on the positive and negative aspects of growing up gifted would be difficult to accomplish in a heterogeneous classroom; yet, in a resource room where gifted students feel comfortable enough to express their feelings toward their abilities, such an activity can lead to intense discussion about the social pangs of growing up gifted.

But, a resource room is just one small piece of the puzzle. Even the popular Schoolwide Enrichment Model (Renzulli & Reis, 1985), although serving the needs of some students, is not a panacea for meeting the needs of gifted students. Unless we allow for the reality that gifted students' needs are more than academic and school-related, we

1. Enrichment in the regular classroom
2. Part-time special class
3. Full-time special class
4. Independent study
5. Itinerant teacher
6. Mentorships
7. Resource rooms
8. Special schools
9. Early entrance
10. Continuous progress
11. Nongraded school
12. Moderate acceleration
13. Radical acceleration
14. Advanced placement
15. Fast-paced courses
16. Concurrent or dual enrollment

Figure 1. Programming Options
for Gifted Children

Note. From *Educating able learners* (p. 30), by J. Cox, N. Daniel, & B. Boston, 1985, Austin: University of Texas Press. Copyright © 1985 by University of Texas Press. Reprinted with permission.

often overlook an important component of their development. Yet, we need only read the comments of Vamir to understand the intensities that occupy his world.

A Blueprint for the Future

In an inclusionary era that assumes that each teacher is responsible for the learning of every student, some students will still be "outliers"—kids on the edges whose academic or emotional needs are such that full-time placement within a heterogeneous classroom does more of a disservice to them than offers a benefit. Gifted students are often these outliers when they exhibit thoughts, behaviors, and educational challenges that require more concentrated services than one teacher can deliver in one classroom.

As individualized educators, we must not apologize if we cannot meet a student's needs in a heterogeneous classroom. Instead, we must realize that, within the constraints of a single day, or a single career, we will face intellectual or emotional issues that would be better addressed by someone whose skills, training, and personality differ from our own. We must realize that "one size fits all," be it in shoes or in academic options, pinches everyone where it hurts and impedes the forward progress of those whose pace is different in speed or style.

If we are truly committed to personalizing learning, we must appreciate that today's panacea—full inclusion for all students with special needs—is tomorrow's bad practice. Without the willingness and the ability to admit that each student's individuality demands something unique, our schools will continue to address only partially the needs of selected students. Gifted students are no exception to this rule.

Educational Leadership
November 1999

Multiple Intelligences

Convenient, Simple, Wrong

Introduction

his short article was my first full-blown attempt to show that the Multiple Intelligences emperor, Howard Gardner, indeed, had no clothes.

Many, many letters came my way once this article was published, and virtually all of them said "thank you." Apparently, there were (and are) a lot of "closet critics" of the MI notion, but too few of them were willing to vocalize their concerns. In many cases, some letter writers stated that there was something they didn't like about the MI theory, but they "just couldn't put their finger on it." This delineation of *convenient, simple* and *wrong* seemed to be the analysis they were looking for.

Whatever your views of the MI idea for teaching gifted students—something Gardner says he never promoted, yet has not been quick to downplay—I do hope you will consider what has happened nationwide to gifted programs as the MI train has chugged forward. Indeed, many gifted students have been left behind at the station, wondering what happened to the specialized services they were getting because of who they were: a gifted kid with special learning needs who is now just one among many who is multiply intelligent.

've always been leery of concepts that absolutely everyone understands. In recent years, the catchphrase "Multiple Intelligences" has become just such a concept. Since Howard Gardner first coined this term in his book *Frames of Mind* in 1983, the MI bandwagon has been bulging with people only too quick to state that they, too, believe that everyone has some intelligence that bears attention.

If only that were true!

It's not that I don't believe that some people who possess strong mathematical proclivities may have lesser abilities in musical areas, or that someone with "naturalistic intelligence" (Gardner's latest category of brilliance) may have trouble trying to explain this aptitude to others (interpersonal intelligence). It's just that the MI theory has two attributes that always arouse suspicion in me: convenience and simplicity.

Convenient

First, convenience. For years, people involved with gifted education have been running scared from the threat of "elitism." Afraid that others might see us as trying to create a small, select group of children who are intrinsically superior to others has caused the field to seek ways to downplay a legitimate truth: Some people, including children, are smarter than others. When MI came along, we rushed to its defense and embraced its egalitarian theme: "See?" we told people. "We're not elitist! Look, Howard Gardner says almost everyone can be intelligent in something! And we agree!"

And so, upon the advice and with the approval of many gifted child educators, MI quickly become the law of the land and in its classrooms. How convenient.

Simple

Second, simplicity. It doesn't take a rocket scientist to understand the difference between being able to construct an eye-catching building (spatial intelligence) and being able to construct a cogent paragraph (linguistic intelligence). Tapping into these individual intelligences has become simple: just purchase one of the many workbooks available on MI and do the icon-coded activity that corresponds to the intelligence you're trying to foster. It's simpler than baking from a Betty Crocker cake mix, and it contains even fewer ingredients.

It seems to me that, in our rush to embrace MI and its democratic ideals, we have left behind one important element: the gifted child. You know who I mean: the child who used to get identified as G/T due to factors beyond his or her control, like the ability to conceptualize at an early age, to manipulate symbol systems like numbers or letters, to empathize with others at a deep, deep level, or to prefer the company of intellectual peers who don't ridicule a kid who has a brain that works overtime. These children—gifted children—are neither convenient nor simple, and, in our decreasing attention to addressing their complex needs, we have done a disservice to both them and our profession. Shame on us.

Wrong

Unfortunately, instead of debating the benefits of MI theory, many educators of gifted children have embraced it warmly and with little regard for the detrimental impact this shift in thinking may have on our field of study. Indeed, an entirely new breed of gifted child educator has been spawned—"talent developers"—psychologists and educators who used to write about gifted children, but who now admonish us to drop out references to *giftedness* and replace that volatile term with its politically sanitized corollary: *talent development*.

The problem with this is that talent developers talk around the issue of giftedness instead of directly at it. They do not discuss how parents can soothe the hidden concerns and quiet fears of children who wonder whether giftedness is a thing to cherish or resist, or how to react to a child who thinks like a 12 year old, looks like a 10 year old, plays like a 6 year old, and argues like a middle-aged, high-priced lawyer. And they ignore the fact that matters of curricula (which are very big with talent developers) do not address the real content of life: self-knowledge, respect for others, and compassion, those vital life skills that never get measured by standardized tests, but are, in fact, the truest measures of anyone as a successful human being.

Ignoring Giftedness

Talent developers and MI fans, in their quest for a new and simpler conception of giftedness, have ignored two important elements in their equation: the developmental nature of giftedness and the fact that giftedness is someone you are, not something you do. Essentially, talent development and MI lack two features that are vital aspects of every gifted person I have ever met: heart and depth.

Growing up gifted is a lot more complicated than merely determining what talents someone chooses to display or which of Gardner's eight intelligences best fits particular behaviors and strengths. There is an added element to all gifted people—the emotional element—that fits neither clearly nor wholly into the MI theory. It never will.

My hope is that someday soon the field of gifted education will emerge from the trendy, Gardner-driven mode in which it now finds itself. Only then, when we are willing to look once again at aspects of giftedness that are neither obvious nor empirically measurable, will we see the myriad elements that combine to create a gifted child, that complex being who is more than the sum of his or her parts and whose inconvenience provides insights that an idea as simple as MI cannot possibly convey.

Gifted Child Today
November/December 1996

Reach Out,
But Don't Touch

Introduction

'm a hugger. Always have been. When a child (or teen) is crying or visibly upset, I am there to serve as a surrogate shoulder, in lieu of Mom or Dad. And, when a student accomplishes a feat that seemed too difficult on first attempt, I am there with a high-five, a firm handshake, or, if I know the child well, a hug. The same happens when one of my students comes back for a visit a year or two after having graduated to the high school. I look in his or her eyes, and, if a hug seems welcome, then a hug is given.

Pretty scary, huh, especially for a guy.

In this era of rampant lawsuits based on suspicions and innuendoes, it is a real risk for an educator to touch a child in any way, shape, or form. Still, I continue to do it and, in my defense, I will add that, if I've been an educator for more than 20 years and haven't abused a child yet, I'm not about to start now.

The profession of teaching is among the most intimate that exists. We get to know many of our students very closely, especially in gifted programs (I have the same students for three years in a row). How can I (or you) not give a hug when Susan was declared winner of the Geography Bee, or Alan got a standing ovation for his rendition of Romeo, or Stevie lost his favorite souvenir from a field trip he took in second grade? It's human nature to want close contact at times of triumph or strife, and this article portrays why I refuse to be as cautious as some of my colleagues advise me to be.

At the National Education Association's convention in New Orleans this past summer, delegates and participants were asked their views on physical contact with students—not corporal punishment, mind you, but rather, the reassuring hand-on-the-shoulder contact that connects one human being, literally and figuratively, with another.

"You're careful about touching a student in any way, even an instructional way," said an art teacher from Montana. "Now what you do is take the pen . . . you don't have any physical contact." In unavoidable situations where he finds himself alone with a student, a Louisiana teacher reported that he will now "open the door wider. I sit more in the middle of the room."

Who can blame these teachers? Given the too-frequent scenario equating accusation with guilt (especially with male teachers), it comes as no surprise that, in the teaching profession, touching has become taboo. Every pat on the back has become suspect, each congratulatory squeeze to the shoulder a source of potential problems. Hugs have been demoted to handshakes. Private meetings with students have regressed to public forums. Teaching, one of the most personal and interactive of all professions, has been sterilized to a point unimaginable even a generation ago.

Working in an elementary school, I come into contact with many children in need of emotional solace. A scraped knee, a bruised ego, or a lost lunch box each brings on the same reaction: a fountain of tears. And, even though the school nurse doles out bandages liberally and kindly, the act of healing is seldom complete without an additional "It'll be all right" kind of hug.

Nothing kinky. Nothing amorous. Just a quick, reassuring connection that indicates our link as two human beings, one who needs comfort and another who is willing to give it.

I'll never forget Mick, a 9-year-old student of mine whose home life was punctuated with frequent moves and even more frequent neglect. A tough kid, Mick eyed school (and teachers) warily, and, even by fourth grade, he had developed a reputation as a trouble-finder. So, it surprised me when, one day, Mick stayed after school purposely to show me the new bike that his "real dad" had just given to him. It was handsome and tall and ready for adventure, just like its owner. Mick and I talked for a while—privately, I'll admit—about both his bike and his dad, and, suddenly, rough-and-tumble Mick dissolved into tears. It seems that Luigi, an even taller and tougher eighth grader, had threatened to steal Mick's bike, and Mick was afraid that he would.

Instinctively, as the father of a son only two years older than Mick, I held him tightly. His sobs and quivers were genuine and strong. Mick was afraid. There was no way that an artificial handshake or an arm's-length sentiment of comfort would suffice.

Mick was 9 years old, he was scared, and he was in need of a hug. If my hug wasn't justified, what would have been?

Perhaps if I worked with high school students, who by then have learned how to suppress many of their overt emotions, I would have responded differently. But, tears are tears, no matter what your age. And fear is fear, even if the dragons that bring it on change over time. I'd like to think that I'd respond the same way with a 16-year-old as with a 9-year-old, despite the "risks" involved, for I refuse to live and teach in fear that each casual or comforting touch will be misinterpreted as something it is not. Experience should count for something, and if I haven't mishandled children in my 18 years as an educator, I'm not about to start now.

I understand that the problem of physical and sexual exploitation of students is a real issue. But, I also understand that such crimes are committed by the tiniest minority of colleagues who share this profession of teaching. Recently, though, the sick few who choose to abuse and demean their students have set the tone for the rest of us: Reach out, but don't touch. In adopting this new philosophy, our profession has quietly but surely taken a step back. Like Mick, we are afraid of an enemy even bigger and stronger than we are—the "enemy" of self-doubt and false accusation.

My heart goes out to that art teacher from Montana who feels the need to expose his students to the beauty of art from a far and safe distance. I feel sorry for that Louisiana educator who believes it is prudent to have a potential witness nearby when discussing a student's personal problem. And I feel worse for the millions of kids who are growing to learn, through our example, that emotions are bad and physical contact is inappropriate unless it is some circumspect handshake. In years to come, today's kids will surely pass on this unspoken message to their own children.

Back to Mick: after drying his tears with my shirtcuff, we devised a plan that would soothe his anxiety about Luigi's avaricious desires. Mick would bring his bike into our classroom, keeping a watchful eye on it until the bike no longer looked new or good enough to steal—about three days! When Mick finally pedaled his treasured bike out of our classroom for the last time, he seemed confident and safe.

"How far one little candle throws its beam," I thought, recalling the words of the novelist John Cheever, "so shines a good deed in a naughty world."

Mick, you deserved this.

How long will educators—us—allow ourselves to be suspects when, in fact, most of us are victims? Victims of a spate of accusations about our personal behavior and professional ethics that has given both parents and students unwarranted fears about what goes on in a classroom. Individually and collectively, we must state unequivocally that our goal as educators is to instruct, not abuse, children. Unless we do so, we may lose one of the last and greatest elements of our profession that has guided it since its inception: trust.

Education Week
September 21, 1994

Mom, Apple Pie, and Differentiation

Introduction

I apologize, in advance, for offending any reader who is growing tired of my slaughtering of sacred cows, but, with curriculum differentiation, I am about to do just that.

If you look up the word *bandwagon* in an educational dictionary, you are bound to find an image of curriculum differentiation in action. Once the bastion (and I'm not saying this was correct) of the gifted education gurus, curriculum differentiation has now hit the big time. Everyone is doing it (or, at least they think they are), and all is now well in the world of gifted child education.

Well, not exactly.

By focusing so many of our efforts on how to improve curricula *for everyone*, we have neglected to mention that even the best differentiated curriculum *still* does not meet the entire range of needs possessed by gifted children. You see, gifted kids are gifted both inside and outside of school, and if we take care only to look after their academic needs, we are dismissing or discounting the most vital part of their essence: the emotional part.

I am afraid that school districts across this great land will begin to say, "Since we are differentiating for all students, we don't need a special program for gifted children." Indeed, this is already happening.

Wake up, folks! While differentiation is a part of our good efforts toward meeting the needs of the gifted, it is but one small aspect of a much greater goal: to serve gifted children's needs that are less easy to decipher than those related to curriculum—their emotional and social needs. If nothing else, this article points out this fact.

There are a few demigods in our culture, icons that demand universal respect. Mothers, apple pie, and the American flag all come to mind as examples. But, a school-based equivalent has recently entered our lexicon, a word and concept that, up until recently, had been the bastion exclusively of gifted child educators. The term? *Differentiation.*

It used to be that differentiation of curricula was the sole property of educators who were seeking to make the mundane offerings of school more palatable for high-end learners (before political correctness, we called these kids "gifted"). Related terms like *critical thinking, Type-III projects,* and *higher order operations* were corollaries of this differentiation concept, and gifted child educators everywhere used this multisyllabic term to distinguish how what they did differed from their classroom colleagues responsible for teaching that most dreaded of beasts, the "regular curriculum."

But then, the Association for Supervision and Curriculum Development (ASCD) pumped up the volume, extolling the benefits of curriculum differentiation for all learners. Given the age-old assumption (erroneous, of course) that "what is good for the gifted is good for all students," the term *differentiation* began to appear regularly in ASCD publications, videos, and workshop descriptions that, in the apple pie, American tradition, encompassed all students under the same instructional umbrella.

There's only one problem: This differentiation bandwagon is getting off track (excuse the mixed metaphor). Here's why:

The most subtle and insidious aspect of this "differentiation for all" idea is the insinuation that a properly differentiated curriculum will fully meet the needs of gifted learners. Although I will admit that curriculum alteration for highly able students is a good beginning, we must remember that we are not just talking about gifted students. We are talking about gifted people; gifted individuals who are filled with some unique social and emotional aspects to their lives that always have, and always will, distinguish them as different from their classmates in unseen, yet important, ways. For proof of this, talk to a gifted child about how he or she is similar to and different from other kids in class. In most cases, you will hear that the needs expressed by gifted young people transcend the realm of academics. Differentiation seldom (if ever) acknowledges these nonacademic distinctions among children, yet they are often the most important components of growing up gifted.

Secondly, this "one-size-fits-all" interpretation of differentiation is as false in education as it is (I assume) in pantyhose. To be sure, differentiation, in theory, means unique forms of instruction and curricula for different students, depending on their abilities or levels of achievement. However, theory does not always translate well, or readily, into classroom practice, and I am afraid that what is happening with differentiation is what happened with cooperative learning more than a decade ago—everyone benefits somewhat, but the gifted child benefits somewhat less than others in the classroom. I do not criticize my colleagues who go from workshop to workshop (as presenters or participants) in search of curriculum's Holy Grail. I only wish they would concentrate more on what is good for the gifted few as avidly as they do for the nongifted many.

The third problem I see with differentiation being offered as this generation's educational panacea is the notion that every single classroom lesson leads to an academic Nirvana for all students. Forgive my naïveté, but are these the same classroom teachers who have recently become responsible for serving special education students' needs through another "innovation," inclusion, while also making sure that all students pass the state's competency/proficiency tests at high enough levels that the statistics published in local newspapers make citizens proud to live where they do? Gee . . . I thought so. Isn't it grand, then, that we are adding differentiation for all students to this ever-growing list of demands for classroom teachers?

Is there a workable approach to this differentiation frenzy that is permeating our nation's schools? Of course there is. The first thing to do is acknowledge that different types of teachers have different types of strengths and that those with the training, experience, and an affinity to work with gifted students should be allowed to do so—both *within* general education classrooms and in *separate* programs or classes designed specifically to meet the academic and emotional needs of gifted children.

Secondly, we can acknowledge that differentiation, while beneficial in a general sort of way, needs to encompass far more thought and insight than merely changing an activity, a lesson, or an assignment. It is a year-long—indeed, a career-long—commitment to matching an individual student with educational options that make sense for him or her throughout the elementary and secondary years. This might entail an 11-year-old attending high school classes, or a 4-year-old skipping kindergarten and entering first grade . . . or second. Do proponents of differentiation for all have this mindset? Some do . . . many don't . . . all must.

With all due respect to apple pie, motherhood, and Old Glory, I am reluctant to elevate yet another item—in this case, differentiation—to sacred cow status. Isn't it time that gifted child educators, and the administrators for whom they work, speak honestly about the limitations of even a good idea like differentiation? Only with this up-front acknowledgment that even the best of solutions will not fit everyone will the needs of gifted children—academic, social, and emotional—be met in our schools.

Gifted Child Today
September/October 2000

A Lesson
From Racquetball

This, my most recent article, came about while I was lounging around a pool at a fancy Las Vegas hotel, thinking I should be doing something more than lounging around a pool at a fancy Las Vegas hotel. The content of the article may be new, but the theme is not; indeed, it is one I have been bantering about for almost as long as I have been involved in this field of gifted child education.

In a sense, this article goes back to the roots of our democracy, when Thomas Jefferson said that "There is nothing more unequal than the equal treatment of unequals." I'm not sure how much we've learned since Mr. Jefferson's time, but I do know this: When we assume that the intellectual needs of gifted children will be met in the middle school—or in any grade level—by clumping everyone together in the name of "equality," we are bastardizing the use of that term. Mr. Jefferson would be ashamed.

Just as Ken needs someone to play racquetball with him who doesn't say "Can you slow down a bit? I can't keep up," gifted students who can race ahead like nobody's business need to be with both teachers and peers who can challenge even their strongest efforts. Anything short of that is wrong and shortsighted, no matter how incorrectly couched in "democracy" the intention appears to be.

You do agree, don't you? Then don't be afraid to say so.

One of my more embarrassing moments occurred several years ago when a new acquaintance and I agreed to play racquetball. After a few minutes of gently lobbing the ball back and forth, the games began. Shortly thereafter, they were over: Ken had won 15–0, 15–0, 15–1 (and that single, feeble point was a gift, I think). Only then did Ken tell me that he was a tri-state racquetball champ and a former instructor of the sport.

Despite this unequal beginning, Ken and I are now more like brothers than acquaintances. But, there is one thing we don't do together, and that is play racquetball. What would be the point? I'd be intimidated, and Ken would be bored. For both of us to be challenged at individually appropriate levels, we'd have to play racquetball with others whose abilities more closely matched our own.

I thought of this situation recently when I read the National Forum to Accelerate Middle-Grade Reform's new policy statement on ability grouping (2000). Couched in all sorts of democratic-sounding ideals, it reads, in part, like this:

> High-performing middle-grade schools are academically excellent, developmentally responsive, and socially equitable. Such schools . . . work deliberately to diminish disparities in students' learning and achievement. . . . In high-performing schools, heterogeneous assignment of students is the norm. . . . When students are grouped and regrouped for purposes of instruction, the assignment is temporary and based on diagnosed needs, interests, and talents of students, not on a single achievement test.

Of course, none of the hot-button terms are defined, so "socially equitable," "developmentally responsive," and "temporary" are all open for interpretation. And, although much of this policy statement is only indirectly critical of grouping gifted students together for instruction, one statement is crystal clear (it's even italicized): "The National Forum believes that students should never be assigned to homogenous groups for all their classes all the time."

What does this National Forum policy statement really mean? What were the intentions of its authors? It contains more *ifs*, *ands*, and *buts* than a teenager trying to explain why he broke curfew, and that is what scares me; for now, people—myself included—will be able to point to this statement and excerpt any portion of it that reinforces their own agenda.

Being a professor of gifted child education for two decades and a part-time teacher of middle school gifted students for the past 10 years, I thought I would take a stab at writing my own unequivocal policy statement about gifted students in the middle school that says what it means and means what it says. Here goes: The Delisle One-Man Forum on Serving Gifted Students in the Middle Grades.

Gifted children exist, and, despite the mistaken notion held by many that "everyone is gifted at something," that is not true. Some children, like some adults, are more intelligent than others.

This having been stated, it follows logically that gifted children exist in the middle grades, although this giftedness is often cleverly disguised beneath hormones, growth spurts, and feigned ignorance in front of friends. When these children are found, through standardized assessments, teacher or parent observations, or classmates who call these kids "brainiacs," they should be placed together with other children of similar academic abilities. For some students, this might be for one class a day. For others, all of their classes (and classmates) will need to be accelerated.

It would be beneficial if teachers who instruct gifted children knew something about their unique learning and emotional needs. They could get this information through coursework, professional magazines or journals, attending conferences, or by simply being gifted themselves. Barring all of the above, the single best criterion to be an effective teacher of gifted kids is to simply like gifted kids.

When critics complain that it is "undemocratic" or "elitist" to group gifted children for instructional purposes, remind these people that neither Harvard University (which is private) nor the University of Virginia (which is public) is democratic either. They admit students selectively, on the bases of strong academic performance and remarkable records of service or sport. Thus, it would be silly to plan middle and high schools around a reality that doesn't exist: that everyone will do well and be challenged when they get tossed into the same pot for English, math, or science.

Finally, when critics of homogenous grouping complain that taking the "cream of the crop" from each class diminishes the intellectual challenge for the remaining students, point out this truth: Every student has the right to be challenged, including gifted ones. If their placement in a heterogeneous class is to enhance everyone's learning but their own, that is unethical, as gifted students are relegated to the role of intellectual indentured servants, paying interest on bills they never owed.

There: terse, tight, and understandable. It may never win me any awards for political correctness, and for that I am grateful.

Back to racquetball to make a final point (figuratively, of course). On the court, Ken deserves to play someone who can match his kill shots. But, off the court, he and I can still be buddies. His attained skill in a sport in which he excels at a level I never will does not make him a better person than I, just a more accomplished athlete. Conversely, I do not think myself to be "stupid" or less of a person just because Ken and I differ in how well we perform on a specific task. We just accept this difference between us as . . . a difference; nothing more.

The sooner we take the grouping of intellectually gifted children out of the sociopolitical arena and put it back into the realm of common sense, the sooner we will give both gifted children and others levels of education that are personally meaningful and challenging. Unlike playing Ken, in this game, no one needs to lose.

Gifted Child Today
Summer 2001

Part Eleven

What Goes Around, Comes Around: Unpublished Thoughts and Ramblings

The thickest folder in my file cabinet drawer is the one composed of rejection letters from magazines, journals, newspapers and book publishers for manuscripts they chose not to print because "it does not fit our publication needs at this time." In other words, the editors didn't like what I wrote.

Eventually, through perseverance and kinder editors at competing publications, some of the articles contained earlier in this book did find a home. But not these. The articles here are unpublished prior to now, yet of all of my previously unpublished works, these are my favorite "rejects."

I did not include professional writings here, in other words, those articles that were more apt for audiences of educators. Rather, I have included here some ramblings that you might find in magazines like *Parents* or *Family Circle*. Of course, you didn't find them there because each of these was rejected by those two fine monthlies.

Enjoy these memories and, through, my words, recall or create some of your own.

Rich

Introduction

When I first decided to return to classroom teaching in 1991, I assumed I would be fine with the fourth graders I was to teach. I wondered (and worried) more about how I would be perceived by my classroom colleagues. I didn't know if I'd be considered an interloper, an outsider invading their turf for some grand educational experiment known only to myself. Or, perhaps some colleagues would think I was "slumming it" for a year to earn back a bit of the professional credibility I had lost by staying out of the K–12 environment for 12 years.

I'm happy to report that my fears were unfounded. Once I established myself as a teacher who looked like a veteran, but had the discipline skills of a novice (and was willing to ask my teammates for help), everything was fine. Indeed, to this day I still visit "my school" regularly and am greeted warmly with hugs by Elaine and Pat and George and Sue and handshakes by many others—including Rich, whose story this is.

I sent this manuscript out three or four times, each time receiving a nondescript, form-letter rejection. I *still* don't understand why, because even today I read it as an honest explanation of the reason it is important to second-guess negative first impressions.

Imagine that: I was harboring the same type of hidden prejudices that I feared others would hold against me! Live and learn—which is exactly what I did, thanks to Rich.

I f any of his students had dared dress this casually on the first day of school, they would have been sent home for a different outfit. But, this was a teacher, a new guy named Rich, one of two new teachers this year at Meadows Middle School. I was the other one.

The principal began with introductions of us to the staff. My new tie was tight and my old shirt was suddenly a half-size too small; a result, no doubt, of both first-day jitters and a summer filled with plentiful food and drink. Rich sat there in a "Save the Rainforest" T-shirt, well-worn cut-offs, and sneakers so old that they hadn't ever been endorsed by an athlete. He seemed very relaxed.

I spoke only briefly, mentioning how pleased I was to be teaching again, my first year in a classroom after a 12-year career as a college professor of education. To a smattering of applause, I then sat down. Rich spoke, too, mentioning his previous teaching experience in a neighboring town.

"They jerked me around for two years," he told us coarsely, "so, I told them what they could do with their contract."

A few snickers, a few gasps. Through sight *and* sound, Rich had *definitely* left an impression.

The meeting broke, allowing extra time for us to prepare for tomorrow's arrival of students. I'd been in for two weeks already, designing bulletin boards that would dazzle and learning centers that would excite my fourth-grade kids. Everything was perfect and original—not a store-bought decoration to be found.

At 1 p.m., I walked by Rich's room, thinking we could go out for lunch before putting the finishing touches on our classrooms. I'd loosened my tie in an attempt to balance our wardrobes, even just a little.

"Oh, Rich has left for the day," the secretary mentioned as I strode by her desk.

"Already?" I asked. I was puzzled, not knowing whether I felt more jealous or angry: Was Rich *that* good that he could just walk in and teach?

The next morning, that very important first day of classes, buses arrived right on time. Assembly was scheduled at 10 a.m. to welcome the kids to their new school year. Rich's class streamed in quietly, like little soldiers, filling the bottom three rows of bleachers. Rich looked different today, his rainforest T-shirt having been replaced by a rainforest tie. A student of his spoke quietly to another one, and Rich pounced on the boy as if he'd committed a felony. Everyone else, even my students, sat up and took notice. He had left another memorable first impression, this time on our school's children.

During the next few weeks, I saw Rich very little, but I thought about him a lot. He was too new at this to have already grown cynical, so I had to assume that he actually *wanted* to teach. Maybe he'd mellowed since those opening days of school, or maybe he just ascribed to that ol' disciplinary dictum that "You don't let them see you smile until Christmas." Whatever the reason, I hoped to have a chance to get to know him even a little better than I did. After all, a guy whose wardrobe is a collection of rainforest regalia can't be all bad.

That's when the magic happened. One November afternoon, due to an adjusted schedule that threw out the day's routine, Rich and I had recess duty at the same time. Generally, we teachers huddled together in conversation, eyes glancing outward at the children, but removed, nonetheless, from their playtime activities. For these few moments, we were as happy to be free of them as they were to be rid of us.

Except Rich: "S'cuse me, Jim," he said. "I have some appointments."

At that point, Rich sped off to the center of the schoolyard, smirking in a way that indicated to me that he had been quite a handful himself when he was in grade school.

"Go out for a long one, Joey!" Rich shouted, planting a perfectly passed spiral into the arms of one of his students.

Next, he ran over to the painted blacktop. "The secret to four-square," he told the girls huddled there, "is to look at one person and knock the ball toward someone else. Like this! Try it." (They did. It worked.)

"Ten jumps is all I can muster up," he said breathlessly to the girls playing Double Dutch. "And don't raise those ropes too high!"

Here was Rich, as animated as I was stagnant, enjoying his students in a freestyle manner that didn't match the reputation I had unfairly given him. Still gruff in tone, Rich was gentle in demeanor. He spoke the voice of Oscar the Grouch, but his actions were those of Mr. Rogers.

When recess ended, he blew the whistle to the tune of a popular song. "Who knows this one?" he asked. "Who knows this one?"

His 26 students clamored around him, anxious for this special attention, suggesting song titles that ranged from "Three Blind Mice" to the latest Mariah Carey tune. Rich then led his students into the building, this Pied Piper of Meadows School setting the tone for an afternoon of learning.

Rich winked at me. "See you again, Delisle."

After that day, I rearranged my recess so Rich and I could be outside together more often. I had a lot to learn from Rich, about both spirals and spirit. Occasionally, we talked, but more often we just played recess as ardently as did any of our students. Us against them, boys against girls (we had an edge there), class against class: I came to know my students better *in* the classroom because Rich taught me how to appreciate them *outside* of it, too.

When springtime came, Rich and I planned a couple of science units together. On Earth Day, though it dawned chilly, Rich wore the same rainforest T-shirt he had worn that first day in August. It brought back memories of how I had misjudged him before I even knew who he was.

"I remember wondering," I confessed to Rich, "how you ever got through the interview process to get this job."

He laughed. "And all *I* could think of was, 'Who's the geek in the tie? Doesn't he know it's still summer?'"

We laughed together that day, and, on June 11, the last day of school, we played that silly men's game called "macho wars," where guys refuse to acknowledge to each other just how sad we are to see something good come to an end. Our students had become closer to us than we ever imagined they could, and, watching them run to the pool party at the recreation center next door, we realized simultaneously that they'd never again be "our students." For each of them, fourth or fifth grade was over. It had been a good year for *all* of us.

"So," I asked Rich, "did you bring your bathing suit?"

He smiled. "No. Did you?"

"No."

"Good . . . then let's go over to the pool party. For once, we'll just watch."

When Did We Stop Being Parents?

Introduction

When I dug through some old files and found this manuscript, I hoped that it would have become anachronistic. It wasn't. In fact, the message of this article may be even truer today then when I wrote it in 1992.

The freewheeling parents of today—yuppies with little ones—may offer more, materially speaking, to their children than could parents of previous generations; but, in terms of guidance and discipline, I believe they offer less than I received from my mom and dad. I know—there I go sounding like that old curmudgeon again, railing against the younger generation the same way that our parents and grandparents complained about kids in prior eras. If that is how this article is perceived, I'm sorry; maybe that's why it was rejected a couple of times before I shelved it. Also, I realize that my example of one family with ill-behaved children looks like an indictment against *all* parents with kids in the little tykes niche, and I don't mean that, either. Still, I've seen enough egregious examples of parents refusing to discipline their children's "cute" (to them) behaviors that I took the time to write down my thoughts here.

About a year ago, I was on a cross-country flight, harbored in an aisle seat in first class—about the closest place to heaven outside of church. A mother got on with two young children—about 4 and 6 years old—and plopped down in the nearby vacant, first-class seats.

"Oh, no," I thought. "It's playtime."

How wrong I was! This mother *talked* with her children. She *explained* about the plane's noises and movements. She'd brought toys and books on board to personalize the five-hour journey and even packed some little "surprises" (like trinkets and Cheerios) that each child got to unwrap every 45 minutes until they had fallen asleep.

Upon landing, I turned to the woman and thanked her for being so kind and sensitive to both her children and their fellow passengers. She looked a bit puzzled, smiled shyly, and roused her children for the trip home. To herself, she had probably done nothing special. How I wish I could say that was the norm.

Last month, my wife and I went to enjoy a relaxing lunch in the pastel, fern-coiffured sunroom of a trendy downtown restaurant.

But, soon after ordering, we were distracted by some rather loud, out-of-context "Cowabunga, dude" statements coming from the table behind ours. There sat six yuppified adults and two children. The kids, a boy and a girl, were around 5 and 7 years old. The grown-ups laughed at this Bart Simpson imitation coming from children so young. My wife and I, both educators, smiled, too.

That was all the ammunition needed by these two young performers.

In a steady succession of louder and louder "Cowabunga, dudes," the children continued for—no lie—three minutes straight. Next came a chorus of "Row, Row, Row Your Boat," equally as loud and monotonous as the previous verbal barrage. Using our best "You're in trouble now" teacher gazes, my wife and I turned around to ogle the offending children and their adult counterparts, none of whom tried even once to quiet down the little ones.

Several minutes later, as the octet prepared to leave, the presumed father of one of the children looked toward us smilingly and said, "Now you'll be able to eat your lunch in peace."

Without batting an eye (my wife is good at things like this), Deb said, "Yes. That will be nice."

Put out by Deb's honesty, the mother (again, a presumption) of one of the tots eyed us both and said, "Well, when you go out in public to dine, you have to be tolerant of children's behavior, you know." Quickly, she stormed into the parking lot, leaving no time for a retort of our own.

So, I think I'll give her one now: "Ma'am, when did you stop being a parent to your child?"

There. I feel better.

* * * *

We've all experienced it. Whether it's a mother trying to reason with her 2-year-old who has staged a sit-down strike in the cereal aisle, or the kid sitting behind you on your US Air connection from Pittsburgh who is using the back of your seat for kick-ball practice, our children are out of control. Change that: They are actually *in* control, with their otherwise-competent parents playing the roles of patsies.

Don't get me wrong: I am not one to stifle individual expression in children. In fact, as both a teacher and a parent, I encourage it when it appears. But, this right to express oneself, as a child, stops when I, as an adult, say it does. I'm sorry if my son is bothered by my asking him to turn down his stereo when it invades my earspace. And I understand that Melissa probably thinks I'm the world's most evil teacher when I tell her to relinquish her seat at the classroom computer to another student who has been waiting patiently for 15 minutes. But, I expect them both to comply and, a minute after they do, any remaining animosity they may have felt toward me is either gone or cleverly disguised behind a smile. By providing limits to our children, we are not sti-fling their individuality, but rather are encouraging them to see it in relation to a pic-ture bigger than themselves.

But, what do many parents of my generation—I'm in my 40s—do when their chil-dren squeal publicly in fake cries, or do some deed that they were expressly forbidden from doing a minute before? The most common response is to ignore the behavior, as if by magic these actions that are attracting attention of every adult except the parents will cease by themselves. The next most frequent response is to overreact badly—a pub-lic slap or shout that does little more than hurt and scare the child. Equally as ineffec-tive is the "well-reasoned response," usually coming from Polo-shirted, two-income parents with lots of trinkets, but no common sense. I mean, really, do they honestly think that it works to say to an overtired, screaming 3 year old, "I'll give you a choice: You can take a nap now or stop crying. Which would you like to do?" *Puh-leese*! Simply pick up the child, bring him or her up to bed, draw the shades, and provide either a bottle to keep him full or a blankey to keep her comforted. Is this so difficult?

As Republican as it may sound from two hardened Democrats, my wife and I won-der more and more each day why people need licenses to fish, to drive, and to get mar-ried, but they need only biological equipment to spawn children. That most important of life's responsibilities—the creation of the next generation—is open season for any-one with a libido.

It seems that the majority of today's parents prefer displaying their children to dis-ciplining them; enjoy listening to unnecessary and exaggerated wailing, rather than reg-ulating these actions early on, when they are much easier to stop; and, then, thank you very much, handing them over to us teachers when the kids are 5 years old and spoiled, demanding that we instill discipline to their conduct.

Back to that sun-splashed restaurant that became, for us, an object lesson in self-control. If the tables had been turned and it had been *our* son who was row, row, row-ing his boat, we would have told (not asked) him, quietly, to stop. If he hadn't, we would have repeated our insistence, this time a bit more sternly. Still singing up a storm? Out he would have gone, away from the situation and its attention for a one-on-one chat with either of his parents. *Now* he would have known we were serious, and, with no one left to impress with his tunes, he would have eventually ceased his misbehaviors.

"Matt," we'd then say, "are you ready now to go back into the restaurant?"

Matt, like 9 out of 10 kids, would whimper a compliant "Yes."

It has worked for us, it worked for our folks, and—surprise, surprise—it can work for today's parents, too. But, if relief doesn't come soon, and Baby Boomers continue to let their loud children rule the roost, I have a suggestion that would revolutionize the restaurant and airline industries: Upon arrival, ask customers for their preference:

1. smoking or nonsmoking section
2. children or nonchildren section.

My ears, like my lungs, deserve a breath of fresh—and quiet—air.

Revisiting a Home I'd Never Left

Afew introductions ago, I mentioned that "The Smartest Kid In America" was my favorite article. I was wrong; this one is. However, since this one never got published (which *floors* me, because it is *so* much better than some of my in-print drivel), I didn't know if it could qualify as my favorite.

I've reevaluated. I'm right. It still is.

The best thing about experiencing rites of passage with my son (which is what this piece is about) is that, as a dad, I often got to reflect on the times when I went through similar situations, similar angsts. First love . . . first B . . . first stood-up date . . . first death—each holds significance that can only be counted in emotions. And the *biggest* first is leaving home to attend college, preceded by choosing where to go. This short story about my son Matt's choice to attend college 700 miles from Ohio, but only 20 minutes from where I had grown up, dredged up many old memories, lost opportunities, and long-buried joys. To this day, I can't read it and not cry. I wish you the same reaction.

When I was 17, I couldn't get away fast enough. Leaving my hometown near Boston, I headed west to college in Michigan. I thought I'd never look back.

For years, I didn't. Except for occasional family visits and my marriage in a barn in Connecticut (that's *another* story), I spent my years living in places that, as a kid, sounded exotic. Now, having just turned 40, I found myself on a flight to Boston with my family. Our mission: to visit colleges that Matt, our 17-year-old son, thought he might like to attend. The irony was easy to spot: Matt was seeking a return to a place I had been glad to leave when I shared his age and innocence.

Our morning flight was comfortable and cloudless. And, even though Matt was a frequent-enough flyer that he'd earned his first free ticket by age 12, he was glued to the window as if he'd never flown before. As we neared Logan Airport, Matt was enchanted by the beautiful sights below: the city to his left, the Atlantic to his right, and, straight ahead, perhaps his home for the next four years.

"Maybe the good weather is an omen," Deb, my wife, suggested. Then, she whispered ever so softly, "How did he grow up so fast?"

Our cab ride to our hotel at Copley Place was a roller-coaster adventure. For 20 minutes, we careened around corners, cars, and pedestrians. It was then that I remembered my father's advice about driving in Boston: Never use a turn signal and, above all, always avoid eye contact with other drivers. Those wise words seemed as appropriate today as they had been 23 years ago.

Matt was oblivious to the roadway mayhem. Trying to act cool and nonchalant—traits that all 17-year-olds seem to desire—his eyes gave him away. For that moment, he was a little kid again, and I took a mental snapshot of his excitement to store away for a time when he wouldn't be as close by as he was right now. *He* was ready for college, I think, but I wasn't sure if Deb and I were quite as prepared.

Our first college stop was Boston University, its campus striding a tree-lined Back Bay neighborhood as old as our nation itself. The Charles River, situated in B.U.'s backyard, was crowded with crew teams from Harvard and Tufts. On this sunny spring day, their silent movement was a stunning contrast to the noise just behind us on Commonwealth Avenue.

Our campus tour guide, a student from Los Angeles, pointed out the notable landmarks—the Rapid Transit ("The T") to downtown, the new student center with a 24-hour cafeteria, and, of course, Fenway Park. When I asked where the library was and how late it was open, I thought Matt would disown me—how *dare* I ask a question about academics on a campus tour!

Just a T-ride away, in the cushy suburb of Chestnut Hill, we visited our second school: Boston College. They, too, talked more about weekend possibilities than weekday classes, but this time I kept my mouth shut. The library hours, Matt reminded me, were posted on the building's entrance.

We jostled our way back to Copley Place on the T, Deb and I being the oldest people aboard. We felt like chaperones on a school field trip.

It was then that it struck me: By going to college in Michigan, I had given up the world's greatest college town: Boston. Matt knew better, I guess, for, as we were enjoying a family meal that evening, he opened himself up with uncharacteristic candor. He explained that he liked where we lived now, but that college was a time for new adventures, new places, new people. He'd find these in Boston, he thought, just the way I thought I'd find them in Michigan. In an odd twist of fate, Matt was returning home to a place he'd never been, while I was going back, through him, to a place I'd never really left after all.

Our evening flight home was as spectacular and clear as had been our arrival. Lights twinkled, both in town and on the water, and Matt gazed longingly out the window once again. Deb and I, in a sad realization that our boy was now a man, looked longingly at him. He had found a new home.

Conclusion

In Praise
of Elitism

Introduction

The *piece de resistance*, I believe: This article represents all I have grown to become, professionally, since I began my Ph.D. studies in 1978. Thus, it gets a category all its own.

Initially, I believed everything I read and everyone I listened to. Like a dry sponge lapping up every available bead of water, I soaked up knowledge indiscriminately, noticing neither inherent conflicts in logic nor opinions that went askew of my own, still-forming beliefs of who gifted children were.

As time progressed and my knowledge deepened, I began to question—and challenge—everything! This brought some pain to me, and to others I had grown to admire and enjoy. I didn't understand (still don't) why I was not allowed to disagree professionally with my advisor while maintaining a strong and rich personal relationship with him. But, it was not to be, and I needed to be true to myself and to the intellect that my mentor had encouraged me to forge. I miss what might have been, but I respect the choices I've made.

So, here it is: 23 years worth of soul searching, thinking about, chewing up and spitting out ideas about gifted kids and what we should do to serve them best. All encapsulated in a brief, 1,200-word essay—which, coincidence or not, is about the same length as my first published article, "Roger and Jim."

To Roger, to Matt (. . . all the Matts!), to Deb, to Joe, to Alan, to Cassie, to Sara, to Alex: Thank you all. May the ride continue for a long, long time!

I n a recent edition of the *Duke Gifted Letter,* a publication sponsored by the Talent Identification Program (TIP) at Duke University, I took part in a so-called "Expert's Forum" about the merits and flaws of the biggest educational misnomer of modern times: the "Theory" of Multiple Intelligences (MI), as proposed by Harvard researcher, Howard Gardner. With its egalitarian insistence that nearly everyone is gifted at something, the MI idea has taken the country, and the world, by storm. Why? Because MI artificially distributes giftedness equally among various talent areas—linguistic, mathematical, spatial, and so forth—which is a politically correct but intrinsically *in*correct notion of what intelligence is. What a shame . . . what a sham, and I am not afraid to say so:

> As a theory, MI is convenient, simple . . . and wrong. . . . So many people have jumped on to the bandwagon with the idea that "everyone is gifted at something" that many gifted programs have been eliminated or watered down. Some people are under the illusion that the needs of gifted students can be met in a setting that allows multiple forms of expression. MI is a simplistic, wishful-thinking approach that seems like a good thing to people who are uncomfortable admitting that intellectual abilities are not equally distributed in American society. (Delisle, 2000, pp. 2–3)

Naturally, my comments have been interpreted by some as meaning that I am an "elitist" when it comes to identifying and serving gifted children. For those who level this accusation, I thank you. For if being an elitist means that I still believe in a distinct quality of giftedness that is the domain of the few, not the many; and if being an elitist means that I believe gifted individuals need to be understood as the complex intellectual and emotional beings that they are; and if being an elitist means that I will advocate for a small percentage of children to receive a level of academic rigor and emotional understanding that transcends the typical, then an elitist I shall be. It is a badge I will wear proudly.

Gardner's sad and incorrect notion that giftedness is as common a behavior or trait as being able to bowl a game of 100 is based on an incomplete and inaccurate interpretation of the mountains of research that proves otherwise. But, this idea of giftedness as a talent, a "thing" is not unique to him. Starting in 1978, with the publication of Joseph Renzulli's article "What Makes Giftedness?" and concluding (as yet) with Gardner's latest incantation of a ninth intelligence, the world of giftedness has been upside-down, to the detriment of gifted children. As a fallout of Renzulli's and Gardner's work, it is now becoming increasingly popular for educators to scrap intact gifted programs and replace them with enrichment options for all children. This may satisfy school officials, who can now proclaim to parents that "the gifted program benefits everyone," but this schoolwide enrichment plan generally fails to provide the sustenance necessary to fulfill the complex lives of gifted children.

The idea of giftedness as being a developmental, lifelong trait that transcends day-to-day achievements has been replaced with Renzulli's "Type III" projects and Gardner's *ad nauseum* intelligences. When this happens, we relegate giftedness to a commodity to be traded and displayed, rather than the unique state of mind and being that it really is. But, in our current era of school accountability, high-stakes testing, and the "win-at-all-costs" approach to education, it is hard to argue against marketplace ethos of Multiple Intelligences. Too few gifted educators and school administrators discuss the obvious: School programs based on Gardner's notion of intelligence or Renzulli's interpretation of giftedness as a product are based more on political expediency than they are on psychological or educational legitimacy. In our rush toward egalitarianism as regards the concept of giftedness, we have lost sight of what should be our primary vision: the gifted child who cries out for attention.

But, argue we must. For if we don't, the gifted children who inhabit our homes and our classrooms will become pawns in an educational shell game that tries to hide giftedness by shifting around notions of what intelligence entails. When this happens— "gifted one year, not gifted the next," "multiply intelligent in math and spatial, but not in verbal or interpersonal"—we dissect the child into a specimen to be examined rather than an entity to be cherished. Sad to say, but the work of Renzulli, Gardner, and other self-titled "talent development specialists" has tarnished the notion of giftedness more than they have shined it. For in proposing their ideas on all-inclusive giftedness, they have left behind the very children they supposedly endorse: those children who are gifted in the mind and the heart 24–7, whether or not their panache in completing projects or in sharing their multiple intelligences in five of the nine possible categories is obvious.

Elitist? You bet I am, because I believe in the sanctity of human differences and the reality that an IQ of 145 *does* earmark you as different at age 10 from your fourth-grade classmates in some important, but unseen, ways. Elitist? You bet I am, if it means taking a child aside and emphasizing that giftedness is a lifelong quality that does not go away when the school years end. Elitist? You bet I am, and it has nothing to do with social or economic or racial classes, but instead is simply an indication that abilities— intellectual and emotional—differ among and between people. Always have, always will. Elitist? You bet I am, for if gifted students need a foot soldier to explain to others that they may be as different from average students, academically and emotionally, as are children with mental retardation, then I will be their man.

Can we as an enterprise—can you, as an individual?—give up the notion that *elitism* is a bad word and an evil concept when applied to gifted children and those who care about them? I hope that is possible, for without our active and vocal support, the gifted children we used to identify and serve in special school programs will wither as surely as do fields of grain without water.

As always, our world and our homes need the richness of spirit and compassion that gifted children provide. To abandon them up in deference to "equity" or "excellence for all" is to make them sacrificial lambs on the altar of egalitarianism. Gifted children deserve better, and who else to champion their cause than a bunch of "elitists" who realize and accentuate an essential truth: Gifted children do exist, as they always have and always will, and to discount their presence and prominence in our society is to be the ultimate intellectual snob who would dismiss reality rather than face it.

Giftedness exists, and not in equal measure across all people. Isn't it time to fess-up the errors brought about by the egalitarian illogic of Multiple Intelligences? Isn't it time to address the inherent inequities brought about by endorsing enrichment for all? Isn't it time to recapture the field of gifted child education from those who have held it hostage for a generation? Our gifted children deserve to be identified and served in ways that capitalize on their unique abilities and qualities. Please join me in being elitist enough to say so.

Gifted Child Today
Winter 2001

References

American Association for Gifted Children. (1978). *On being gifted*. New York: Walker.

Anthony, E. J. (1970). Two contrasting types of adolescent depression and their treatment. *Journal of the American Psychological Association, 18,* 841–859.

Betts, G., & Knapp, J. (1981). Autonomous learning and the gifted: A secondary model. In A. Arnold (Ed.), *Secondary programs for the gifted* (pp. 29–36). Ventura, CA: Ventura Superintendent of Schools Office.

Blaine, G. B., & McArthur, C. C. (1971). *Emotional problems of the student*. New York: Appleton-Century-Crofts.

Bloom, B. S. (1977). Affective outcomes of school learning. *Phi Delta Kappan, 59,* 193–198.

Blos, P. (1962). *On adolescence*. New York: Free Press.

Calhoun, L. G., Selby, J. W., & Faulstich, M. E. (1980). Reactions to the parents of the child suicide: A study of social impressions. *Journal of Consulting and Clinical Psychology, 48,* 535–536.

Colangelo, N., & Davis, G. A. (1991). *Handbook of gifted education*. Boston: Allyn and Bacon.

Colangelo, N., & Pfegler, L. R. (1979). Academic self-concept of gifted high school students. In N. Colangelo & R. T. Zaffrann (Eds.), *New voices in counseling the gifted*. Dubuque, IA: Kendall-Hunt.

Cox, J., Daniel, N., & Boston, B. (1985). *Educating able learners*. Austin: University of Texas Press.

Cutts, N. E., & Moseley, N. (1957). *Teaching the bright and gifted*. Englewood Cliffs, NJ: Prentice Hall.

Delisle, D., & Delisle, J. (1996). *Growing good kids: 28 activities to enhance self-awareness, compassion, and leadership*. Minneapolis: Free Spirit.

Delisle, J. R. (1980). Preventative counseling for the gifted adolescent: From words to action. *Roeper Review, 3*(2), 21–25.

Delisle, J. R. (1982). Learning to underachieve. *Roeper Review, 4*(4), 16–18.

Delisle, J. R. (1984). *Gifted children speak out*. New York: Walker.

Delisle, J. R. (1992). *Kidstories: Biographies of twenty young people you'd like to know*. Minneapolis: Free Spirit.

Delisle, J. R. (1998). Zen and the art of gifted child education. *Gifted Child Today, 21*(6), 38–39.

Delisle, J. R. (2000). Expert's forum. *Duke Gifted Letter, 1*(1), 2–3.

Delisle, J., & Galbraith, J. (1987). *The gifted kids survival guide II*. Minneapolis: Free Spirit.

Delisle, J. R., & Renzulli, J. S. (1982). The revolving door identification and programming model: Correlates of creative production. *Gifted Child Quarterly, 26,* 89–95.

Doorly, A. (1980, September/October). Microcomputers for gifted microtots. *G/C/T, 14,* 62–64.

Educational Products Information Institute (EPIE). (1981). Grant progress report (NIE-G-790083). Stonybrook, NY: Author.

Emerson, R. W. (1883). *Respecting the pupil: Essays on teaching able students.* (D. Cole & R. Cornett, Eds.) Exeter, NH: Phillips Exeter Academy Press.

Feldhusen, J. F. (1995). Talent development: The new direction in gifted education. *Roeper Review, 18,* 92.

Feldhusen, J. F., & Kolloff, M. (1978, September/October). A three-stage model for gifted education. *G/C/T, 1*(4), 3–5, 53–57.

Finch, S. M., & Poznanski, E. O. (1971). *Adolescent suicide.* Springfield, IL: Charles C. Thomas.

Fisher, E. (1981). Being a good model for your gifted child. *Gifted Children Newsletter, 2*(6), 1–2.

Galbraith, J. (1983). *The gifted kids survival guide.* Minneapolis: Free Spirit.

Galbraith, J., & Delisle, J. (1996). *The gifted kids survival guide: A teen handbook.* Minneapolis: Free Spirit.

Gallagher, J. J. (1975). *Teaching the gifted child.* Boston: Allyn and Bacon.

Galton, F. (1869). *Hereditary genius.* London: Macmillan.

Gardner, H. (1983). *Frames of mind: The theory of multiple intelligences.* New York: Basic Books.

Garfinkel, B., & Golombek, H. (1977). Suicide and depression in childhood and adolescence. In H. Jalinek (Ed.), *Psychological problems of the child and his family.* Toronto: Holt, Rinehart, and Winston.

Glaser, R. (Ed.). (1971). *The nature of reinforcement.* New York: Academic Press.

Goertzel, V., & Goertzel, M. (1962). *Cradles of eminence.* Boston: Little, Brown.

Gowan, J. C. (1972). *The emotionally disturbed gifted child: Implications for school people.* Westmoreland, PA: Westmoreland Intermediate Unit.

Grollman, E. A. (1971). *Suicide.* Boston: Beacon Press.

Grueling, J. W., & DeBlassie, R. R. (1980). Adolescent suicide. *Adolescence, 15,* 589–601.

Heckinger, F. (1981). Expediency vs. creativity. *Gifted Children Newsletter, 2*(6), 3.

Hesse, H. (1974). *Steppenwolf.* New York: Bantam.

Hollingworth, L. S. (1926). *Gifted children: Their nature and nurture.* New York: Macmillan.

Hollingworth, L. S. (1942). *Children above 180 IQ, Stanford Binet: Origin and development.* Yonkers-on-Hudson, NY: World Book.

Holtzman, W. H. (1960). Some positive and negative aspects of schooling. In K. E. Anderson (Ed.), *Project on the academically talented student.* Washington, DC: National Educational Association.

Husain, S. Y., & Vandiver, T. (1984). *Suicide in children and adolescents.* New York: Spectrum.

Irvine, D. (1987). What research doesn't show about gifted dropouts. *Educational Leadership, 44*(6), 79–80.

Jacobs, J. (1971). *Adolescent suicide.* New York: Wiley.

Jones, C. F. (1991). *Mistakes that worked.* New York: Doubleday.

Kulik, J. A., & Kulik, C-L. C. (1991). Ability grouping and gifted students. In N. Colangelo & G. A. Davis (Eds.), *Handbook of gifted education* (pp. 178–196). Boston: Allyn and Bacon.

LaRusso, R. S. (1980, October). *A multi-level educational approach to the high-IQ underachiever and/or underproducer.* Presentation given at the annual meeting of the National Association for Gifted Children, Minneapolis.

Laufer, J., & Laufer, M. (1984). *Adolescence and developmental breakdown: A psychoanalytic view.* New Haven, CT: Yale University Press.

Leder, J. M. (1987). *Dead serious: A book for teenagers about teenage suicide.* New York: Atheneum.

Lickona, T. (1991). *Educating for character: How our schools can teach respect and responsibility.* New York: Bantam.

Lombroso, C. (1891). *The men of genius.* London: Robert Scott.

Manes, S. (1983). *How to be a perfect person in just three days.* New York: Dell.

Marland, S. P., Jr. (1972). *Education of the gifted and talented: Report to the Congress of the United States by the U.S. Commissioner of Education and background papers submitted to the U.S. Office of Education*, 2 vols. Washington, DC: U.S. Government Printing Office (Government Documents, Y4.L 11/2: G36)

McKenry, P. C., Tishler, C. L., & Christman, K. L. (1980). Adolescent suicide and the classroom teacher. *Journal of School Health, 50,* 130–132.

Mehrabian, A. (1970). *Tactics of social influence.* Englewood Cliffs, NJ: Prentice-Hall.

Morgan, L. B. (1981). The counselor's role in suicide prevention. *Personnel and Guidance Journal, 59,* 284–286.

Multimedia Program Productions. (1981). *Donahue transcript #01161.* Cincinnati, OH: Syndication Services.

National Forum to Accelerate Middle-Grade Reform. (2000). *National forum policy statement: Student assignment in the middle grades: towards academic success for all students.* Retrieved May 10, 2001, from http://www.mgforum.org/policy.asp

Newland, T. E. (1976). *The gifted in socio-educational perspective.* Englewood Cliffs, NJ: Prentice-Hall.

Parrish, H. M. (1957). Epidemiology of suicide among college students. *Yale Journal of Biology and Medicine,* 585–595.

Peck, M. (1968). Suicide motivation in adolescents. *Adolescence, 3,* 109–118.

Pirsig, R. (1974). *Zen and the art of motorcycle maintenance.* New York: Bantam.

Povey, R. (Ed.). (1980). *Educating the gifted child.* London: Harper and Row.

Poznanski, E., & Zrull, J. P. (1970). Childhood depressions: Clinical characteristics of overtly depressed children. *Arch. Gen. Psychiatry, 23,* 8–15.

Purkey, W. W., & Novak, J. M. (1984). *Inviting school success* (2nd ed.). Belmont, CA: Wadsworth.

Purkey, W. W., & Novak, J. M. (1996). *Inviting school success: A self-concept approach to teaching, learning, and democratic practice.* Belmont, CA: Wadsworth.

Raph, J., Goldberg, M., & Passow, A. H. (1966). *Bright underachievers.* New York: Teachers College Press.

Renzulli, J. S. (1977). *The enrichment triad model.* Mansfield Center, CT: Creative Learning Press.

Renzulli, J. S. (1978). What makes giftedness? Reexamining a definition. *Phi Delta Kappan, 60,* 180–184.

Renzulli, J. S., & Reis, S. M. (1985). *The schoolwide enrichment model.* Mansfield Center, CT: Creative Learning Press.

Roberts, S., & Wallace, B. (1980). The development of teaching materials: Principles and practice. In R. Povey (Ed.), *Educating the gifted child.* London: Harper and Row.

Robinson, A. (1990). Cooperation or exploitation? The argument against cooperative learning for talented students. *Journal for the Education of the Gifted, 14,* 9–27.

Robinson, K. G., & Samek, R. (1981, June 6). Teen-agers' deaths shock friends. *Hartford Courant,* C-1.

Roeper, A. (1990). *Educating children for life.* Monroe, NY: Trillium Press.

Roeper, A. (1995). What I have learned from gifted children. In *Annemarie Roeper: Selected writings and speeches* (pp. 133–143). Minneapolis: Free Spirit.

Roets, L. (1985). *Understanding success and failure.* New Sharon, IA: Leadership Publications.

Rogers, K. B. (1992). *The relationship of grouping practices to the education of the gifted and talented learner* (Report no. 9101). Storrs: The National Research Center on the Gifted and Talented, The University of Connecticut.

Rosenshine, B. V., & Furst, N. (1971). Research in teacher performance criteria. In B. Othaniel Smith (Ed.), *Research in teacher education* (pp. 44–54). Englewood Cliffs, NJ: Prentice-Hall.

Rowe, M. B. (1969). Science, silence, and sanctions. *Science and Children, 6*(6).

Sargent, M. (1984). Adolescent suicide: Studies reported. *Child and Adolescent Psychotherapy, 1*(2), 49–50.

Schoolar, J. C. (1973). *Current issues in adolescent psychiatry.* New York: Brunner/Mazel.

Seiden, R. H. (1966). Campus tragedy: A study of student suicide. *Journal of Abnormal Psychiatry, 71,* 389–399.

Teicher, J. D., & Jacobs, J. (1966). Adolescents who attempt suicide: Preliminary findings. *American Journal of Psychiatry, 122,* 1249–1257.

Terman, L. M. (1905). A study in precocity and prematuration. *American Journal of Psychology, 16,* 145–183.

Torrance, E. P. (1961). Problems of highly creative children. *Gifted Child Quarterly, 5*(2), 31–34.

Whitmore, J. (1979). Identifying and programming for highly gifted underachievers in the elementary school. *GATE, 1,* 56–75.

Whitmore, J. R. (1980). *Giftedness, conflict, and underachievement.* Boston: Allyn and Bacon.

Winebrenner, S. (1992). *Teaching gifted children in the regular classroom.* Minneapolis: Free Spirit.

Zadra, D., & Moawad, B. (1986). *Mistakes are great.* Mankato, MN: Creative Education.